Industrialized
Building
Systems
for Housing

The MIT Press

Cambridge, Massachusetts,
and London, England

Industrialized Building Systems for Housing

A compendium based
on *Industrialized Building*,
MIT Special Summer Session,
August 18–29, 1969,
and *Systems Building
and Industrialization
for New Communities,*
MIT Special Summer Session,
June 16–20, 1970

Edited by
Albert G. H. Dietz
Laurence S. Cutler

This book was designed by
The MIT Press Design Department.
It was set in Univers,
printed on Finch Textbook Offset
by The Colonial Press Inc.
and bound by The Colonial Press Inc.
in the United States of America.

ISBN 0 262 04034 4 (hardcover)

Library of Congress catalog and number:
71-158160

Contents

Acknowledgments

The two conferences from which the papers in this volume are drawn included a number of other presentations which are not printed here. Without these additional papers, the summer sessions program would have been a donkey without a tail and legs. To these other speakers, we would like to express our sincere gratitude.

The effort in assembling data, graphics, and the manuscripts, as well as the transcriptions, could not have been completed without the untiring efforts of Christine D. Cosmopoulos, Carole A. Beals, and Daphne A. R. Wiggins. Sherrie Stephens Cutler of ECODESIGN assisted by reviewing the manuscript several times and by offering her candid comments, criticism and constructive suggestions. For all this we thank her.

Our thanks to Dean Lawrence B. Anderson of the School of Architecture and Planning at MIT and Professor James Austin of the Office of the Summer Session for suggesting these special summer sessions and for encouraging future sessions.

Professor Forrester's paper was first presented to the National Academy of Sciences—National Academy of Engineering. We extend our thanks for permission to reprint this paper. The paper by Dietz was first presented at the joint international meeting of the American Institute of Architects and the Royal Institution of Canadian Architects in Chicago, June 1969. Large portions of that paper were published in the AIA Journal, November 1969. Robert Platts carried out his research on European systems for the Building Research Division of the Canadian National Research Council.

Finally, our sincere appreciation to the audience — or, rather, participants — of these sessions, for it is their personal experience as architects, engineers, professors, builders, manufacturers, and developers which created the ambience of excitement concerning housing systems which is so difficult to capture on paper.

Albert G. H. Dietz
Laurence S. Cutler

Professor Arthur D. Bernhardt	Assistant Professor, Department of Architecture, Massachusetts Institute of Technology
Mr. Charles Biederman	Vice-President of Technical Services, Levitt Technology Corporation
Mr. Charles H. Blitman	President, Taylor Woodrow-Blitman, Inc.
Professor Charles Brewer	Department of Architecture, Yale University
Mr. Bernard H. Breymann	Vice-President, Building Systems Development, Borg-Warner Corporation
Professor Ing. arch. Vladimír Červenka	Director, Research Institute for Building and Architecture, Republic of Czechoslovakia
Mr. Philippe Charat	Componoform, Inc.
Professor John F. Collins	Consulting Professor of Urban Affairs, Massachusetts Institute of Technology
Professor William H. Correale	Technical Director—Code Project, Polytechnic Institute of Brooklyn
Professor Laurence S. Cutler	Assistant Professor of Architecture, Massachusetts Institute of Technology; Principal, ECODESIGN, Inc.
Mr. Edward Diehl	Architect and President, Edward Diehl & Associates
Professor Albert G. H. Dietz	Professor of Building Engineering, Department of Architecture Massachusetts Institute of Technology
Mr. S. Porter Driscoll	Director, Architectural Division, United States Department of Housing and Urban Development
Mr. John Dunnan III	President, Corporate Structures Inc.
Mr. Ezra Ehrenkrantz	President, Building Systems Development, Inc.
Mr. Ellis Ellwood	Manager, Architectural and Construction Services, United States Gypsum Company
Mr. Calvin Felton	Chief Architectural Designer, Urban Planners Incorporated
Mr. J. W. Ferenc	President, Architectural Products, Inc., Feran Industrialized Construction Systems
Mr. Urs Gauchat	Architect, Carl Koch & Associates
Mr. Reese Hammond	Director of Research and Education, International Union of Operating Engineers
Mr. Wayne C. Hart	President, Stresscon Industries, Inc.
Dipl. Ing. Dr. Milan Hrncirik	Foreign Trade Department Executive, Republic of Czechoslovakia
Mr. Timothy E. Johnson	Research Associate, Department of Architecture, Massachusetts Institute of Technology
Mr. John D. Lang	Vice-President and Director of Research and New Investments, H. B. Zachry Company

Mr. Henry O. McElyea	Manager for Design, Engineering, and Technical Service, Johns-Manville
Mr. Riccardo Meregaglia	President, Impresa General Construzioni, MBM, Milan
Mr. Neal B. Mitchell	President, Neal Mitchell Associates, Inc.
Ing. Pavel Mrkvan	Superintendent and Construction Engineer, Bureau of Buildings, Republic of Czechoslovakia
Professor Nicholas P. Negroponte	Department of Architecture, Massachusetts Institute of Technology
Mr. Joseph Newman	Vice-President, Tishman Research Corporation
Mr. Calvin Opitz	Research Associate, Department of Civil Engineering, Massachusetts Institute of Technology
Mr. Robert J. Pelletier	Research Associate, Department of Civil Engineering, Massachusetts Institute of Technology
Mr. Robert E. Platts	President, Scanada Consultants, Limited
Mr. Roderick Robbie	Consultant, The Metropolitan Toronto School Board
Mr. Thomas Rogers	Vice-President for Urban Affairs, Mitre Corporation
Mr. Norman Rutgers	Assistant to the President, Lennox Industries, Inc.
Professor Jerzy Soltan	Chairman, Department of Architecture, Harvard University
Mr. Fred J. Stephenson	Consultant, Butler Manufacturing Company
Mr. Donald Stull	Architect and President, Stull Associates, Inc.
Mr. Jack R. Warner	Construction Research Analyst, United States Department of Housing and Urban Development

Participating Lecturers	Systems Building and Industrialization for New Communities	MIT Special Summer Session, June 16–20, 1970
Professor Arthur D. Bernhardt	Director, Program in Industrialization of the Housing Sector, Urban Systems Laboratory, Massachusetts Institute of Technology	
Mr. Bernard Breymann	Vice-President, Building Systems Development, Borg-Warner Corporation	
Professor John F. Collins	Consulting Professor of Urban Affairs, Massachusetts Institute of Technology	
Professor Laurence S. Cutler	Assistant Professor of Architecture, Massachusetts Institute of Technology; Principal, ECODESIGN, Inc.	
Professor Albert G. H. Dietz	Professor of Building Engineering, Department of Architecture, Massachusetts Institute of Technology	
Mr. S. Porter Driscoll	Director, Architectural Division, United States Department of Housing and Urban Development	
Mr. Ezra Ehrenkrantz	President, Building Systems Development, Inc.	
Mr. Harold Finger	Assistant Secretary for Technology and Research, United States Department of Housing and Urban Development	
Professor Jay W. Forrester	Sloan School of Management, Massachusetts Institute of Technology	
Mr. Urs Gauchat	Architect, Carl Koch & Associates	
Mr. Reese Hammond	Director of Research and Education, International Union of Operating Engineers	
Mr. Hans Harms	Department of Architecture, Massachusetts Institute of Technology	
Professor John Myer	Department of Architecture, Massachusetts Institute of Technology	
Mr. David Pellish	Housing Technology Officer, New York State Urban Development Corporation	
Mr. Roderick Robbie	Systems Consultant, Environment Systems International Inc.	
Mr. Guy Rothenstein,	Vice-President, Balency-MBM-US Corporation	
Mr. Norman Rutgers	Assistant to the President, Lennox Industries, Inc.	
Professor Jerzy Soltan	Chairman, Department of Architecture, Harvard University	
Mr. Frank Sparks	Executive Director, New England Mobile Home Manufacturers Association	
Mr. Charles Topping	Consultant to the Building Industry	
Professor Wilhelm von Moltke	Professor and Chairman of the Urban Design Program, Harvard University	

Industrialized
Building
Systems
for Housing

Introduction

The United States today—at a time when housing more than ever is needed—does not exploit existing building technology to the fullest. The technology is available, but the constraints are an obstacle. The latter can only be overcome by a determined, concerted effort by all elements of the building industry.

As stated in the first of the papers collected here, when the talk is about the large volume of building—particularly housing—projected for the balance of this century, it is often said that we have the necessary technology and that no great improvements are either necessary or likely, but that other factors prevent its full application.

It is also said that costs of building, especially housing for low- to moderate-income families, are too high but that technology cannot substantially reduce them and that costs, as reflected in rents, must be brought down in other ways—mainly by financial means, such as interest subsidy, preferential tax treatments, and so on.

There seems to be a contradiction here. If costs are too high and technology cannot substantially reduce them, then technology is inadequate. It may be true that no great improvements are possible; it may also be true that we need only to utilize fully our existing technology.

To find out whether we can make full use of existing and potential technology, we must (1) see what that technology is; (2) examine the complex interaction of technology with social, political, and economic constraints; and (3) determine what must be done to remove those constraints so that technology can achieve its full potential.

There is, of course, no single technology; there are many, and none universally applicable to all building situations. We have the traditional methods of construction developed during centuries of trial; methods which, when well organized and efficiently carried out, often still offer the best available solutions to given problems. Nevertheless, we are acutely aware of the shortcomings of traditional methods.

Americans are presently taking a long, hard look at *industrialization* as an answer to some of the housing problems. It has been suggested that there are any number of appropriate industrialized building systems which are useful for a wide range of specific uses and situations. To match the solution to the problem, to adapt the technique to a flexible need and demand, to create a decent home and a better total environment: these are the goals that may be achieved with the help of industrialization.

Industrialized Building Systems

There are many industrialized systems technologies, but no one of them is applicable to all construction cases, no one is the panacea.

They are dependent upon, and influenced by, many other aspects of the housing situation, such as land use, density, volume, environmental conditions, user needs, continuity, codes, and labor.

Thus, *industrialized systems building* may be defined as those incorporating a total integration of all subsystems and components into an overall process; one fully utilizing industrialized production, transportation, and assembly techniques. This integration is achieved through the exploitation of the underlying organizational principles. Once this is understood, industrialized housing systems may be classified in a variety of ways, of which the following are the major categories:

I. *Monolithic Unit: Boxes*
Monolithic units (Figure 1) are generally factory-produced and preassembled volumetric elements with a high degree of finish and a minimum amount of required site erection time (utility connections). They may be further categorized as a function of their relative degree of self-containment.

A. *Lightweight units or mobile-home types*: Totally self-contained housing units which can retain their mobility, or be permanently installed and grouped or stacked with the addition of a demountable frame. In most cases mobile homes are completely preassembled and finished, and require only site utility connections for occupancy.

B. *Heavyweight or volumetric components*: Room-size (or smaller) volumes of concrete, steel sandwich, wood- or fiber-reinforced plastic, which can be grouped horizontally and/or stacked vertically (if bearing) and dry connected to form single-family or multifamily attached or detached housing. In some cases, these volumes may be incorporated in traditional structural/mechanical space grids to provide high-rise multifamily housing. Stacked bearing units often avoid the necessity of producing six-sided volumes by wall and slab sharing, and, in some cases, bonus room units are acquired by checkerboard stacking. Other types of systems employ discontinuous room units to provide for mechanical chases, sound insulation, and structural fireproofing.

Basically, monolithic units are restricted by travel radius from the plant (action radius);* they are also extremely costly to handle. They are usually to be considered "closed" systems because it is not possible to mass the volumes in very many different ways; thus, monolithic systems restrict the flexibility of urban designs dependent upon them.

---

*See the Glossary for definitions of the technical terms used throughout this volume.

II. *Total Systems: Panels*

Total systems (Figure 2) are usually large concrete slabs or otherwise panelized units not made in the form of a box, but often large enough to constitute entire walls, partitions, and floors, or substantial parts of floors and roofs, which form boxes when put together. They are fabricated in a shop and assembled at the site. In some cases, the components of different manufacturers can be incorporated within the same system if the components are "open" in that they provide for modular coordination options for subsystems. Panels come in a variety of materials; some examples are heavyweight (concrete) or lightweight (sandwich) pieces.

A. *Open Production*: Mold sizes and incorporations are modified to specification per project of about 300 dwelling units or more. A typical example would be a concrete panel incorporating any desired finish, and the panels are usually either room-size or in manageable strips (semiheavy, cast on-site or at a remote factory).

B. *Closed Production*: The components produced are usually bearing panels and are relatively light. The system is based on a small number of standardized components. There is usually a limited number of components; thus, floor plans and architectural expression are restricted. Generally, panels require a huge aggregated market (about 1,000 dwelling units) to justify the use of systems building at all. The market required is usually about 1,000 dwelling units per project.

III. *Structural Systems: Frames*

Frames generally constitute parts of the structure (Figure 3), such as beams and columns, fabricated off-site but assembled on-site. Into these are fitted infill units, such as walls, partitions, floors, ceilings, and roofs. These latter elements are also usually fabricated off-site and assembled to the structural elements on-site. The primary advantage is the reduction of on the site work in favor of quick component assembly. Transportation is economical because the components are small and light, and because central factories can enjoy large market areas (action radii). However, the increased number of joint connections and materials somewhat complicates the total process, increases the cost, and, alas, may result in acoustical characteristics not conductive to privacy.

IV. *Special Construction Techniques*

"Special Construction Techniques" express the application of machine technology to traditional craft procedures (Figure 4). Most of these techniques are characterized by on-site construction using special machinery and, usually, cast concrete. It would serve our purposes well to give several examples in order to illustrate some of these techniques in more detail.

Figure 1
Monolithic unit. Factory-produced, heavyweight boxes stacked together in checkerboard fashion in order not to be redundant in the wall structure. These units provide a high degree of finish and require a minimum amount of on-site erection time. Courtesy of *Engineering News-Record.*

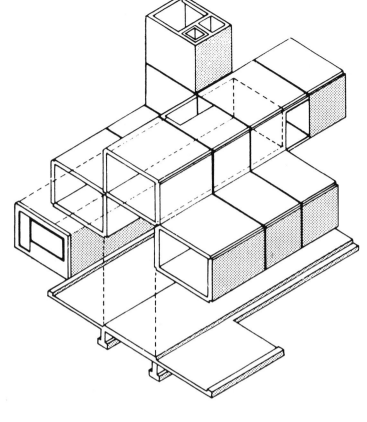

Figure 2
Total system. Large heavyweight panels integrating subsystems and utilizing prefabricated grade-beam foundations. On-site assembly allows for solution of construction problems peculiar to the site. Courtesy of *Engineering News-Record.*

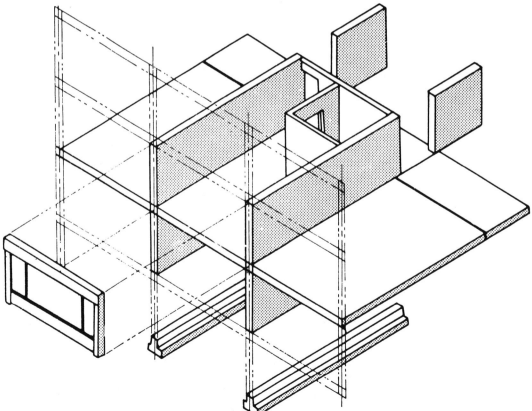

Figure 3
Structural system. Functioning as parts
of the structure such as beams and columns, this lightweight concrete frame
employs rationalized traditional infill
panels, window and roof sections, and
other elements. Courtesy of *Engineering
News-Record.*

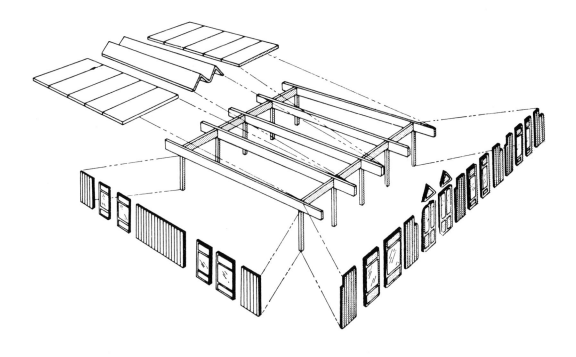

A. *Lift slab*: Slabs are cast-at-grade, one over the other, with sleeves designed for slab connections to previously erected columns. After curing, the slabs are lifted into place and bonded.

B. *Slip-form*: Vertical steel forms 4'0" high are arranged in the intended configuration (this system is often used only for service cores.) Concrete is poured into the top of the forms while they rise vertically at a rate (conditioned by temperature) which permits the concrete to reach initial set at the bottom of the form. Slabs are cast conventionally at each level.

C. *Tunnel forms with accelerated curing*: Precision-made volumetric steel forms with integral heating equipment are placed next to one another on a slab, and floors and walls are cast in one single operation, in one- or two-room widths. After casting, the heating accelerates the curing of the concrete and the formwork is easily removed by crane to a new position for immediate reuse. By accelerating the concrete curing process, the cycle is reduced to only 13 hours curing time and 11 hours preparation.

V. *Components*
The industrialized production of materials and components (Figure 5) is nothing more than the rationalization and the application of modular coordination and assembly line techniques to traditional craft technology (windows, floors, panels, etc.). Such coordination is applicable to the grouping of units that had previously been produced and distributed separately (heart units or utility cores), with a greater portion of production accomplished at the factory. It is generally accompanied by the use of new materials.

VI. *Mechanical units*
The term "mechanical," as used here, comprises plumbing, electrical components, and heating or air conditioning units (see Figure 3 of Chapter 7). They may be assembled on-site in the traditional manner, or subassemblies may be fabricated off-site and connected together on-site. The degree of subassembly may vary from "plumbing trees" to completely preassembled bathrooms, kitchens, and similar components.

VII. *Performance specifications*
These decree full compatibility of the subsystems, in order to provide a market ample enough to guarantee the manufacturers a suitable exposure. Totally flexible, the design standards regulate the compatibility in such a way that one manufacturer is able to join with others and to offer competitive bids with higher quality and integrative design.

The Summer Sessions

The increasing importance of industrialized building as the demands for building accelerate and the capacity of traditional construction

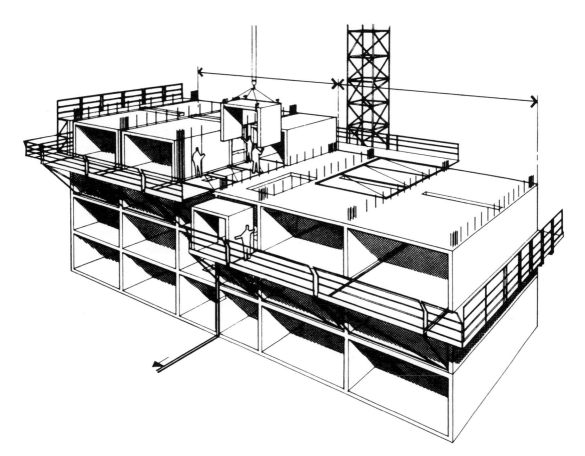

Figure 4
Special construction technique. The application of machine technology to traditional craft procedures, illustrating
a "building that builds itself" by utilizing precision-made volumetric steel
forms with integral heating equipment to
accelerate the curing of the concrete.
Courtesy of John Laing Construction Ltd.

Figure 5
Components. The total integration of
different manufacturers' building elements that can be combined, by virtue of
their dimensional and functional integration, to create a unit. Courtesy of
Engineering News-Record

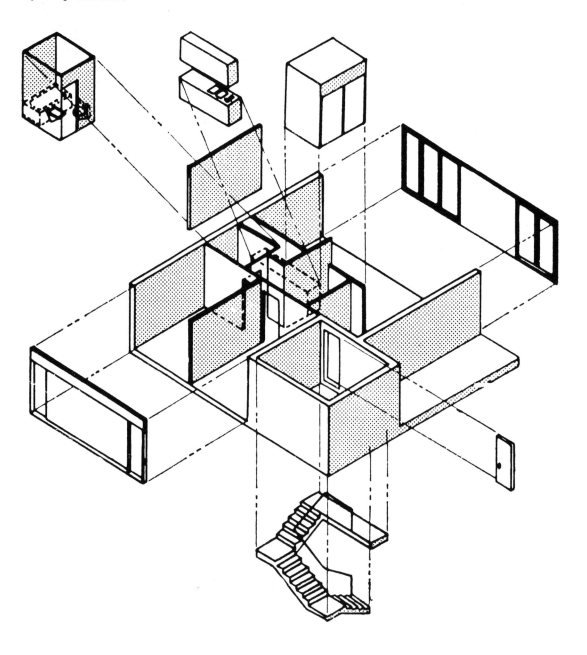

methods to provide is severely strained caused us to develop a summer session program to clearly identify the value and role of industrialization in all aspects of building. The Summer Sessions were intended primarily for practicing architects, engineers, developers, and builders, as well as for teachers of architecture and building engineering and development. In the first session (Industrialized Building, August 18–29, 1969), a strict examination was made of the underlying principles leading to industrialization; the types of building systems evolving in accordance with those principles, particularly in housing, were investigated in detail. The second session (Systems Building and Industrialization for New Communities, June 16–20, 1970) examined not only the technology but also the morphology of systems and urbanization. The basic policies which, we hope, will be set at a national level to implement housing in consonance with local needs were brought out during the second session. Both sessions examined the developing urban requirements and, in this light, the principles of design, performance standards, the effect of building codes, volume production, the problems of introduction and evaluation of innovation, governmental policy, labor, building modules, and finally, the necessary organization for production. Examples of industrialized systems were described and illustrated by participants familiar with American and European practices. Graduate students from MIT and Harvard also volunteered to participate by setting up and conducting a "User-Needs Workshop" during the 1970 session.

We feel that we can fairly say that all those who participated in these sessions came to agree that "to meet the building requirements of urban communities in the decades ahead, advanced concepts in design and production must be closely correlated with user needs and the needs of communities as a whole." This statement expresses the goal of the two summer sessions. It is with this goal in mind that we offer here selections from but a few of the presentations.

Albert G. H. Dietz
Laurence S. Cutler

Spring, 1971
Cambridge, Mass.

1
Building Technology: Potentials and Problems

Albert G. H. Dietz

In discussions of the large volume of building—particularly housing—projected for the balance of this century, it is often said that we have the necessary technology and that no great improvements are either necessary or likely, but that other factors stand in the way of its full application. It is also said that costs of building, especially housing for low- to moderate-income families, are too high but that technology cannot substantially reduce them, and that they must be brought down in other ways, mainly by financial means such as interest subsidy, preferential tax treatments, and so on.

There seems to be a contradiction here. If costs are too high and technology can not substantially reduce them, then technology is inadequate. It may be true that no great improvements are possible; it may also be true that we need only to utilize fully our existing technology. Perhaps we are in the position of the dirt farmer who refused to send his son to agricultural school because, "we don't farm as good as we know how right now."

To determine whether we can make full use of existing and potential technology we must (1) see what those technologies are; (2) examine the complex interactions of technology with social, political, and economic constraints; and (3) determine what must be done to remove those constraints. This is obviously an enormously complicated subject, only a few facets of which can be touched upon here.

Elements of Industrialization
Existing Technologies

As this audience well knows, there is no single technology; there are many, and none universally applicable to all building situations. We have many traditional methods of construction developed during centuries of trial, and based upon diverse materials, structural principles, and methods of environmental control. When well organized and efficiently carried out, these often still offer the best solutions to given problems. Nevertheless, we are acutely aware that they have their shortcomings in the face of today's situation and tomorrow's demands. The search for improved technologies moves forward on a worldwide scale. We hear much about industrialization, building systems (also called systems building and the systems approach), the performance concept, organization and project control, and how these promise to help solve our problems. We may examine them briefly to see where they stand today, and where they appear to be going.

Industrialization

"Industrialization," as is true of many commonly used words, means different things to different people. To some, it is merely a subterfuge to avoid the bad odor of "prefabrication." To others, it is the panacea for all building ills. As used here it means not only shop

Presented to the 1969 session. Albert G. H. Dietz is Professor of Building Engineering, Department of Architecture, Massachusetts Institute of Technology.

fabrication, but also the efficient organization of construction that combines shop fabrication with orderly site assembly.

There is no dearth of industrialization schemes. The Patent Office is full of them. In many respects they are more advanced (that is, more widely employed) abroad than in the United States. Some are based almost entirely on traditional technologies adapted to shop fabrication, some employ moderately advanced ideas, some are exotic. They can be classified in various ways. One such classification is into boxes, big panels, and pieces.

Big Boxes

Boxes are room-sized or larger enclosures that may constitute the entire building, as in trailers and mobile homes, or they may be assembled into larger buildings such as apartments and hotels. They may comprise only the structural shell—indeed, some walls may be fitted in only after the major portion of the building has been completed—or they may be completely prefurnished with all utilities, carpets on the floor, and pictures on the walls. In one publicity stunt, a "tenant" and his family rode their hotel room from the ground to its place in the building.

Big boxes may be heavy or light. Some concrete boxes weigh 80 to 100 tons. Others, such as those built by the mobile home industry, are extremely light and can be towed long distances on wheels. In at least one instance, wood-frame boxes were hauled 600 miles to their final destination, where they were stacked by a light mobile crane to provide dwelling units. Some boxes unfold from a compact arrangement, conforming to highway restrictions, into full-sized units. There are many variations. Most strive for the fullest possible prefurnishing and the incorporation of all utilities. This is the attractive feature of the big-box approach, and one of the reasons for the spectacular growth of mobile homes.

Big Panels

Big panels are wall-sized slabs and large floor units that are assembled at the site into the finished configuration (Figures 1, 2). A single panel may form part of several rooms. Panels may or may not be finished on both sides: it is common for both surfaces of concrete panels to be so finished, whereas wood-based or other framed panels may have only one finished side to allow for easy joining and the field incorporation of utilities. As in the case of boxes, big panels may be heavy or light, depending upon materials and method of fabrication.

The obvious advantage of big panels over boxes is that boxes are bulky, while panels can be efficiently stacked for transportation. Panels, on the other hand, call for many more joints to be made in the field and seldom permit the degree of prefinishing and shop incorporation of utilities and equipment possible with boxes. Many of

Figure 1
Industrialized concrete building panels.
Thamesmead.

Figure 2
Concrete-panel construction. Prague.

the advanced European systems are based on big panels, usually concrete.

Pieces

The term "pieces" refers to smaller units than big panels, usually columns, beams, and floor slabs, assembled at the site to provide the structure into which are inserted nonstructural panels or field-fabricated parts such as partitions. The line between industrialization and traditional construction can easily become blurred. The objective may be greater flexibility of arrangement with a smaller number of different units than might be possible with big panels, or it may be simpler fabrication equipment in the shop, or simpler and lighter erection equipment, or pieces small enough to be handled by man-power alone. More joints are usually required than with boxes and large panels, but the joints may be simplified by being put at points of low stress. The amount of field finishing and field incorporation of utilities is generally greater than with boxes and big panels, but this can be reduced by careful and ingenious design.

These approaches are not mutually exclusive, nor do they preclude mixtures of industrialized and traditional methods. The latter is the rule; few, if any, of the new technologies make no use of traditional procedures. Box construction is likely to employ some panels and pieces; the dividing line between big panels and pieces is not sharp; foundations are almost certain to be field fabricated; and it is often more economical to cast floors in place than to use precast slabs, especially when plans are irregular and nonrepetitive.

European Practice

In Europe, industrialized housing is much more widely practiced than in the United States. There are many reasons. The devastation of war created an enormous demand at the very time that the depletion of skilled manpower left traditional handicraft methods incapable of coping with it. Government involvement in housing is much more extensive than here and provides a large single market that makes industrialization both possible and attractive.

Most of the European systems are based upon big panels (Figure 3), although some use has been made of boxes in various countries, in-cluding the USSR, and boxes may find increasing favor in the future. Big panels are predominantly concrete, although, as will be seen, there are some notable examples of other materials and of com-posites. Big panels have spread throughout Europe from methods originating in various countries. The notable innovations originating in Scandinavia and France in Western Europe parallel extensive large-scale development in Eastern Europe.

Materials

Advances in materials technology range from modest to exotic. Some are already in use, others appear to be promising for the near future, still others are in the distant future or may not find their way into buildings at all. Only a few can be mentioned here.

Figure 3
Simultaneous erection of precast wall
panels and site casting of floors. Milan.

Expansive cements and controlled-set cements are recent additions
that promise to overcome some of the problems with concrete—
notably, shrinkage and cracking upon curing—and that may
provide the ability to control the cure time of concrete to meet
varying conditions. If questions respecting long-time stability, creep,
and related aspects of expansive cements are answered to the satisfaction of building users, and if the set of concrete can be closely
controlled under site conditions and in the shop, these materials
can provide valuable additions to the existing array of cements and
their modifiers. Self-prestressing may be possible; if so, it will obvi-
ate the necessity for much of the equipment now associated with
prestressing or posttensioning. The usefulness of concrete, already
great, may be enhanced even more.

Steels stronger than the old reliable structural steel so long used in
building have already found uses, as have high-stress bolts and the
consequent virtual disappearance of hideously noisy rivets. More
steels can be expected, leading to still more flexibility in design.
Sprayed-on fireproofing has created a minor revolution and has help-
ed steel to regain some previously lost applications. Steels that form
tenacious rust surfaces have appeared. New design concepts, such
as the staggered truss and greater use of cable-supported structures,
can help to provide economy and flexibility.

Enhanced dimensional stability, increased hardness, and integral
finish are being supplied to wood by deep impregnation with plastic
monomers subsequently polymerized in situ by chemical means or by
penetrating high-energy radiation.

Plastics continue to provide one of the fastest-growing sources of
material for floor and wall coverings, durable finishes, high-performance engineering adhesives, tough transparent enclosures, piping,
hardware, film, insulation, and many other uses. The number of these
applications will undoubtedly expand; new uses will be found as designers become more familiar with the various plastics and questions
respecting their performance are resolved.

Sealants, although a small item, have already become critical in
building, and increasing industrialization, with its need for field joints,
will step up the demand. Problems still remain; chiefly, quality control of workmanship in the field.

Photochromic glass is expected to help solve the old problem of sun
control. By darkening as light intensity increases, and vice versa,
such glass can assist in maintaining fairly uniform levels of light and
in overcoming glare. Chemical tempering should help to remove the
present limitations of tempered glass.

High-strength mortars and adhesives that provide joints at least as strong as the masonry units themselves have already resulted in thin masonry walls, brought about changes in techniques, increased production, and made prelaid masonry panels possible.

Among the possibilities being explored in laboratories are the combining of inorganic materials, such as concrete, with organic materials, such as polymers, in an attempt to marry the hardness, compressive strength, and durability of the former to the toughness and resilience of the latter, and thereby to gain most of the advantages and overcome most of the limitations of both. Thin toppings for floors and strong stuccos have already resulted from such combinations.

Composite Materials

Composite materials are among the most promising of all developments. The increasingly severe demands imposed on materials by our building practice often cannot be met by simple single-component materials; they call for the combined behavior of several materials acting in concert to provide properties not attainable by the constituents acting alone. An example may serve to illustrate.

The Greater London Council recently decided to construct a number of high-rise apartments in which industrialized components should be employed to the greatest practicable extent. Utilizing its power to set its own building standards, it decided upon a series of performance requirements for the exterior walls. These should be factory-produced panels able to withstand 80-mile-per-hour winds, having a U-factor not greater than 0.20, an average acoustical attentuation of 35 decibels, zero flame-spread on the surface, one-hour fire penetration resistance, minimum weight, minimum thickness, and should require only minimum maintenance.

After several years of development, a composite wall panel emerged that had an outside shell of mineral-loaded molded glass-fiber-reinforced plastic with a durable, renewable, baked-on polyurethane finish; a 3- to 4-inch thick filling of wire-reinforced foamed concrete weighing only 20 pounds per cubic foot and attached to the shell by a flexible bond layer, and an inner facing of reinforced gypsum plaster bonded to the core with a layer of bitumen that simultaneously provided a vapor barrier. This panel easily met all requirements, weighed less than 20 percent as much as traditional masonry or precast stone concrete, and was one-third the thickness. Foundations and steel frame were lighter than for traditional construction. The builders could assemble panels to the supporting steel and place them so rapidly, with an ordinary tower crane, that the manufacturer could not keep pace with them. In-place cost was competitive with standard construction, even though the first shells were made in the United States and shipped to London for completion.

This is only one example of the growing use of composites in building. Many more can be expected. The building industry may borrow from developments in space-vehicle design, such as filament-wound structures and high-performance fibers, filaments, and whiskers.

Filament winding makes maximum use of high-strength filaments, mainly glass, by winding continuous filaments impregnated with a matrix, such as synthetic resin, upon a simple mandrel of the desired shape, the orientation of filaments being controlled to meet the expected stresses. Extremely high strength-to-weight ratios are achieved, and the only limitation on size is the size of the relatively simple equipment required. Some limitations on shapes attainable and on openings for windows and doors exist, but the technique is feasible. The idea of winding on a form deserves further attention.

High-Strength Fibers

The attainment of high strength by drawing materials into fine filaments is not confined to glass, the strength of which rises from about 5,000 psi for massive glass to better than 500,000 psi for commercial filaments, and still higher in the laboratory. Materials capable of being formed into filaments commonly exhibit comparable strength increases. It is for this reason that space-vehicle research is concentrating on such materials as boron, beryllium, silicon carbide, carbon, and graphite. These are not only light and extremely strong, they are in many cases much stiffer than glass fiber and steel. This is an important factor because stiffness, rather than strength, is often the determining factor in design. The glass-fiber-reinforced plastic "House of the Future," for example, was designed for stiffness; strength was more than adequate.

Still more exciting from the technical viewpoint are the "whiskers," extremely fine single-crystal fibers of materials such as aluminum oxide (sapphire), whose strength and stiffness, measured in millions of pounds per square inch, approach the theoretical maximum attainable values.

Costs of most of these materials, ranging as high as several thousand dollars per pound, are at present completely prohibitive for building, and may continue to be; but projected costs of carbon and graphite and some of the carbides are not unreasonable, and these latter materials may soon become economically competitive elements of high-performance composites for building.

Composite Structures

We are not fully exploiting those composites that we have, such as glass-fiber-reinforced plastics, nor are we fully utilizing the possibilities of composite structures. For example, in a study carried on by two graduate students, it was demonstrated that in a 150-foot ribbed lamella vaulted roof, concrete ribs could be combined with diamond-shaped, double-curved, eight- by eighteen-foot reinforced-plastic infilling panels, one-tenth inch thick, capable of carrying the imposed wind and snow loads, and transmitting daylight into the interior, at a saving of one ton of weight per panel. The concrete ribs would provide the primary structure, and the panels would first act as forms and then as lightweight, light-transmitting secondary structures; concrete and plastic each making its best contribution to the whole.

The future for composite materials and composite structures—in which several functions are combined to attain superior performance —seems bright, but there are real problems that must be solved, as will be brought out later.

Systems
Systems Analysis

Much is heard today about systems, systems analysis, and the systems approach. The building fraternity is accused by systems-oriented space practitioners of not employing the systems approach. The building designers retort that they have always designed whole systems, that this is the essence of building design, and that buildings are complex systems involving the interaction of human and technical factors, whereas space systems are largely technological devices, complicated in detail, but simple in essence, upon which human whim and prejudice have little influence. The form and functioning of a jet plane or a lunar vehicle are determined almost entirely by technological requirements; the form and functioning of a building are dominated by human attitudes and requirements.

There is much truth in both viewpoints. The superb functioning of the lunar probes is the result of an extremely sophisticated, total systems approach in which the interrelationships of all the parts, including the human occupants of the capsule, are carefully studied and correlated in detail and in combination, and sophisticated mathematical procedures, employing the most advanced computer technology, are employed to optimize the resulting intricately related requirements. It is recognized that the human brain, superb computer that it is in many ways, is incapable of solving or keeping track of more than just a few simultaneously reacting factors at a time, and that mathematical tools must be relied upon to handle multifaceted problems.

To a limited extent, those systems tools are being utilized in building design. Structures are commonly analyzed and designed by computer; so are many mechanical subsystems. Traffic studies use mathematical models. There are other instances in which a start is being made. These usually have to do with portions of the whole problem.

The crucial part of the design of buildings and building complexes is the conceptual stage in which the many requirements of the owner (often badly formulated, only vaguely understood, and subject to change), economic factors, political and legal constraints, social influences, the site, and technological limitations of materials and equipment must somehow be put together into a coherent optimum design. This has not to any noticeable extent made use of the tools of formal systems analysis.

Perhaps the problem of building design, with all its complexities and human uncertainties, is not amenable to solution by systems analysis and synthesis. What seems to be true at the moment is that a combination of formal systems analysis and the empirical intuitive approach of the master designer must somehow be combined to the benefit of each. Having struggled through the mass of requirements and found a workable solution, it is difficult for the designer to divorce himself from it in his search for other possible solutions; furthermore, he may not have time. A considerably better approach is for him to set down the important relationships among the various aspects of his design problem in such a way that they can be handled by a computer, which can then provide many alternative solutions. Space allocation is one distinct possibility. The crucial point is that the computer, certainly as matters stand now, will not distinguish between acceptable and unacceptable solutions. This must be done by the human designer; his judgment and sense of fitness must lead to the decision. What the computer can do is provide him with more choices.

Parenthetically, there seems to be a curious contradiction in the attitudes of many architects toward the computer. It is dismissed as a mere mechanical tool, utterly incapable of doing the creative work of design and therefore of no consequence; at the same time, it is feared as a monster that will take over. The truth lies somewhere between, and it seems more likely that the computer, properly employed, holds the promise of relieving the architect of drudgery, freeing him for the creative tasks that are beyond the computer's capacity. But this will not happen until the profession makes a determined effort to understand and use the computer.

Complex Systems

One of the dangers in the manipulation of large complex systems is that decisions made and actions taken on the basis of even the best judgment and greatest experience can often be disastrously wrong. This is true because the human mind simply cannot comprehend or visualize the intricate, hidden, but extremely sensitive interactions that occur in such systems. Industrial dynamic analysis has shown that violent fluctuations in industrial processes may easily be brought about by the very steps taken to avoid them. A recently completed study of urban dynamics has shown that steps advocated to provide housing and to rescue the decaying central cities may easily hasten that decay and worsen the housing problem (see Chapter 5). It is entirely likely that the decisions taken to avoid unwanted situations in the design of large complex buildings may lead directly to similar situations. If systems analysis can help to avoid such errors, then designers should make every effort to avail themselves of this new technology.

Even a relatively simple example may illustrate. All too often when a lighting problem arises the obvious answer is to increase the level of illumination. Indeed, this idea has become so firmly fixed that code requirements have constantly been rising. What is actually wanted is better visibility, which may be only marginally related to light level. Contrast, glare, direction, and subtle psychological effects—the quality of the luminous environment—may be much more important than the level of illumination, which, in any event, gains nothing when raised beyond a certain point, and may bring about undesirable secondary effects such as overloading of the cooling system. Only by considering the total system and its interactions can an optimum answer be found.

Illumination is only one aspect of the whole subsystem of environmental control. Relatively little study has been made of the combined effects of light, sound, temperature, humidity, and other factors acting simultaneously, as they do, upon human beings. Each factor by itself has had extensive research, but the combination of all of them has had little (Figures 4–6).

Building Systems

When the many actual and proposed building systems are examined, it becomes evident that the vast majority, both here and abroad, concentrate on structure. As we all know, in today's buildings, structure is an important, but not overwhelmingly important, part of cost. Control of the internal environment—light, sound, temperature, humidity, odor, air movement—is a major factor, and the associated costs are high. Yet, the total systems approach seems all too often to be neglected. The structure and envelope are carried to the point of no return, and then environmental controls are added, sometimes, it seems, as a cosmetic unskillfully and perhaps futilely applied.

The whole system of structure and environmental controls must be considered together; it is their combined action that governs the quality of the environment. Simple changes in structure can often enormously affect the acoustical environment; advance consideration can simplify and increase the efficiency of mechanical systems, and illumination can be made effective or difficult by structure and envelope. The technology of integrated environmental control systems and the technology of coordinating such integrated systems with structure and envelope have not advanced far; much more must be done if efficient cost-reducing overall building systems are to be achieved.

It often happens that if all aspects of a system are not carefully considered together, seemingly insignificant details suddenly become important. I can give a simple example. In a large European industrialized housing project, it was noted that, by careful planning, a large precast floor panel could be lifted from the special truck by an efficient traveling tower crane and put into position on the eighth

Figure 4
Preassembly of reinforcing steel, radiant-
heating coils, and utility lines. Milan.

Figure 5
Heated casting bed for concrete wall
panels; foamed plastic insulation in
place. Milan.

Figure 6
Precast stairs.

floor in four minutes. To place the necessary additional reinforcing steel in the joint for structural continuity and to fill the joint with grout by hand took at least as long. Later finishing of the joints in the ceiling, and finishing of wall and partition joints with moldings or other devices, all took much additional time. In such schemes, it often turns out that the cost and time involved in handling the joints is a major factor. This is one reason why skepticism is often voiced respecting the superiority of industrialization over traditional field construction. Clearly, a total systems approach must find better answers if industrialization is to fulfill its promise.

A total systems approach must integrate the functions carried on in a building with structure, environmental controls, internal transport, utilities, and efficient construction, operation, and maintenance into an optimum solution. That it must also be visually acceptable goes without saying.

An example of what may happen when more than one aspect is taken into account may illustrate. In connection with a study of component construction in single-family detached dwellings, various modular sizes of wall and partition panels were compared with respect to flexibility of arrangement and cost. The conclusion reached was that many combinations were about equally acceptable and that the module should be based, not on structural requirements but first, upon the most efficient use of dimensions dictated by heating, plumbing, and kitchen equipment, and second, best panel sizes for windows and doors. Plain structural panels could be virtually any modular size that met the first two criteria. If these modular requirements were met, great flexibility in arrangement could result, that is, many efficient unstandardized plans could result from a small number of standard components.

In spite of all attempts to allow for every contingency, innovative technologies may run into unforeseen situations, with far-reaching consequences. When a gas heater exploded and blew out the corner panels halfway up in a panelized industrialized building, allowing collapse of that corner, the results reverberated throughout the industrialized building community. It was realized that although the design conformed to all code requirements, this particular contingency had not been anticipated. New regulations have meant extensive and expensive strengthening of existing panelized buildings and redesign of new ones. In one instance, the ensuing delay in construction resulted in the piling up of components at the fabricating shop and forced a disruptive temporary shutdown.

Constraints
Public Attitude

So far the discussion has centered mainly upon hard and soft technology; some aspects of physical structure, and some exploratory ideas respecting systems. What about constraints, those factors that may obstruct the further use of better technologies?

There are many, and some, at least, are rooted outside the building industry per se. For example, the intensive study phase of the late In-Cities Program of the Department of Housing and Urban Development brought to light some revealing public attitudes toward new and unfamiliar technologies. Typical reactions were "OK, so long as it's brick," "No Bucky Fuller," "No more concrete prisons," "We don't want skyscrapers," "No crackerboxes," "No ticky-tacky." These attitudes clearly reflect suspicion of, and reluctance to employ unfamiliar technologies, as well as distinct disenchantment with unsuccessful applications, of which there have been more than a few.

Still another aspect of the importance of public attitude is found in the decaying inner city, where inhabitants have forcefully proclaimed that "If we don't build it and control it, we will burn it."

These expressions, extreme though they may be, cannot be dismissed out of hand but must be taken into account as new or different housing technologies are explored.

Rehabilitation poses the greatest need, the greatest challenge, and has so far been the most stubbornly intractable field for new technologies. It entails the most direct contacts with the public. The most starry-eyed and unrealistic promises have been made and broken, and the greatest disappointments and suspicions have resulted. The technology immediately most useful here is probably the application of advanced, sophisticated, efficient organization and control, utilizing mainly traditional building methods, but introducing, as rapidly as possible, new technologies in centralized compact mechanical and electrical systems. Here, new ideas are urgently needed. For example, if new plumbing devices such as dishwashers, laundries, and garbage grinders simply result in overloading already inadequate sewerage systems, little progress will have been made. Ways of reducing water consumption and of more efficiently disposing of wastes are badly needed. This, of course, is not restricted to the ghetto.

Industrial Organization

An innovation that does not conform to established industrial patterns may have a difficult time in finding a home. For example, the wall panels for the Greater London Council described earlier were not made of only one material, nor was any one material preponderant. Their use therefore did not coincide with the primary interests of any one manufacturer, and no materials manufacturer took on either their development or fabrication. This was undertaken by a small entrepreneur engineering firm in London, which had to pull together the necessary design, development, and production skills on both sides of the Atlantic to accomplish this modest task. It required an arduous, protracted effort.

This example illustrates a situation that constitutes a serious constraint

on technological progress, when that progress calls for the coordination of materials, equipment, or both, into an efficient system or
subsystem. The composite panel of the Greater London Council, not
perfect by any means, was able to accomplish by the combined
behavior of its materials what no component by itself could do. More
advanced and sophisticated systems than the London panels are
feasible. They will call for coordinated production involving several
industries. But, when a composite component appears that calls for
closely coordinated production, we find that industry is not really
organized to carry on the necessary research, development, and
production.

This is understandable. The principals and research directors of a
materials-producing firm find their hands full with their own problems, with which they are at least familiar, without taking on completely new ones. If an innovative idea embodies equipment (such as
electrical or mechanical items) as well, the reluctance of manufacturers to participate is even greater.

There are other reasons for reluctance to proceed with systems
development that cuts across traditional industry lines. Collaboration
on the part of several industries, especially if they are closely related,
may expose the participants to action under the antitrust laws. If a
composite component comprises several items that are traditionally
handled by several crafts, unions may insist that representatives of
each craft be involved in the installation, even though they may not
actually be needed. Codes may not recognize the virtues of composite behavior and may, therefore, insist that the components be
considered separately, thereby negating the objective of the composite.

These impediments notwithstanding, some progress is being made.
There is research and development in composite materials and
combined systems and subsystems. It is not as rapid or extensive
as it should be.

Our system of bidding and awarding contracts can be a strong de-
terrent to innovation. When the requirement is for three or more
suppliers of a given item on an "or equal" basis, and an innovation
is produced by only one, that innovation can be effectively blocked.
Something else, such as a cost-benefit analysis, should be available
to allow single-source innovations to be employed.

Design-Production Organization

Innovative technology may not only affect materials and equipment
manufacture and the organization of the producing industries, it may
significantly affect the organization of the design and building processes. An example may illustrate.

Careful and detailed analyses lead to the conclusion that efficiency, economy, and speed in the construction of high-rise frame buildings can be achieved by constructing them from the top down: building the penthouses, roof and top floor at ground level, pushing them up, building the next lower floor under it, pushing that up, and so on, until the building is completed. The obvious advantages lie in the elimination of much of the traditional hoisting equipment and the convenience of doing work at ground level, where components can be delivered directly, workmen do not have to travel far, and the job can be readily enclosed to avoid delays due to weather. The push-up equipment, though rugged, is practicable. The technology is feasible; economy stems from efficient working conditions resulting in speed of erection.

Here the principal problem is organization and control. Before any given floor is pushed out of reach, everything that that floor will need for completion must either be built in or must at least be stored on it, except for small items that can be transported on the building's elevators. Extreme care in scheduling the job must be exercised to make sure that nothing is omitted that may later have to be hoisted a long way, thus defeating the whole system. Items calling for a long lead time, such as elevator equipment that must be installed at the very beginning, may have to be ordered long before the design of the building is finished. This, in turn, means that the builder must be brought in early in the sequence, so that commitments can be made as soon as possible. To achieve the benefits of this particular new technology may, therefore, call for a revision of the usual design-bid-build sequence and certainly calls for much more sophisticated organization and control of construction than are ordinarily found.

Management Technology

The more closely the new and advanced building technologies are examined, the clearer it becomes that they demand sophistication in the technology of management, organization, and project control. It has often been remarked that the successful European industrialized systems are the well-organized and managed ones. There is no technical magic in any of them that gives a distinct lead over the others. Economics and cost reductions are achieved mainly by efficiency and speed, not by some mysterious low-cost material. Speed calls for close coordination from the very inception of the project; great care must be taken to foresee all contingencies so as to forestall expensive and time-consuming changes, orders must be given for items requiring long lead times, and the design-production schedule must be carefully worked out, showing the sequence of steps and interdependencies. Only a well-coordinated and managed team, representing all aspects of design and production, can accomplish this.

Obviously, such careful coordination and control can be and has been applied to traditional construction with most salutary results. It has been claimed that this emphasis on organization, management, and control is really the only "new" technology needed in building, and that all else is secondary. While this is patently an exaggeration, it does emphasize the importance of complete control. No matter where this kind of managerial ability comes from—traditional architects, the building fraternity, engineers, or elsewhere—the individual with the capacity will fill the position. As one architectural dean remarked, the man with managerial ability, no matter what his background, will be the architect. Hopefully, he will be sensitive to and sympathetic with good design.

Prediction

Any innovation entails at least some uncertainty respecting its expected performance. It does not have an extensive proved history, therefore, its long-time behavior is unknown, and everyone waits for someone else to try it first.

Here is one of the most difficult and urgent technological problems. For many purposes, there are no short-time tests that will reliably predict long-time behavior. This is particularly true of weathering, where the problem is compounded, first, by insufficient knowledge respecting the actual microclimate surrounding a given building; second, the complex physical and chemical interaction of the constituents of the microclimate upon the behavior of building materials; and, third, the lack of generally available knowledge concerning the actual behavior of buildings under the many diverse conditions to which they are subjected. We tend to build our buildings and forget them.

The same situation is true of many other aspects of building behavior. Although a given building's maintenance department may have a good idea of what ails it and what has to be done to keep it going, systematic study of such information is generally lacking, and, consequently, it is not easy to devise ways of predicting behavior because the actual conditions are not clearly understood.

This is not to decry the efforts of such organization as the American Society for Testing and Materials (ASTM) and the American National Standards Institute (ANSI). Their test methods and standards provide the basis upon which the building industry largely depends for control of the quality of its materials and components. However, these organizations are the first to recognize that the basic information upon which their tests and standards depend is far from complete, especially in the areas of prediction of long-time behavior from short-time tests. The building fraternity must assist in providing that understanding.

It is a peculiar situation, to say the least, that the very people who depend most upon ASTM and ANSI standards for building components participate very little in preparing them. They are written mostly by materials specialists rather than by the architects and engineers who specify them and, inevitably, reflect the viewpoints of the materials specialists. This is not the fault of ASTM and ANSI; they have long been vainly trying to enlist the active participation of the designers in drawing up those standards. As advanced technology moves more and more in the direction of industrialization and the total-systems concept, it is even more imperative that the designers and producers of buildings become actively engaged in drawing up the basic standards that govern them. The agencies are there; they need only to be employed.

Evaluation and Certification of Innovation

In the United States there is no established procedure for evaluating and certifying technological innovations in building materials or components. True, as already stated, the ASTM and the ANSI have many widely employed test methods and specifications, and one prominent laboratory issues labels respecting degrees of fire resistance, but none of these constitutes complete evaluation of a new component.

As matters stand, if a major manufacturer brings out an innovative item and tests it in his own laboratories, the results are suspected of being biased. A developer of a new idea who wants to obtain independent tests must find a commercial laboratory, a university experiment station, or some similar testing agency and have such tests run as may appear to be applicable. In any event, when the tests are finished and the report is in, it is quite likely to be met with considerable skepticism. Bias in the selection, conduct, or interpretation of the tests is likely to be suspected, or the testing agency itself may either be unknown to or deemed incompetent by architects, engineers, building officials, and other interested parties. The result is that the innovator has a hard time getting his idea evaluated and accepted. Progress is often agonizingly slow, and a good idea may die before it can prove itself.

This problem has been recognized in Europe, and many countries have set up a system of evaluation and certification patterned after the original French agrément procedure. A board of experienced and knowledgeable people, drawn from government and nongovernment backgrounds, reviews carefully all innovative ideas brought before it, examines the supporting evidence, prescribes what tests, if any, shall be run, examines the results, and, drawing upon the experience of its members, issues a certificate setting forth its findings and judgment respecting the item, how it may be employed and how it may be expected to behave in use. The sponsor of the innovative idea is free to use his certificate in advertising and when approaching architects, engineers, building officials, builders, financial people, owners, and any others. By and large, the agrément boards have established themselves so well that their certificates are accepted by the building fraternity and by officials as impartial expert evaluations. In France, where buildings must be guaranteed by designers and builders for ten years instead of one, insurance companies frequently demand an agrément certificate for any new components and will not insure unless it is forthcoming.

The agrément system as practiced in Europe may or may not be directly transplantable to the United States, but some such central, generally accepted agency could be extremely beneficial in breaking down the existing barriers to the adoption of innovative technologies.

Performance Codes and Specifications

In an era of rapid technological development, codes and specifications based upon detailed descriptions of how to build can seriously hamper progress, whereas a carefully reasoned statement of objectives or performance can be a stimulus to innovation. Much is heard about performance, and rightly so, but the accompanying problems must be recognized.

First comes the question of what performance is wanted. Clear, hard, and deep thinking is needed to make certain that the performance called for will result in a building that will actually behave as wanted.

It is not enough merely to specify performance, it must also be possible to evaluate it, to see if a component actually behaves as it should. This calls for a clear understanding of what is to be evaluated and may demand extremely sophisticated evaluative techniques. In many instances, these have not been developed.

When applied to building codes, officials must be much more sophisticated and knowledgeable about the performance to be expected. It is much harder to determine whether a given design will meet a two-hour fire requirement than to see if it calls for eight inches of brick.

Designers must assume much greater responsibility for their designs, along with the freedom that design based on performance may allow them. They cannot hide behind a code that tells them they must build thus and so.

These responsibilities and problems notwithstanding, the objective of basing design upon performance is inherently sound and can provide much of the impetus toward technological innovation.

Labor

This discussion would be incomplete without some reference to labor, but this is an area in which such strident claims and counterclaims, accusations, and assertions with no discernible solid foundations are made, and the field is so full of conflicting statistics, that one hesitates even to touch upon it. Builders vociferously point to the shortage of skilled labor, and labor equally vociferously points out that the unemployment rate in the building trades is twice that in manufacturing, and both are right, because of fluctuations in building activity.

It is undoubtedly true that labor wage rates in building have risen much faster than costs of materials and equipment, but labor insists that annual average take-home pay is not out of line. The craft-union type of organization does not fit the trends toward industrialization, offsite fabrication, and components combining several materials and functions, but organized labor claims that it can and will accommodate to this trend. The ultimate power of the locals to determine local working conditions does not accord with building technologies that depend upon broad regional or national application. Labor says it can conform.

Traditional skills and the long apprenticeships associated with them may not be applicable. One large-scale European industrialized housing producer prefers to start with unskilled labor; he can train operatives in the simple manipulations needed in short order, and they need not unlearn anything. Building agencies in Eastern Europe say that erection requires not more than 25 percent skilled labor, the rest can be unskilled. Clearly, the training programs for new technologies need to be examined. Shortages of the right kind of manpower may yet be the most serious constraint and at the same time the most powerful impetus toward new technologies.

Government Policies

Government policy strongly affects building and building technology both directly and indirectly. Most advanced technologies require fairly heavy investment in plant, whether fixed or movable. This, in turn, requires at least a reasonably even production schedule, but building is subject to fluctuations caused not only by weather but by economic and political factors beyond its control. Industry is going to be wary of investing in plant that may stand idle. To appreciate the basis for such caution, one need only recall the disastrous drop in housing starts caused by the 1966 and 1969 credit squeezes.

The announced federal government goal of an additional 600,000 dwelling units per year for ten years, to be superimposed upon existing housing starts, can be either a vastly unsettling or a stabilizing influence upon the building industry. It can, therefore, either stimulate or stifle innovative technology. If the government program is carefully planned and phased into overall building, it can help to fill in the gaps, smooth out the fluctuations, and lend stability; if it is not, it can accentuate the existing swings and defeat its own purpose. Here is a staggering problem in dynamic analysis.

Considerable sums will be needed for research and development to bring existing and potential technology to bear on the production of 600,000 units per year, a figure which will be closer to 800,000 or 1,000,000 per year when the inevitable delays and lead times needed to gear up production are considered. While private industry can and will absorb much of this cost if there is an assured, steady market, as indicated above, some of the developmental costs will

Research

have to be borne by government, just as it has assumed those costs in other fields such as space exploration and national defense.

To help find answers to the unsolved problems of technology and its constraints will require research. The building field is notorious for its uneven, relatively low level of research. Research is extensive in materials and equipment but spotty or nonexistent in areas that have to do with the total building, its functional and physical behavior, design as a total system, and other aspects not directly related to component manufacture.

Dissemination of information respecting research is equally unsatisfactory. There is no central agency that collects information respecting all research, digests it, and makes it available to the field. The result is that we do not really know what is going on, where work is being done, and what the gaps are.

Our government efforts at building research are small and scattered. European governments, whose countries have much smaller building programs than ours, have centralized building research agencies with larger budgets than ours. One Japanese building firm has a larger annual research budget than the principal United States government agency carrying on building research.

This is not a plea for all research to be carried on by the United States government, but it is notable that the very large research programs that have made possible the advances in space, defense, and agriculture, to mention only a few areas, have been supported by government funds. In those important areas that do not justify privately supported research, government should step in. There should be a well-organized central research facility that carries on in-house research, collects and disseminates research information, and supports well-coordinated research at universities, private research agencies, in appropriate industrial facilities, and by other government agencies. It can assist in the work of standard-setting and code-writing organizations. It should in short, act as a focal point for the encouragement of research, without itself preempting the field.

From the foregoing discussion it should be clear that building technology is uneven, relatively advanced in structures and envelope, but still requiring considerable improvements in integration of all systems and subsystems, especially the close coordination of all aspects of environmental control with structure. In a general way, the routes that should be taken for improvement are discernible, but the advances possible are not yet off-the-shelf items. They will require much research and development before they are ready to incorporate into buildings.

Building technology is not independent of nontechnological constraints rooted in social, economic, and political factors; it is strongly sensitive to and deeply influenced by them. Only if those constraints are taken into account can building technology make its full contribution. The full potentialities will not be realized unless all segments of the building field are determined to find solutions and put them to use. No one segment alone can accomplish it

2
Constraints

John F. Collins

When I conceived of viewing housing as a production process, as a means of developing sensible policies to encourage the adoption of technology in housing, I noted that there were two ways to generate improvement and efficiency. The first was to change the relationship of inputs (capital, labor, and materials), while the second was to determine the constraints which operate on the production process and develop ways and means of relaxing these constraints so as to effect an increase in output and a decrease in cost.

I discarded the first, a purely technological view of the problem, as being inadequate because housing is much less a problem of technology than it is a social process. Many people ask why we can employ technological resources and systems analysis to get us to the moon in a relatively short period of time and cannot similarly apply these resources to the problem of efficiently housing the people of the United States.

The constraints on the moon flight were almost exclusively resource constraints: money and trained personnel. Economists have known for a long time that an increase of resources in a particular area will relatively quickly develop the required technologically competent people to earn the high wages.

Improvements in the housing process do not depend on the commitment of resources alone. They depend on the ability of the government to provide *sufficient incentives* along with the required resources to encourage the people who comprise the political and social institutions, whose behavior constrains efficient housing, to change their actions to those which will enhance efficient housing development.

Housing Development: Constraints and Incentives

Analysis of housing must proceed from the constraints that impede the production of low-cost housing and inhibit the development and application of technology to improve efficiency. These constraints not only impede production and inhibit technological progress, but they also account for the substantial variability of the costs of various aspects of the housing process because of their local character. These constraints include, but are not limited to:
1. Industrial organization of the housing industry
2. The inability to interpret the preferences and behavior of home users
3. The multiplicity of ownership of available sites
4. The inability of the design professions to deal with building technology on a performance basis
5. The inefficiency of the marketplace
6. Federal and local government rules and regulations
7. Environmental considerations

Presented to the 1970 session. John F. Collins is Consulting Professor of Urban Affairs, Massachusetts Institute of Technology, and former mayor of Boston.

8. Restrictive work practices
9. Financing

Industrial Organization of the
Housing Industry

Some of these constraints are more readily relaxed than others, but
no changes happen accidentally. Either the natural processes of
economic growth provide appropriate incentives for the industry
to change its methods, or these incentives must be implanted from
outside. The appropriate incentives do not exist at present, so it falls
to the national government, particularly to HUD, to formulate and
implement an appropriate incentive system. In place of disincentives
like the relatively low returns at high risks that now face potential
mortgage lenders for low-income ghetto housing, the long pay-out
periods, the uncertain and highly cyclical demands for construction:
a set of positive incentives to progress is the order of the day.

The inability of the housing industry as presently organized to develop, modify, and accept for regular use sensible technological innovations is limited by the scarcity of trained managers who elect housing
as a career. The high level of instability in the construction industry in
general and in the housing industry in particular is derived directly
from the use of monetary as opposed to financial policy as a means
of regulating the economy. This high level of instability has made it
necessary for firms to minimize their fixed overhead with the obvious
consequence that little or no technical staff capability has been developed in the industry, except where the demand for housing has
been somewhat isolated on an individual or regional basis.

Most building systems derive economies when the scale of the project itself is large (Figure 1). It would appear that unless a project
consists of four or more structures, conventional construction is likely
to be no more expensive than systems construction. Since most
home builders erect low-rise housing, their actions are obviously
prudent and sensible.

The few large-scale home builders who have derived economies of
scale have done so as a result of their ability to purchase the required
inputs for housing at low costs and to schedule the delivery and
allocation of resources on the job in as efficient a manner as possible.
These firms, such as Ryan Homes, Levitt, Bob Schmitt Homes, and
others, derive managerial, as opposed to production, economy. Many
home builders, for the aforementioned reasons, are unable to obtain
these savings.

What should concern us is not so much the present organization of
the construction industry, but its likely future organization as a result
of having to satisfy the new housing needs of the American city. It is
clear in this respect that much of the new housing which will be built
in urban areas will be higher rather than lower in density, and in addition is likely, on the basis of cost considerations alone, to be high-

Figure 1
"Most building systems derive economies
when the scale of the project itself is
large." Bison Wall Frame Flats at Druids
Heath, Bells Lane, Birmingham, England.
Courtesy of Concrete Limited.

rise. High-rise technologies lend themselves nicely to the use of building systems and, in fact, experiences in other countries clearly show that systems may be obtained where they are employed for these purposes.

What then must be asked is whether the present organization of the industry is capable of accepting technological innovation and whether or not it is likely that these innovations will develop the desired result of low-cost construction. At present all the incentives for efficient performance in this business have rested with the developers, and they have been largely insulated against high costs, and in fact, in a large part, have been encouraged to spend the maximum mortgagable amount as a result of the fee structure employed by the Department of Housing and Urban Development. It is clear that one of the first serious examinations of the present systems of incentives and disincentives should occur with respect to the role of the developer.

In no sense do I mean to minimize the importance of this responsibility, nor to suggest that developers should not be well compensated. What I mean is that the system for compensation of developers should not impose on them incentives which are in the absolute worst interest of the public at large.

The appeal of the mobile home is its low cost, and the prevalence of such homes is evidence of the fact that if a low-cost alternative is available, the market will accept it. This does not mean, however, that low-cost housing should be confined to low-income groups. What it does mean is that the public at large should have the opportunity to benefit from cost saving and to economize on housing as they see fit. The present organization of the housing industry militates, to some extent, against heterogeneous demand for housing in a particular area. High-cost housing may let in many middle- or upper-income persons. Most private development reflects the general pattern of income segregation in housing. There must be an incentive developed to insure that developers do not continue this practice when it may be avoidable. At present, there are few opportunities for profitable development on industrialized building systems. The experience of the prefabrication industry over the past several years illustrates this in their low rates of return. Efficient industrialization of housing requires large and continuous production. At present, the market is not yet organized to encourage firms to make investments in these systems. It is clear that, unless firms begin to make investments in these systems, national housing goals will not be satisfied. So the question then becomes, "How and in what way can an incentive plan be developed which will encourage firms to invest in these systems?" The behavior of the members of most large organizations suggests that if risks (i.e., the level of uncertainty associated with acceptance of a system production) were minimized, the members might be interested in sponsoring investments. A measure of business risk insurance is needed, unless the profit opportunities in this area become more clearly indicated.

The Inability to Interpret the Preferences and Behavior of Home Users

Housing developers are at a complete loss when asked to comment on the tradeoffs perceived by potential housing consumers between an amenity, or group of amenties, and lower or higher rental levels. No well-established procedure for determining the preferences of potential inhabitants of housing exists. There are several reasons for this.

First, anybody who has built low-cost housing has had no trouble renting it; this is a result of the condition of the housing stock in American urban areas. What is clean and new will be very highly valued over that which is filthy and old. In the future, however, it will be very important to be able to make these determinations sensibly, as the features that are or are not included in housing will determine its rental level on the one hand and the cost to the community which provides public services on the other. In this respect, what I am suggesting is that the users of housing are *not only* the residents of the units themselves, but also the neighbors and other citizens of the community at large.

User analysis then should include the mechanisms for evaluating individual demands as well as the means of understanding how and in what way the cost of community opportunity can be affected by the decision of the developer. With respect to the former, the present practice of not reimbursing developers for analyses of this type should be discontinued and a mechanism for performing these analyses in particular market areas should be developed. Under no circumstances, do I mean to suggest that wholesale interviewing should begin immediately. There are innumerable technical difficulties associated with obtaining useful information of this type and these must be dealt with before any regular program can be sponsored.

Another very important aspect of this constraint is the present inability to involve useful members of the community in the management and operation of real estate and construction. There is a shortage of skilled persons from the various minority groups of concern to policymakers who have the required training to become contractors, developers, or real-estate managers. Some formal mechanism is necessary here in order to involve them meaningfully in the process. Large developers and contractors should be encouraged, as some have already done on a regular basis, to train ghetto residents in these skills.

The Multiplicity of Ownership of Available Sites

The scarcity and multiplicity of ownership of available sites for large-scale industrialized housing projects imposes a substantial constraint on the willingness of anyone to invest heavily in industrialized housing factories. For efficient operation, a building-systems factory must be able to produce several thousand units per year. Few American cities have available appropriately zoned sites for a production schedule sufficient to permit the operator of the factory to write down his investment. As a result, when a building system is considered for a particular project, frequently the entire fixed cost is allocated to the single project with the obvious consequence that the building system appears to be more expensive than conventional construction. If large-scale housing is to be developed in American cities, much of the speculative uncertainty associated with land must be eliminated. Here, either the federal or state governments will have to play a role, for only they can offer a sufficient commitment to a prospective housing-factory builder that a given number of sites will be available over a given time period.

The Inefficiency of the Marketplace

From the standpoint of industrialized housing, the marketplace is inefficient in that demand in the United States is not homogeneous. Ideally, from the standpoint of cost minimization, everyone should be willing to live in the same type of structure. This would promote the maximum level of purchasing economies and technological efficiencies. It is completely clear, however, that people wish to individualize their homes, and unless cost savings which could be offered to them were enormous, it is highly unlikely that this individualization would be sacrificed.

Additionally, the demand for housing is structurally diverse in that the requirements of young persons differ from the elderly, those of large families differ from small, and certain ethnic groups may wish special features to be included in the structure itself. By the time one gets through chopping up the housing market into all its relevant pieces, one finds that the number of housing units in demand in any particular metropolitan area for which any given technology is applicable may be below the minimum efficient size for a production facility.

The building economists need not worry about this problem as they can legislate the available housing stock. Once again, some incentive must be developed to encourage people to give up perhaps structural individuality. An exchange for individualized interiors might provide a sufficient incentive, but low cost is more likely to effect a behavior change.

Other Constraints

The remaining constraints, government rules and regulations, environmental considerations, restrictive work practices, and financial institutions have been discussed elsewhere by myself and others concerned with the housing process. Most of these problems seem to be working themselves out.

Zachry system. Monolithic unit made of heavyweight boxes stacked against a slip-formed end wall. Built for the San Antonio Hemisfair, this was a first and successful try at industrialization by an American heavy-construction firm. Photo by Tell-Pics, San Antonio.

Labor unions in many places have a commitment to participation in improving the efficiency of the housing process. Here, the incentive is more jobs and higher wages. Few union men in construction are unemployed in America today. A substantial increase in the number of housing units built, especially when many of them will be constructed in urban areas, will increase union membership and union wages far beyond any time loss as a result of productivity changes.

The Department of Housing and Urban Development has begun to encourage communities to shift to performance codes. If they are intelligently developed, these will substantially alleviate many of the difficulties created by local rules. Environmental considerations both add to and decrease the cost of housing. Pollution control provides an example of the former, while increased densities are an example of the latter. People's standards for environmental quality change their preferences. Where it is important to house low-income families, zoning changes can be effected. Where there is hostility to the persons of low-income families, densities will not be reduced without changes in the law.

The last constraint with which I deal is the financing of the proposed housing construction. Low-income families have lately been unable to live in new housing in urban areas, except when there was a commitment to produce cheap housing, such as the New York tenements that provide immigrant and worker housing. At present, there is no incentive to build housing which low-income families can afford unless the development is accompanied by some form of subsidy. Even with efficient operation of building systems, subsidy will be required. If it is a matter of public policy to house low-income families in new housing, then subsidies will have to be substantially increased in order to encourage the development of a large number of units. Technology can pay part of the subsidy bill, but it can't pay all of it. Efficient assimilation of technology will require the development of incentives which must extend beyond the construction industry itself. Improvements must focus on the relationships of all the costs of the housing process, and a system of incentives must be similarly directed.

3
Housing Research in the Federal Government

Thomas F. Rogers

Prior to joining the Mitre Corporation, I had been the Director of Research in the Department of Housing and Urban Development (HUD) for two years. Recounting my experiences as a director of HUD is one of the more useful ways by which I can attempt to pass on to you some of the observations which I made while in that office.

First, I would like to give some of the history of research and development (R&D) at HUD, and then make some general observations. I shall describe the R&D situation that existed immediately prior to mid-1967, when I joined the Department. I shall then illustrate some of the initial steps which we took within the department to relate some of the antecedent programs to the now large general research programs within HUD. I shall also outline, in comments on a few specific projects, some of the more important lessons which were learned. Then, I would like to talk about the most recent happenings. Finally, I shall make some projections or estimates for the future. These latter, of course, since I am no longer with the Department of Housing and Urban Development, are personal opinions only.

Prior to mid-1967, there was very little of what most of the professional world would describe as sound research and development activities within HUD. Not that there weren't activities of a technical nature, but they were very small, indeed, and usually not very closely managed by professional R&D personnel. The reason for this can only be seen, in my view, through observing the state of research and development in many of the domestic departments and agencies of the federal government as a whole. By this, I would include, certainly, much of the Department of Health, Education, and Welfare, the Department of Labor, the Post Office, the Department of Transportation, and so on. Some two to three years ago, by far the vast bulk of professional scientific and technical attention in this country was directed first to commerce and industry, and then to agriculture, defense, space, nuclear energy, and medicine. Some areas which had received relatively little useful attention were those such as housing, transportation, labor, delivery of the mail, and delivery of medical services.

HUD, you will recall, was formed from many individual agencies only four short years ago, and it did not differ in its understanding and support of R&D from most of the other domestic agencies. Whether or not this is an acceptable state of national affairs — in my view, it certainly is not—is something that the country has been discussing for the past several years as a part of our growing concern over our national goals and national priorities. In the case of housing and urban development, the situation was further complicated by a great ignorance concerning the activities, applications, and value

Presented to the 1969 session. Thomas F. Rogers is Vice-President for Urban Affairs, Mitre Corporation.

of housing-related research and development by Congress, by the housing industry, and by the department itself. The department, by and large, was (and still is) a financially oriented organization. Except for the public housing program, it is not required to build houses; rather, it is required to encourage others to build houses — a truly significant difference.

The housing industry (and others attending this summer session can speak to this matter more eloquently than I) was, and to a very great extent still is, quite fragmented—again, relative to other industries with which I am familiar. Its R&D activities were, to a good first approximation, materials oriented, i.e., the "brick people" were learning to make better bricks and to make them less expensively; the "glass people" were learning to make better and less expensive glass, and so on. There was very little expressed interest in looking at entire housing systems and subsystems. In fact, there was more than a little apprehension on the part of the materials and components people that, if something new and useful were invented, and they did not invent and control it, they might find themselves at a competitive disadvantage; they did not support those broad R&D activities that were addressed specifically to increasing the volume and decreasing the cost of housing where this implied unconventional methods and solutions. This atmosphere is gradually dissipating, but it was extremely influential in the R&D area some three years ago, and even a year ago.

This situation, coupled with the fact that on the national scale of things, housing for low- and moderate-income families was not listed very highly as a priority, resulted in Congress not giving much attention to sophisticated R&D arguments and activities in the housing field. (One further observation should perhaps be mentioned. When, in my past positions, I have spoken to people in Congress and elsewhere about rockets, or satellites, or electronic memory devices, oftentimes the eyes of many of my listeners would glaze over—but not so in housing. *Everybody*, seemingly, knows how to build a house; *everybody*, seemingly, is quite experienced in this particular field.)

Three years ago, this very new department was extremely sensitive — in my view, overly sensitive — to extradepartmental interests, observations, and concerns, and this sensitivity greatly influenced, and even inhibited, the type, scope, and pace of R&D activities it conducted. Without any exaggeration, I would say that, except for Professor Robert Wood, director of the Harvard-MIT Joint Center for Urban Studies,* who was then the undersecretary of the department, there was hardly anyone in the department on the assistant secretary or staff level, in Washington or in the regional offices, who was usefully conversant with either the R&D "universe" or such

---

*Now President of the University of Massachusetts—eds.

sophisticated industries as electronics, space, etc. Some of the
people then had been close to the technical community and had
some appreciation of the work that could and should go on, but in
this federal department, where employees are numbered in the tens
of thousands and where the budget is at a level of several billions of
dollars per year, you could literally count, on the fingers of one hand,
the people who had useful professional research and development experience — and have a few fingers left over. There was no
PPBS (Planning-Programming-Budgeting System) or anything approaching the type of policy, documentation, and atmosphere that
this would imply in a department. To this point in time, in practically
every state government, and in, perhaps, almost every city government I can think of, there is a lack of commitment to the objective
and quantitative definition of socially and politically related goals; a
lack of definition of the specific problems that inhibit the attainment
of these goals; a lack of the measurement of individual program
efficiency and effectiveness in terms of its output. In the domestic
departments and at state and local government levels, by far the
greater attention is placed on studies and measures of program input: how many people are working at a certain type of activity, how
much money is going into it, how much time is spent on it — rather
than paying explicit attention to how efficiently and effectively
their stated operational goals were being met by turning (dollars
times people) into goods and services.

There were no general research appropriations in the department;
activities concerned with study and innovation were funded under
congressional authorizations which were quite specific in nature,
and there were no funds available to the department to do the
things which *it* thought were important in light of its operational
program deficiencies and difficulties. There were a number of so-
called "Demonstration Programs": the Urban Renewal Demonstration Program; the Comprehensive Metropolitan Area Planning
Demonstration Program; the Federal Housing Administration
Technical Studies Program; the F.H.A. Experimental Mortgage
Insurance Program, etc. I mention these, particularly, because all
of these bear on housing to a greater or lesser extent. There were
some other demonstration programs in the department dealing
with open land, transportation, and so on.

Let me, for a moment, speak of the word "demonstration," which I
found to be a most frustrating word to live with — as I'm sure many
of the people in the department and elsewhere also came to appreciate. There were research and development activities in the
housing field sponsored by the federal government in the early
1960s. However, for reasons upon which I can only speculate, but
which I believe to be the ones that I touched upon earlier, those
activities stopped after two to three years. In the interim, some
people who were quite perceptive and quite positively and honestly

motivated, quite innovation-minded, began to appreciate that the urban scene in general, and the housing field in particular, was seriously limited in knowledge, in experience, in technique, in analysis, in components, etc. Knowing, therefore, that R&D did have to go on, they were able to convince Congress to support certain "demonstration" activities. When carried through to successful completion, such activities could be expected to act as exemplary activities for others in the housing field. Now, in the political world, I am informed that "something beats nothing every time" — or, in mathematical terms, the ratio of something to nothing is infinite. By the time I arrived at HUD, though, I was faced with having to cope with an exasperating atmosphere and type of activity that had built up around the word "demonstration," and which had resulted in the demonstration programs yielding little of value or relevance to the important problems of the department. The reason for this is as follows: If you do try to do something outside of the regular operating programs then, by definition, it *must* be innovative. Now, if you try to do something that has not been done before, there is a finite likelihood that it will not work out entirely as you had expected. However, if you undertake to conduct a "demonstration," and the funds have been obtained so as to "demonstrate" something which is truly innovative and potentially helpful, what do you do when that project begins to produce unexpected effects or nonuseful results? It was a disconcerting thing to watch bright, honest people attempting to grapple with the very difficult situations arising in this context. Suffice it to say that I spent a great deal of my time trying to understand this very simple matter of the inherent incongruity of attempting to accomplish professional R&D objectives through the use of "demonstration" programs and then, when they failed, to try and turn things about.

A final comment concerning "demonstration": in the department, program funds were given out on the basis of grants, and this is a most inefficient and ineffective way of enlisting the brains and talents of the country to solve other than basic research problems. This administrative procedure related to the lack of a departmental PPBS structure and, consequently, to a lack of problem definition and priority.

Aside from "demonstration," there was another key word: "evaluation." One of the most important areas of activity in which scientists and engineers can learn how to assist the government is that of learning how to measure the efficiency and the effectiveness of various governmental programs, and how to put what they learned— the data, the experience, the hypotheses, the analyses, etc. — before the elected and appointed officials at the federal, state and local levels in a form that can assist these officials to make the evaluations which their positions require of them. I found, though, that the department was funding scientists, engineers, and other professionals to examine certain questions, and then having these professionals, on the basis of that expenditure and their professional judgment, returning to the department and saying: "We've made the following analysis, or we've made the following measurement. This is what we've found, and these are the conclusions that can be drawn from it—*and*, in our judgment, therefore you ought to 're-organize the whole department,' or 'reorganize the executive branch,' or 'stop the war,' or 'decrease the taxes' or 'increase the taxes'," etc., etc. I feel sure that it came as a shock to some of these men who would so conduct themselves to learn that I expected them to restrict themselves to speak as scientists and as engineers in their capacity as departmental contractors. There now exists a much better understanding of this matter than there was a few years ago.

I would add one more thing. Within the department some three years ago, there was essentially a complete lack of appreciation of the cost in time, dollars, and professional effort required to conduct major, useful R&D programs. There was a general understanding that, if the country found that it had been required to spend three billion dollars a year for some ten years to reach its goal of going to the moon, and if it were trying to improve an entire major industry's efficiency and effectiveness in order to provide housing for the nation's lower-income families, but to do this latter only a few million dollars a year were being spent—then, this latter effort probably was "off the pace" by two or three orders of magnitude. Again, the people in the department, not having had the experience of having to deal with very large R&D programs, just had little useful appreciation of the methods that would have to be used, the skills employed, and the tremendous amount of money, talent, and time required to solve major and complex national problems.

HUD adopted a competitive process and began announcing, in professional terms, those problem areas that it judged to be the most important. They asked all the architectural, scientific, and engineering talents in the country to respond. As far as the universities are concerned, a balanced judging among many of the universities and colleges in addressing more basic and longer-range problems was originated. Within the department we reorganized to bring R&D more fully to the attention of the assistant secretaries. The department inaugurated PPBS activities. (The R&D people worked at least as hard at this as any other group in HUD, and found out that it was a terribly difficult thing to do—much more difficult than in defense and in space; one knows more or less "where the moon is," but articulating the goals of the Urban Renewal Program in objective and quantitative terms is a much more difficult task, indeed.) Congress was asked for a general research appropriation; for the position of an assistant secretary of Research and Development; and, also, for longer time extensions for R&D contracts. All these requests were granted. HUD was made a member of the Federal Council, the preeminent group of people within the federal government who speak for R&D with the President's Special Advisor on R&D. The department then began to work with other departments and agencies on R&D matters quite consistently—particularly Commerce, Defense, and Agriculture. HUD worked with the Kaiser Committee and the Douglas Commission and contracted with the National Academies of Science and Engineering to think hard about its R&D needs and to advise it about the strategies that might be adopted in trying to enlist the scientific and engineering communities in the universities and industry to the solution of its problems.

Let me mention a few features of some of the projects which resulted from these efforts and were carried out under the various "demonstration" programs:

First, "rehabilitation"—more specifically, the "Instant Rehabilitation" Project conducted in New York City, widely publicized as "instant rehabilitation." This project's developmental stage culminated in a 48-hour period during which the tops of some "old law" tenements on the Lower East Side were cut open, kitchen-bathroom "core units" were inserted down through this opening, and the buildings generally were rehabilitated up to quite an acceptable level of physical quality.

We learned two or three important things in carrying out and reviewing that project. One is that it is very difficult to undertake anything innovative that is truly public in a large city; also, that it is very difficult to do anything rapidly. Yet, in this project, the department was trying to show that something innovative could be done publicly, in a city, in 48 hours!

The travail that the people in the department went through to prepare for, to conduct, and to report upon that project was almost unbelievable. For instance, while the R&D costs involved were quite reasonable—and, in my judgment, it is remarkable how much was done with the amount of money that was spent—to many people in the department the costs were unbelievably large, since they had never been involved in spending a few million dollars on a single research project.

Another part that was not fully appreciated within the department and in the housing industry is that applied research and development projects are not undertaken to demonstrate what already has been done—things that are clearly and demonstrably in hand—but, rather, to verify (you trust) useful working hypotheses. Oftentimes, therefore, in the verification process one is bound to be surprised. The people conducting this project were surprised at times, and they were then criticized for not having been sufficiently prescient to have anticipated these surprising occurrences beforehand.

The Project also introduced me to the hazards of conducting experiments in the only laboratory that makes sense in the urban field—the city itself. The hazard is simply that of the expressed views of the local population: from the people in the actual physical area of the experiment all the way up to, and including, "city hall"—elected and appointed officials, industry, commerce, and so on.

For instance, one of the things that I did not understand then, and frankly, still do not appreciate, is that there is a persuasive group of people in New York City who believe that the rehabilitation of some of the city's older buildings simply is not admissible activity—it just should *not* be done. Many of them, therefore, found it impossible to view this experiment as exactly that: an experiment—a way of finding out what it would cost and a way of obtaining confidence about the advantages and limitations of various techniques. They couldn't help but view this professional activity as an "opening wedge" into doing something that could, eventually, take place on a major scale—something that they frankly and honestly believed should not be done. It was literally impossible for some of these people, emotionally, and perhaps intellectually, to stand off and look at an experiment in this area objectively—they just couldn't do it. Unfortunately, some of these people were responsible, in many important ways, for the conduct of the experiment. Suffice it to say that when the experimental-developmental activities were completed, the local newspapers reported that the experiment had failed because it encountered costs that were "too high." The facts, though, do not square with this view, since a proper distinction had not been made between the cost of eventually rehabilitating any buildings in large volumes in this fashion from the cost of conducting this first novel development-test.

There was then, and to some extent there still is, a lack of appreciation of the fact that important and sound research and development activities and development tests simply cost a great deal of money. The hand-built automobile that is the prototype for production in Detroit is made at a price that very few of us could afford. The same holds true for the color television set that is developed in the electronics laboratory. However, scientists, engineers, and other professionals perform these laboratory exercises in order to learn *how* to do them—they are quite prepared to pay the initial cost to learn, to experience, to obtain data and information. Therefore, later, when in production, the product will be improved, the costs will be reduced, and the production schedules will be met. This "way of professional life" still is not fully appreciated in housing R&D—at least within the cities themselves.

Another thing that we learned was that it is very difficult to find out what housing actually costs. We found that when one asked "What is the cost of housing?" one person would respond in terms of the cost per gross square feet; another, the cost per net square feet; another, the cost per living unit; another, the cost per tenement;

another, the cost in 1964; another, in 1968; another, the cost in Manhattan; another, the cost in Staten Island; etc., etc. It was, and is, difficult to obtain sound information in an objective way and on a basis from which one could make useful comparisons. Consequently, personally, with two or three other people in my office, I examined the cost of the "Instant Rehabilitation" Project and other rehabilitation projects in the city in careful detail. We also examined the cost of some new construction activities in the city. We arrived at a basis of reasonably objective comparison between rehabilitation and new construction and, also, some reasonably sound projections as to what each would cost in volume. The department has issued two reports regarding these studies.

Second, let me make some observations regarding the "Phoenix Project" in Detroit. A Cambridge architect was convinced that one ought to be able to design and construct some good quality, low-cost living units in a city such as Detroit, the characteristics of which would be appreciated—and in fact contributed to—by the people who were going to reside in the buildings and in the local neighborhood. Further, it would be the type of housing that had the fundamentally attractive characteristic that would enable it to be placed upon city lots of various sizes and shapes. I do not know whether the construction for the Phoenix Project finally is under way in Detroit or not; it has been at the point of actually beginning for some time. But, in the process of getting as far as it has, we certainly learned one thing: it will be very difficult to bring into being, at least in our larger urban cities, a large volume of appropriate low-cost housing unless there are radical changes in the present methods employed there to do so.

I shall never forget the first meeting that I attended in the city of Detroit dealing with the building of these few R&D living units. There were people from the mayor's office; from the architect's office; from the developer's office; from the nonprofit sponsor's office; from Washington; people from the neighborhood; the state; etc., etc. Without exaggeration, there must have been thirty people sitting at the table, and if we could have turned all of the acoustical pressure and the paper generated there into bricks and mortar we would have been halfway there.

The second thing that we learned about in "Phoenix" is that there is a way to assist people at the local level who are willing, in principle, to see novel building processes adopted, but who, faced with the rigors of their local code, do not have a straightforward and acceptable way of assuring that the resulting structures are safe, sanitary, and of sound general quality. In the Phoenix Project we reviewed the systems design in Washington, had it analyzed there, had the system itself measured at the Department of Commerce's National

Bureau of Standards under circumstances agreed to by the city professionals in Detroit and their advisors; with some ensuing modifications, it then received a construction permit. I believe that, as a result of the lessons learned in that cooperative activity of a very fundamental nature between the city of Detroit and the federal government, some steps now can be taken by the new Administration to assist the local code, engineering, and inspection people in a most useful way.

Finally, I appreciated, again, the difficulty of accomplishing experimental activities in the city. Such experiments are not going to be able to be accomplished in the way that experiments heretofore have been conducted, i.e., either within the laboratory (as mentioned) or at isolated field sites, and in an entirely amiable, understanding, sophisticated, professional atmosphere. And, yet, the experiments, the development tests, must go on, and we must learn, on the basis of such experiments and development tests as "Instant Rehab." and "Phoenix," how to obtain useful, objective data and experience with which to increase our confidence about how to form and manage our housing-related federal programs.

Now, let me put myself on the other side of the fence for a moment, and let me mention an experience in trying to enlist people from my own previous professional community to assist with housing problems. One example was that of a small analytical study supported at a large Department of Defense "think tank"—one in which HUD funded an inquiry (along with the Department of Defense) as to how one could aggregate large, long-time housing markets. Now, while the men in that organization are very bright, educated, energetic, sophisticated thinkers, it soon became plain that they simply had great difficulty in understanding that they were dealing with a situation that was so primitive and, yet, so complex, that they had to proceed very carefully and sensitively, and that they had to learn a great deal in order to do so effectively. They had difficulty, also, in appreciating the fact that the amount of money that they had received under the contract was about all the money that the departments could afford to give them and that it could not be considered a "down payment" on a long-term total study cost. All of the parties involved learned a great deal. We learned again at HUD (and this is, in a sense, the complementary situation with respect to the difficulty of conducting experiments in the city) that trying to "wrap around" the experience and the talents in the aerospace industry, let's say, to the fruitful study of urban problems, is a nontrivial matter. In fact, I read an article just the other day that quoted the new head of a major Department of Defense "think tank" as saying that his particular organization found it very difficult to work on urban problems because there are no people in the domestic agencies with whom they can communicate easily.

Let me speak briefly about what our fundamental strategies in HUD were:

1. To stop the poorer projects, those that were poorly conceived or poorly managed, and to truncate or taper off those in which good work was being done but which were, nonetheless, addressing second- or third-order priority areas; to turn around our R&D activities to face the more important HUD problems;

2. To obtain understanding in the Congress, in industry and in labor, of the necessity for doing urban-related R&D;

3. To lay the groundwork for obtaining a major, long-term commitment on the part of the federal government to subsidize activities in the lower-income housing field in a major and consistent fashion.

My judgment was that this third element was the keystone. If we could obtain such a federal commitment, all other things would become possible—not necessarily likely, and certainly not easy—but without it we would be "pushing uphill." That is, we wanted to attract nationwide professional RDT&E (Research, Development, Testing, and Evaluation) talent to the housing field; we wanted to learn how to aggregate housing markets; we wanted to encourage the housing industry to become more capital-intensive, and to look at the *industrialization of housing production*; we wanted to begin to conduct major professional housing development tests; we wanted, for various reasons, to interest the Department of Defense in doing military housing R&D work. But, to begin to do all this, we had to have a national commitment for the long-term federal subsidization of housing for our nation's poorer families.

Now, let me mention some recent history and make some projections. The Housing Act of 1968 is a truly extraordinary document. Personally, I would not have judged two years ago that it would come into being. In my view, the Housing Act did one thing beyond all else; it stated the country's goals for housing our lower-income people in what I call "operative" terms. The country no longer simply asked for "a decent home in a suitable living environment for all Americans."

It said that 26 million living units are needed within the next decade and that 6 million of these, for our lower-income families, will have to have some level of federal support. The act states the problem's magnitude and presents a time span for its solution. However difficult it may be in getting there from here, now there is a goal statement and a commitment of attainment in quantitative, operative terms.

The Housing Act, in general, reaffirmed the need for housing-related R & D on the part of the department; it established the position of an Assistant Secretary for R&D; it extended our R&D contract lifetime to four years; it wrote, in Section 108, a truly extraordinary piece of authorization that encouraged large-scale housing R&D. HUD received $10 million for general research in fiscal year '68 and a modest, but unique, R&D increase of $1 million to $11 million in fiscal year '69. The Johnson Administration asked the Congress for $25 million for R&D in fiscal year '70 and, while I was still at the department, the Nixon Administration decided to ask for $30 million—by far the bulk of which would go into housing-related R&D. The department started the "In-Cities" Project; the Department of Defense started to do R&D work on military family housing; my office formulated a detailed plan for the implementation of Section 108 and, based generally upon this initial plan, and with Secretary Romney's keen interest in encouraging the industrialization and mass production of housing, HUD's "Operation Breakthrough" has been inaugurated.

Let me close by stating a conclusion or two and a problem or two. My judgment is that we have overcome the fundamental inertia regarding the conduct of professional R&D activities in the housing area. How rapidly these activities expand will depend upon two things: the availability of federal funds and, at least as important in my judgment, the ability of the R&D community to demonstrate to Congress that they are accomplishing useful things, and that these useful things are being applied to affect HUD's operating practice. The department and the R&D community must be able to say to itself and to Congress for a few cents of R&D money on the eventual production dollar, this is what we did to our operating programs; we spent this money on R & D, and then we reduced the cost and the time, and we increased the volume in our operating program as a direct result.

Let me say that, in my judgment, we still are faced, in the entire urban field, with a "zero-order" problem. Let me explain this to you in terms of my past experience in the Department of Defense. When Secretary McNamara thought that he had an operating problem, he could turn to literally thousands of people to help him to determine whether or not he in fact had this problem. These were people in industry, in the universities, in the foreign service, and in the intelligence community. If he then concluded that he had a problem, and that he was responsible for solving it, and if it were an R&D problem, he had some 7 to 8 billion dollars a year (with all that that implies in terms of talented people, equipment, energy, institutional arrangements, etc.), available for its solution. If he obtained a useful solution, and if it bore up under test, then he could place it into production, he could buy it, and he could train his defense department people to use it. Note that essentially all of these people worked directly for, or under contract to, the Secretary of Defense. That is *not* the way things are done on the urban scene. The Secretary of Housing and Urban Development does not build houses; the people who *do*, do not work for the secretary. What the secretary does is to encourage the Congress to provide him with the funds which, in turn, he can provide to governors, mayors, nonprofit organizations, local housing authorities, etc., who, in turn, provide it to other people to produce, operate, and maintain housing. Only in some strange, nearly random, osmotic, ground-current way, "is the loop closed," eventually. Unlike the defense area, unlike the space area—in the housing area, the head of HUD is responsible for seeing that housing is satisfactorily built and occupied, but he doesn't have the direct authority over the people responsible for doing so. Rather, he must depend on the experience, judgment, and integrity of the people who are turning the funds he obtains from Congress into satisfactory goods and services in an efficient and effective manner. HUD cannot fire the mayor!

The department is faced with the simple fact that the country just doesn't have enough energetic, flexible, experienced professional people in our city halls and in our state capitols. And, until we have adequate professionalism there, this country will continue to attempt to solve major complex problems under a very difficult set of circumstances, indeed. The university R&D people should be able to help in certain ways. They can try to couple themselves more closely into the offices of the planners and the decision-making people in their cities to help them so that in the longer run, by understanding what new knowledge and what new techniques are necessary in the sound conduct of local affairs, they can develop appropriate texts, curricula and R&D programs.

I have already touched upon the matter of the difficulty of conducting truly useful experiments within the city. I have seen good professional men fail in this type of activity. These are men who, by an objective criteria, appear to have the professional ability required, but who fail when it comes to trying to conduct an experiment under the public eye, in the sensitive, complex laboratory of the city, instead of doing it as they had done it in the past, in the privacy of their laboratory, with the comfort of their professional colleagues and the large resources available to them.

Finally, I would say that another difficulty underlies all of these, which, I hope and trust, will be alleviated in time with the termination of the war in Southeast Asia and the halting of inflation. More money, more talent, more resources must be made available to the housing area. No matter how energetic we are, large problems require large resources for their solution. The country must obtain them and put them to work in the housing area.

Tracoba system. A precast-panel system, developed in France, and almost prototypical of all such systems. Note the reinforcing steel between panels prepared for grouting with concrete, and the erection struts used to "stay" the vertical panels lying in position. Courtesy of Société de Travaux pour la Construction et l'Habitat Industriels.

TO8B system. Several large-scale precast-panel buildings marching in redundant fashion, exemplifying unimaginative planning yet illustrating structures that offer an excellent resource to designers. Courtesy of Ing. V. Stephan, Stavebni Zavody Praha.

4
A Requirement for Change: Operation Breakthrough

Harold Finger

I find it very hard these days to come to a university campus without making some comment or at least recognizing the general feeling of disenchantment, of discontent, of concern, of protest, and impatience with established institutions. And I have felt for a long time that, although there may have been some extreme elements involved, that basically there was an underlying idealism that generated these concerns that things were not the way they should be.

As we look at almost any element of our domestic or foreign scene—for that matter, as we look at our urban problems—it is very clear to those of us involved in the business of trying to develop services, improve functions, and provide better living environment for our people, that we must accept at least part of the argument that change is really needed. Our institutions have neither grown nor changed as our way of life and the demands placed upon our society have changed. Also, I think we have to admit that there is some truth to the argument that we have not actually accepted the total commitment that was established in the Declaration of Independence, the Constitution, and in almost every statute that relates to the development of a proper way of life. We have been hypocritical in implementing some of those commitments.

That fact is that we have not actually assured that every individual has an equal opportunity to share the benefits of our society. If we have a problem, it relates to that reluctance to change. If Operation Breakthrough has any focus, it is a requirement for change—change not for its own sake, but to improve the process by which we provide housing and develop good living environments for our people.

The emphasis in this conference is on industrialized housing as it applies to new communities, but I want to caution that change does not mean abandoning the old. It does not mean and should not mean abandoning the cities that exist in order to take on the new, saying, "Well, we cannot do anything with those, so let us start afresh and we will develop the real living environment that will satisfy all with equal opportunity in these new areas." The fact is we do not really know how to do that. If we knew how to do that, we would know how to solve the problems of our cities today. If we knew how to do that, we would know how to change the institutions that have kept us from providing a decent way of life in our cities and urban areas.

However we do note some changes that are needed and Operation Breakthrough took an approach that said, "We know some of the weaknesses which are in our system. Let us develop a program that really does try to change them." There was a previous program and some of the people here, I know, were involved. They called it "In Cities," which was really aimed at finding out what factors precluded

Presented to the 1970 session. Harold Finger is Assistant Secretary for Technology and Research, United States Department of Housing and Urban Development.

the opportunity for developing all the housing that was needed, where it was needed, to give people the equal opportunity for decent living. It was an investigative program aimed at defining those constraints.

Breakthrough says, "We know there are constraints; we know generally what they are; let us instead implement a program that tries to break through those constraints." We think that must be done whether you talk about a new community or about established, residential communities. We do have to rebuild large parts of our cities. We do have to recognize that as our population grows a large part of that population will still end up crowding into existing metropolitan areas, and we must overcome some of the restrictions that keep us from developing effective and efficient living situations in those metropolitan areas. We do have to develop some new communities to take some of the load off that growing population at the same time. These are really the goals of Breakthrough.

I think it is heartening to see that there is now in student protest a very strong movement that was reflected by the thousands of students who came into Washington, met with congressional representatives and senators to argue their point, and actually had good receptions. They had good receptions because they indicated the depth of their feeling, and that it was not a passing fancy and that the students that followed them would at least have the same feelings about the need for change. In fact, it may have an even stronger feeling in that direction if their efforts to get change in an orderly way are not really considered and heard and implemented.

Many of us, I think, are very comfortable with the system as it is. As an example, the present Administration has proposed a Housing and Urban Development Act for 1970 which does not set up major new programs, but tries to put together the many, many different programs that have grown with time in the housing and urban development area into a hodgepodge that makes it hard for anyone really to plan a good living environment. There are many who say, "We do not want to drop the old, because we are not sure how the new will work." But the new, without any question, can operate a lot more effectively. It is a much simpler program, replacing something like 40 separate arrangements with eight, thus reducing the administrative costs. It would make it easier for people to understand what assisted housing is, getting more people involved and covered by assisted housing, because there is a steadily increasing group that just cannot get the housing they need because costs have risen so rapidly.

And yet, there are many established organizations that say they like the old because they have learned how to operate that way, and they do not want to change. That happens constantly. Even the National Association of Real Estate Boards recently came out with a statement saying, "Look, let us try to go to the new communities and we will try to develop things the way they should be there." It sounds an almost desperate abandonment. I have not got the written version of that text and I am trying to recall it. All of it related to a feeling of "you are not going to get change." We have to get change. That is what Breakthrough is trying to do. That is what Operation Breakthrough is really aimed at.

It should be made very clear, too, that many of the obstacles have been generated by federal programs. One of our major problems is that many people cannot get housing in areas in which they can find jobs. Jobs are moving to suburban areas, such as around Route 128; central city people have difficulty getting out there, but there are jobs there. The problems of finding housing in that area are considerable. But that is the case not only in this area, but in almost all of our major Northern and Western cities, and, increasingly, in the large Southern cities. We have a separation of jobs from housing opportunities for the people who are needed.

That problem was generated by old discriminatory practices, practices that pervaded our society, but were, in fact, encouraged by federal policies and practices. Let me give you an example. We recently pulled together an old FHA (Federal Housing Administration) underwriting manual. This was a guide for the underwriter—the man who goes out to appraise property. One of the major sections relates to protection from adverse influences. This was in the late 1930s when the manual was written, but the practice continued for a long time. And as we try to force these concepts out, we end up trying to change society because these concepts have so permeated our society that it is tough to change them.

Under the title of "Protection from Adverse Influence," it said, "Recorded, restrictive covenants should supplement and strengthen zoning ordinances, and to be really effective, should include the provisions listed below." It then goes on to say, "Recommended Restriction"—and it calls them "restrictions"—should include provision for the following; and in a long list, it includes prohibition of nuisances or undesirable buildings such as stables, pigpens, temporary dwellings, and high fences. The very next item is "prohibition of the occupancy of properties except by the race for which they were intended," and that was at a time, I will have to admit, when the schools in the District of Columbia were segregated.

The point is, these things are written down, and as we try to change them we have to change the whole philosophy of people who say, "When we move out to a suburban area in a new community, we want all the people there to be like us. After all, if they are not, the value of our property will be diminished."

Another example is the section on the quality of neighboring developments. "Areas surrounding a location must be investigated to determine whether incompatible racial and social groups are present for the purpose of making a prediction regarding the probability of the location being invaded by such groups. If a neighborhood is to retain stability, it is necessary that the area should continue to be occupied by the same social and racial classes. A change in social or racial occupancy generally contributes to instability and decline in values."

If we have a problem anywhere in any of these communities, which we do, it relates to the community reaction developed through statutes, policies, practices, and concepts like this. Another one I wanted to read to you was on natural physical protection. This talks about trying to make sure that the geographic location is in an area that has protection from the outside. "Usually protection from adverse influences is afforded by various means like established geographical or physical barriers, parks, things of that sort. It includes prevention of the infiltration of business and industrial uses, lower-class occupancy, and inharmonious racial groups. "A location close to a public park or area of similar nature is usually well protected from infiltration of business and lower social occupancy coming from that direction." Now, this is just like a great big invasion. That is the word used, and this is the tone that is used throughout the description.

Well, that is one of the barriers that we have to surmount. What we are finding is that our suburban areas are so restrictive in their zoning, in land-use regulations, that people of lower means, lower income, moderate-income people—and more and more, middle-income people—are not able to find houses where jobs are, are not able to find houses in a living environment that our ordinances have stipulated we have to provide to all of our people.

From 1939 on, there were grand phrases that referred to the obligation to assure that every American had a suitable home and a decent living environment. But we have not implemented them. The housing act of 1968 reaffirmed it, and it is very tough to turn things around to make the change needed to implement those statutes, ordinances, and basic commitments of our system in the face of practices that have become our way of life.

Another problem that I think all of you know about is that we do have thousands of separate districts each of which has its own building code. We have tens of thousands of standards written by several hundred standard-setting groups, and these standards are usually referenced in most of the codes that are developed. They are referenced in the FHA Minimum Property Standards to indicate standards that are acceptable to the FHA. In the codes, they are referenced to indicate what is acceptable in each of these areas.

Among these various standard-setting groups are governmental bodies, semipublic bodies, nonprofit organizations, standard compilation groups such as the American National Standards Institute (ANSI). There is the ASTM (American Society for Testing Materials), and there are also very many industrial associations that set standards for their products. The point is that there is nobody managing that whole system. It is very tough to get those standards reviewed and approved. They are actually implemented several years before they go through any kind of a review process, and there is almost no follow-on check, almost no quality-control program to assure that the standard is being used as intended, or to assure that innovations are quickly fed into the standard so that they can be incorporated into the codes that are supposed to reflect those standards.

What we are doing in Breakthrough is trying to change that process. With several hundred institutions or organizational units involved in the standard-setting function, that, too, is a tough job. There are, perhaps, ten major ones. But even working among those ten, or even working with the four model code groups, is not easy, because there are so many differences to be reconciled that the tendency is to reconcile at the highest level of all of it, thereby increasing the cost of housing unnecessarily, because the required performance exceeds what is really required for the housing.

What we are doing is working with the National Bureau of Standards and the National Academies of Science and Engineering to develop a performance basis for codes. We already have a set of preliminary performance criteria that we will use to judge the adequacy of the test results or of the tests that we conduct on the various building systems that we select in Operation Breakthrough. I should mention that those criteria are not complete, and it turns out that there is not an absolutely clear basis for many of the performance specifications that we would like to write into codes. Therefore, testing will have to be done to develop those performance criteria fully. But in many areas, it does provide the best engineering practice and judgment that we can specify at this time.

Most of the codes, also, are incomplete. They set arbitrary requirements in areas where the performance intended by a code is not necessarily the criterion by the time building is done in accordance with specifications. For example, if we had a specification that a structure had to stand a 90-mile-per-hour wind, we would find by many of the specification codes that are written, the actual load that could be withstood would be three or four times that. In other words, the basic structure would have a safety factor significantly beyond what was initially intended. This came up, incidentally, in tests that the Bureau of Standards ran on the Neal Mitchell Framing System, where the performance actually went way beyond what the code intended. The City of Detroit was adamant and they insisted

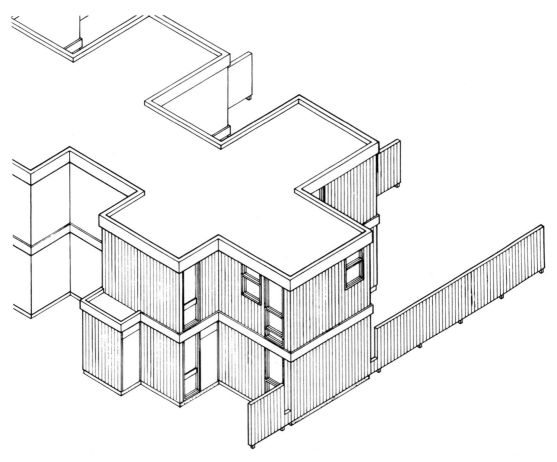

System Ecologic. This townhouse configuration is one of several system
prototypes developed primarily for
designers and developers as a time- and
cost-saving tool. Courtesy of ECO-
DESIGN, Cambridge, Mass.

that they had to follow their code, and that meant that they could not use thin columns, they had to use the standard thick columns that were specified. But the thin columns in the total system far exceeded the performance intent of the codes.

That has to be changed, and we think that by the performance approach we will make those changes. But beyond that, there are many, many other changes related to local governmental operations

System Ecologic takes advantage of building elements presently available on the market by using two modules: a structural module (SM) to integrate components and materials, and a planning module (PM) to integrate spatial relationships and functional layout. One of the many possible elevation treatments is shown here. Courtesy of ECODESIGN, Cambridge, Mass.

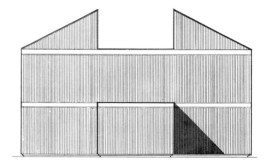

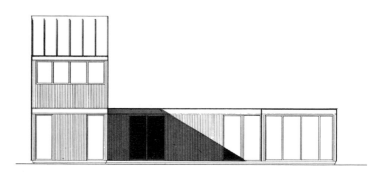

System Ecologic. The planning technique of this system utilizes generic monolithic units comprised of "living units" and "sleeping units," which form "total units" when combined. These units may be shipped as panels for on-site assembly, or they may be assembled at the factory and shipped as completed boxes. Courtesy of ECODESIGN, Cambridge, Mass.

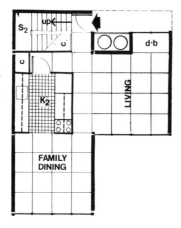

LIVING UNIT   SLEEPING UNIT

and a multitude of organizations that have to be involved in any residential development. That will be the case in the new community development, too, unless you go out into a totally unincorporated area remote from existing development.

HUD, in Operation Breakthrough, for the first time is acting like an entrepreneur. We are going through the process that most entrepreneurs go through when they develop a residential subdivision. We do have greater flexibility because the cities with which we are dealing and the counties with which we are dealing have given us some immunity from zoning and building code requirements, but we still have to work with each of the many bodies that are involved.

We also have to work within HUD rules, and in some ways that is tougher than working with each of the other bodies involved. As we have gone over each of the sites, I find that we do have representatives from other parts of HUD's operating programs and every few minutes, somebody says, "That is not our policy." What we are saying is we had better record every time somebody says "That is not our policy" to find out if that policy is a valid one, because we are going through the process of finding that many of the stumbling blocks are of our own administrative making, not even statutory in many cases.

As an example, we are finding it very hard to develop an economically viable residential community of good design in an inner-city location. And the reason is that you have to provide for so many amenities within that total development in a limited area that you cannot get that under the ceilings set in various of our housing bills. For example, the biggest problem that we have in inner-city sites is what to do with all the automobiles. We cannot simply keep adding the burden of automobile parking to the streets and then transfer the cost to the whole community, or cut down on traffic mobility, but that is what happens. No one developing inner-city sites provides enough parking unless he is building a luxury development, because that is the only way he can charge off to rents all of these additional services needed. It is a major problem. We are looking at factors like that in Breakthrough that we would not really be faced with if we were not going through our own HUD process.

What I am saying is that our whole process is built around methods that we have used, and that at every step of the way change is required in order to recognize the fact that as we develop new approaches, new techniques, those practices are no longer valid. I might mention another one that is of concern to us right now. And that is that appraisals on housing units go with the location in which the appraisal is made. In other words, you work on the basis of existing costs in an area. Certainly the Southern tier of the United States has lower costs in housing, generally, than the Northern tier. Production in a factory is going to result in a set cost of the delivered product so that there will be an FOB price. Now, that FOB price, if the plant is in the North, is going to result in a product that will not readily compete with the appraisal values in the Southern part of the United States. And the question is, overall do we have a benefit by saying, "Let us now begin to treat the United States as a whole, to do appraisals on the basis of the total advantage rather than the circumstances in each area."

The important thing is that the appraisal determines the mortgage— and if the appraisal is low, the mortgage is low and the down payment has to be very high—and you just cannot get a competitive situation in low-cost areas where you might get a very beneficial situation in high-cost areas. But you might not have enough market in high-cost areas to get all the benefits of the production process. Therefore, there may have to be some changes in the appraisal process to recognize where the product came from, what has been put into it, what the overall advantages are. On the other hand, it is possible that the point of delivery will determine what the FOB price is. That is a factor that we have got to think through.

But you can see the problem in delivering industrialized housing throughout the country from a few factories. You can do that with light frame structures where you can ship over large distances. With heavy structures, concrete structures, economical transportation distances are short.

Another change that I ought to recognize before it ends up being asked as a question is the one that relates to the unions, organized labor's response to industrialization. A year ago, when Breakthrough was introduced, HUD Secretary George Romney had a series of meetings with labor and industrial leaders, mayors, and governors. The unions indicated that they were prepared to continue to meet with him. Several of them indicated their support. And I think that what has happened since goes beyond what many of us would have hoped at that time. The fact is that major unions—the Carpenters, the Plumbers, the Electricians, the Laborers—have signed agreements with people in the housing business to build these housing units or components or panels in a plant, operating there at rates more like industrial wage rates. They would have to be negotiated, but they have been worked out like industrial wages rates. And then, to assemble those panels and units on site, the work would be at the normal building-trades salary scale.

Another important element is that they have agreed that in plant situations they would accept some crossing of craft lines. In other words, a plumber could drill a hole and put a pipe through. He does not have to wait to call the carpenter over. In addition, along with that, in plants, the skilled people would be foremen and they would have operating under them people of lower skill levels. And this is one of the important, in fact, major benefits of industrialization, for we already know that we have a shortage of skilled labor. As time goes on, that shortage will be greater, particularly as we increase the production of housing that is needed to satisfy our growing population and replace the deterioration of existing structures. In order to be able to build all the housing that we need, we must provide a greater or more effective use of the labor force available to us. That means we have to train more people to work in housing and to take on the skilled discipline. But we also have to find ways of using the lower skill levels that are not being effectively used today. And that is what industrialization provides. Without it, we probably could not build all the housing that we need, and, because of the deficits that would result, the cost curve for housing would continue to rise rapidly. Just the sheer shortage of housing would lead us to that situation. I think that there can be a greater stability of cost with industrialization by virtue of the fact that, if nothing else, we can provide more readily for the housing needs of the nation.

But the unions have taken, I think, very constructive steps in the direction of agreeing to these processes. It remains to be seen how the unions' local business agents respond to this action of the internationals. It is not clear. In some areas there should be no problem. In others, there will be. I do not want to point out places, but it is clear that some of our cities will lag in the application of new approaches and new ideas. The only approach we can take in that situation is to try to get everything that surrounds them to use the new approaches and display their benefits, and put pressure on the restrictive organizations or cities in such a way that their citizenry says, "We had better change, too." I think that is actually what will happen.

Now to indicate very quickly what we have done so far in Breakthrough—we have evaluated almost 240 proposals of full housing systems and selected 22. We are near the end of evaluation and selection of proposals from 365 companies which proposed various advanced elements of housing systems, software and hardware. We have selected 11 of 218 sites proposed on which to build this advanced housing. We have selected 11 of 82 planners, engineers, and architects who propose to design these sites. These are the demonstration sites for these housing systems; and when I say "housing systems," let me emphasize that we are thinking not only of the building itself or of the technology of the house, but also of its land-use pattern. Interestingly, all of our planners have come up with the very flexible versions of Planned Unit Development. To indicate how concepts have to be changed, we met with a group of the city council of Macon, Georgia one time. There were five members of the council and the mayor. And we started going through the plan that we were developing for the Macon site. One of the councilmen kept asking, "How big are the lots?" though that is not really important. The really important thing is what the total arrangement of units is and what common areas and recreational space are made available to those units in a total living environment. That is the kind of concept that I think we have to get to.

I might mention that I have some concern about that kind of an approach. Because I think what we are going to find is that people who have gone through the individual lot—standard subdivision arrangement will be prepared to accept these approaches, but that those who have been deprived of any opportunity to own a house, to own a piece of ground, may very well want to go through that step. And they may have great difficulty in accepting the concepts that go into planned unit development that requires not only maintenance of the strip of ground around their house and the maintenance of their house, but also a contribution to the maintenance of common areas. That may be a tough concept to have set up. I am getting now to some of the sociological aspects of these developments which, I think, are really critical.

I mentioned earlier that I do not think we know how to develop new communities to give us the way of life we would like. As we go through the designs on these 11 sites which are small residential communities, they rely on services largely outside—schools, transportation, commercial facilities—all outside. Even for those small residential subdivision developments there are major social questions. We are prepared to say that we will use the best judgment we have to try those, but I am not sure we would be prepared to say we are confident enough about our judgment to say that we would also know enough to develop 10 total communities, total cities. We do not know how these residential communities will end up in years to come if they start with an income mix, a housing-type mix, and a racial mix. We intend to follow that carefully. That is a significant part of the experimentation that is involved in this development. It may be that we will find that those communities stabilize out at some income level or some social level or some racial situation. We really do not know. What we are going to try to do is make them fairly stable with a variety of people. In these residential communities, we are really trying to simulate old, small towns that had to provide services and therefore had to have a mix of people for their existence. The fact is, of course, that it may be easier to go to new communities where you have that mix in order to make the town viable, but this is one of the significant problems that we face in Breakthrough.

An important part of this is that the housing is not changed by the financing program that is going to be applied or by the subsidy program. What we shall do is have the family come onto the site and determine what unit it wants. We must have the flexibility then to determine if they can pay the fair-market rent or price for the house; if it is a home ownership situation and they cannot, we will then apply the subsidies to the family, not to the house.

We are trying to get around the idea that housing is inferior in any way if it has a subsidy attached to the family that lives in it. We are trying to encourage a situation where anyone can come onto a site and pick a house and through that means get a mix of families. That means that we may very well end up with people adjacent to each other or fairly close to each other, but of quite wide income differences.

But houses will not be marked by that. Houses will be the same quality, they will have the same amenities within some reasonable limits. We will have variations in price, but we will not have a wide variation in price in neighboring units. Overall, there will be a variation in price. I expect a question as to whether you can build a $15,000 house next to a $50,000 house. In a single cluster there can be some variety of housing prices, say from $15,000 to $22,000, and then any family can go out and live in them.

Question   Can you explain the mechanics of who owns the land right now and who is going to own the house?

Finger   We are going to select a site developer for each site. In some cases we have already taken an option on the land. We will transfer that option to the developer. He will become, in fact, the full developer for the site and the housing system producers will probably be subcontractors to him, although they may also have direct contracts with us. We will arrange for him to get normal private mortgage and construction financing. In addition, we will pay overcost directly out of federal funds. But he becomes our vehicle to develop the site. Some of those developers will probably want to own the sites themselves on a continuing basis. In other words, they may say we stay here, own, manage, operate the site and so on. We may agree to that. On the other hand, we are requiring that they be our agency for disposal of the site. We do not want to be landowners or landlords forever. We want eventually to dispose of the site, and it will be their job to make arrangements with nonprofit organizations or local organizations to take over the site. Or, individual families may buy some of the housing units. We will review and approve and lease in that process.

There are exceptions that can be made and it is my understanding that the regional office of HUD has made many, many exceptions in New York, to overcome those limits; there is a flexibility that is left for unusually high-cost areas.

Question   Can you explain how the tenant-owner selection process will work—how the developer has to operate?

Finger   We have not really set up the tenant-owner evaluation and selection process yet. Until we get the developer, we are hesitant to set up that kind of system. The developer has to be someone who really understands the community, what it needs, and how it would normally operate. I keep saying to people who express concern about this, "You cannot very well bus people to their homes; that is the other way around." But that is one of the things that they tend to worry about—that we will try to import people from all over the community in order to force the mix we were talking about. We think the mix will occur. So, I want to emphasize that we have not yet developed that detailed tenant selection process.

Question   How will HUD know whether Breakthrough has been a success?

Finger   We will be setting up an evaluation process with the site developer that will go on even after we dispose of the site. Our proposal is that we not only maintain the physical records on the systems or on how the area is maintained when repairs are needed, but, also, that we maintain records as to what happens to the families in that community when they leave. Where do they go? If there are vacancies, how do they vary month to month? We want that to follow on for years after the site has been built. It is not until you do that that you really know what the consequences are. We are trying now to collect all the background data on that community so we will have a feeling for what the surrounding community is as well, because the effect might not result from what we have built on the site, but what the surrounding community impact is on the site. We have to try to accumulate the information that will let us analyze those situations.

Question   Will there be an opportunity for the people, the tenants, to express their feelings to the saviors from Washington?

Finger   I have tried to emphasize whenever we have had a discussion on Breakthrough with any of the people we meet that it is very important for them to criticize us point by point in any area where they think there may be a weakness in the program, a potential problem in the program. Unless we understand all of those, we will never be able to be sure that we will be prepared for them. That does not mean that we are trying to solve every problem before we start. We have a host of problems. As we move along, new ones keep cropping up all the time. I am not requiring that all of them be solved now, before we move.

For example, we must have this evaluation program. We do not have it now. We do not now have a tenant selection program. We must have that, but we have set the schedule up in such a way that we know when we will need them. Associated with this, I think, is the need to recognize the things we do not know, so that if things happen later, we can criticize ourselves. But the approach I am defining is, in fact, the approach that has been taken in the space program, and most of the research and development work that has been done in hardware programs. Therefore, I am saying we had better do it in this program, which has a very strong sociological content as well. To give you an example that this can be done: a board set up by NASA, with its own people, ended up criticizing NASA. The fact is, it has to be done if your survival depends on that situation. I think that it is really what we are facing, as we talk about the environment. The environment of living is far more important and more difficult to solve than the physical and natural contamination, the pollution that we generate. I think we can use dollars, but it is not what we need to solve the people-to-people problems that we have which are a lot tougher to understand and to change.

Question   Is there any local community opposition to Breakthrough?

Finger   We have community reaction in almost every suburban site. Some community reaction opposing development exists in almost every suburban site. This is what it is: it says that there is a federal program, therefore, it must be public housing. There is some reaction like that, and, even when we overcome it, there is some reaction that says we do not want anybody around here that earns less than we do, particularly if they are black. They do not really come out with that, but that is the fact. So, there is some community opposition, but there is no official opposition. In fact, there is official support.

For example, in Wilmington, Delaware, there is some division in the ranks of officialdom, but the governor and the county executive are strongly pushing the program. That was one that was mentioned. In King County, there is some local opposition. In fact, it happens to be from a policeman who owns slum property in Seattle and who does not want any residents of that slum coming into King County where he lives. That is the kind of situation that exists, and he has generated some opposition, but also, I think, I have to be very fair about it. We picked sites before we had plans, before we had the systems identified and finally selected, and before we had those designs finished, and, therefore, people really did not know exactly what they were getting. They did have to go on the basis of some confidence in the program that we are laying out.

Question   What is the timetable for Operation Breakthrough?

Finger   I am confident we will have buildings this year, but I do not know how many and on which sites. It varies a great deal from site to site because there are involvements with local approvals, local reviews. I should not say approvals as much as reviews; just the process of submitting something to a planning board and talking with them. We have said that they cannot approve for us, because we have an ordinance from the city that says we can build whatever we want and they will give us all the approvals we need. The point is that the planning board still says, "We want to look at it." We think that it is reasonable, but it takes time. We are trying to develop a schedule where processing is not a "stretching element." We want action orientation. The design process, the testing process, the building process—we want those to be the schedule-determining items.

Question   Is there an arm in the federal government such as the National Building Agency in England, which has an overview of the whole industry, its needs, its morphology, and its new directions?

Finger   There is no group, no official group that is trying to examine the total construction industry, with a view to changing it, and I think you are implying that. We, the Department of Commerce and the Department of Labor, did sit together to try to analyze what the construction industry does. Really, is it an industry or isn't it? There are two parts to it; one portion is the general contractor who builds big structures, public buildings, roads, things like that; and the other one is the home building business. They are really quite different from each other. We have done that kind of analysis. I would say, if you are looking for an interface, we are probably the ones that should be interfacing with you because we are examining the total industry in order to know what the problems are in that industry.

The big one, I think, is the fragmentation that develops as a result of the fragmentation of our markets and institutions, regulatory policies, and practices, not because they want to be that way, but because that is the way the market is structured. Also, they are undercapitalized, generally. What we are finding right now is a very obvious movement in the direction of conglomeration of smaller groups, or of acquisition of these housing people by larger corporations. It is not just an ad hoc kind of occurrence; it is really a trend. The important thing is that we find that those aggregated companies or the acquired organizations, after that has happened, produce more housing than they did before. For example, in 1969, which was a bad year, all of those companies produced more than their companies had produced in the year before. That is a surprising development. What they have done by that process is to take over a bigger part of the market. Still trivial, still only 3.5 percent among at least 19 companies that have been acquired, compared to 2.2 percent, I believe it was. Still a very small percentage of the total number of units built, but it is a movement that is growing.

Question   What is really meant by the well-worn term "market aggregation?"

Finger   We are trying to change the market. We are trying to assemble a market, identify and assemble land. We are trying to change building codes. We are trying to get around zoning approaches that are restrictive. We are trying to encourage investment by organizations, long-term investment in the housing business, by showing them that there is an incentive in the market demand that is available so that, perhaps, through these means they can get more financing into the housing business. We are trying to develop improved management methods within our own organization and encourage such methods in the housing business. It is not simply a matter of saying, "I have got a better way to build a wall." The critical element is really a total attack on the business.

Question   Is the cutting of budget appropriations going to have an effect on this?

Finger   What has been referred to here is the House Appropriations Committee and the House of Representatives who cut the research and technology budget from a request of $55 million to $30 million. Our hope is that the Senate will restore it. I do not know what is going to happen, but it would have an effect on Breakthrough. Incidentally, I have mentioned that the total HUD budget is less than half the Department of Defense research and development budget. That includes all the subsidies and everything else in the program. The total research and development budget in the federal government is $15 billion. The total research budget for Housing and Urban Development, for all the responsibilities in that department, was $55 million, and we were cut to $30 million.

Question   Can you comment on how you arrived at the goals in number of units?

Finger   Is it the 26 million you mean? Let me try to reconstruct that as well as I can. As I recall it, there were 13 million new family formations anticipated, a net addition to the number of families that required household units. There were 9 or 10 million existing substandard structures and structures that would become substandard during the ten-year period, giving the total of about 23 or 24 million units. There was a need to loosen up on the vacancies in order to provide a mobility factor. There was a need to reduce the overcrowding that existed and that is where the extra 2 million came in.

Question   In view of the disposition of various agencies' problems and humanistic consideration, is it feasible, in your opinion, to establish a central repository of information on all aspects of the housing problem, where interested agencies can draw out information?

Finger   I am not sure. One thing we know is that we need a way to record what the need for housing is. That has to be done by local areas. It just is not enough to say we are going to build 26 million housing units, without worrying about where the need is for each element of those 26 million. So, there has to be a system that does record the need. There has to be a system that also records the availability of land in those areas and the effect of existing restrictions on that land. Incidentally, I should tell you that this is the system we are trying to get established as part of what we call our "market aggregation process." And I would say that if there is a critical part to Breakthrough, that is it.

If we cannot develop that market and aggregate that market, we have not set in motion the factors that would encourage the kind of investment and encourage the efficiency of factory operations that you can get only by continuous output for production process. That part we are trying to do. We are working with state and local governments to try to encourage, and are trying to develop our own models. At the same time, we are working with the Building Research and Advisory Board of the National Academy to have the proposals— there were about 600 proposals submitted to us—abstracted. We are trying to have those proposals which were in response to our housing request abstracted so that the systems and the concepts can be widely disseminated. At the same time, we are trying to set up a computer program that will record all of those abstracts and be in a position to add other systems to it. What I am really saying is I think we ought to start accumulating the data by trying to break it into logical pieces. Let me give you another example. The National Bureau of Standards has tried to put into a computer all of the building code requirements that exist and all of the standards that have been developed; very frankly, when I asked them how many standard-setting organization there were and what types there were, and in what codes they were referenced, they said that their computer will not give that information very easily. So they have gone back to work to try to make it a usable device. But I think it is only through that approach of taking pieces that we will end up with something that will give us a total picture.

Question   Really, what exactly is the situation with labor regarding industrialized building systems?

Finger   The important thing about labor cooperation is that there is an agreement by the laborers to precast those concrete panels, the electricians to preinstall electrical work, and, incidentally, the laborers in concrete plants actually do install the conduits themselves.

Dynaframe system. The lace framework
of this Ocean City, Maryland, condominium manifests its design flexibility in the
gentle curve of its facade coupled with
ease of erection and many cladding alternatives. Courtesy of Wayne Hart, Stress-
con Industries.

Camus factory. A British precasting
plant with horizontal casting beds that
can be modified to integrate electrical
and mechanical arrangements, windows,
doors, and various wall textures at the
client's request. The overhead cranes
not only assist in the construction of the
building elements, but also deposit them
on trucks or in storage yards beyond the
walls. Courtesy of Higgs and Hill, Surrey,
England.

I think it is a valid thing to also ask the question as to what the reaction of industry is. Because, as you can expect, there is no universal acclaim for the changes that we are talking about; they will certainly have some effect on the makeup of the industry. Thousands of home builders are worried, and I do not know any of the big producers who intend to do the whole job by themselves. I refer to the big producers of the industrialized housing element and module producers. That is to say, to go out on to the site and assemble by themselves and erect by themselves. They all plan on working with local organizations as franchised operators or licensed dealers, or to sell to independent builders. I think it will be a great advantage to those local builders to buy something from a factory that they know is at a set price. They could eliminate some of the risks that they now have to take by trying to go around and contract the job themselves or go from the bare supply process to the final assembly. In addition, I think there is a good chance for development, if this proceeds, of a new factory-licensed, trained service industry in housing. Clearly, if you install electrical supplies and plumbing in panels in the factory, no ordinary serviceman is going to be able to do the repair job and there is going to have to be a service industry that develops along with this. We have got some indications of this now from some of our producers, and I think it may be a real opportunity for new service establishments to get into this business in an entirely new way.

5
Systems Analysis as a Tool for Urban Planning

Jay W. Forrester

New ways are becoming available for analyzing our social systems. These permit the design of revised policies to improve the behavior of the systems within which we live. Many of the ideas discussed here are treated more fully in my book *Urban Dynamics** which shows the city as an interacting system of industry, housing, and people. The book presents a theory, in the form of a computer model, that interrelates the components of a city. It shows how the interacting processes produce urban growth; and cause growth to give way to stagnation. Various changes in policies are examined with this laboratory model to show their effect on an urban area. A number of presently popular proposals are tested—a job training program, job creation by bussing to suburban industries or by the government as employer of last resort, financial subsidies to the city, and low-cost-housing programs. These all are shown to lie between neutral and detrimental in their effect on a depressed urban area. The evolution of an urban area from growth into stagnation creates a condition of excess housing. Housing is excess compared to the population and compared to the availability of income-earning opportunities. To reestablish a healthy economic balance and a continuous process of internal renewal, it appears necessary to reduce the inherent excess housing of depressed areas and to encourage the conversion of part of the land to industrial use. By so doing, a large enough wage and salary stream can be brought from the outside economy to make the area self-sustaining.

As you can see, these results are controversial. If they are right, it shows that most of the traditional steps taken to alleviate the conditions of our cities may actually be making matters worse. The book first appeared this last May; it is already in the second printing. Although it has so far received little public notice in this country, it has become the center of a political tempest in Canada. North of the border, newspaper headlines, editorials and radio and television panel discussions are debating its merits.

Urban Dynamics is based on methods for studying complex systems that form a bridge between engineering and the social sciences. Although I will present here some results from the book, my principal emphasis will be on the importance of the methods to all social systems.

Over a decade ago at MIT we began to examine the dynamic characteristics of managerial systems. The field known as "industrial dynamics" resulted.† Industrial dynamics belongs to the same general subject area as feedback systems, servomechanisms theory, and

Presented to the 1970 session. The paper was first delivered at the National Academy of Engineering symposium, "The Engineer and the City," Washington, D.C., October 22–23, 1969. Jay W. Forrester is Professor of Management, Sloan School of Management, Massachusetts Institute of Technology.

*Jay W. Forrester, *Urban Dynamics*, MIT Press, Cambridge, Mass., 1969.
†Jay W. Forrester, *Industrial Dynamics*, MIT Press, Cambridge, Mass., 1961.

cybernetics. Industrial dynamics is the study of how the feedback loop structure of a system produces the dynamic behavior of that system. In managerial terms industrial dynamics makes possible the structuring of the components and policies of a system to show how the resulting dynamic behavior is produced. In terms of social systems it deals with the forces that arise within a system to cause changes through time.

A design study of a social system seeks changes in structure and policies that will improve the behavior of the system. Some people recoil at the thought of designing social systems. They feel that designing a society is immoral. But we have no choice about living in a system that has been designed. The laws, tax policies, and traditions of a society constitute the design of a social system. Our available choice is only between different designs. If we lament the functioning of our cities, or the persistence of inflation, or the changes in our environment, we mean that we prefer a social system of a different design.

The design process begins with observation of the behavior modes of a system to identify the symptoms of trouble. Second, the system is searched for the feedback structures that might produce the observed behavior. Third, the level and rate variables making up that structure are identified and explicitly described in the equations of a computer simulation model. Fourth, the computer model is then used to simulate in the laboratory the dynamic behavior implicit in the identified structure. Fifth, the structure is modified until components of the structure and the resulting behavior agree with the observed conditions in the actual system. Sixth, modified policies can then be introduced into the simulation model in search of usable and acceptable policies that give improved behavior.

This design process brings the essential substance of a social system into the laboratory where the system can be studied. Laboratory representation of a social system can be far more effective than most people would expect. Anything that can be stated or described about a social system can be represented in such a laboratory model. The major difficulty is the rarity of skilled professional talent. There are very few men with a knowledge of the proper guiding principles and with experience in perceiving the pertinent feedback structure of complex, poorly defined systems. Whatever one may say about the shortcomings of the process, there is no comparably effective substitute.

Surprising discoveries come from this combination of theory and laboratory experimentation. We observe that relatively simple structures produce much of the complex behavior of real-life systems. We find that people's skills in perception are very different from those commonly supposed. It is often asserted in the social sciences that people are unreliable in analyzing their own actions, yet we find time and again that the policies and practices that people know they are following are the ones that interact to produce the most troublesome consequences. Conversely it can be clearly demonstrated that the vaunted powers of judgment and intuition usually deceive the person who tries to guess the time-varying consequences that follow even from a completely known system structure. We find that the modes of behavior which are most conspicuous in managerial, urban, and economic systems are produced by nonlinearities within those systems. The linearized models which have been used in much of engineering and the social sciences can not even approximate the important modes of behavior in our social systems. The most visible and troublesome modes are manifestations of nonlinear interactions. We find that it is relatively easy to include the so-called intangible factors relating to psychological variables, attitudes, and human reactions. Again, if the influences can be discussed and described, they can be inserted in the policy structure of a model. Any person who discusses why people act the way they do, or explains a past decision, or anticipates a future action is relating the surrounding circumstances to the corresponding human response. Any such discussion is a description of decision-making policy. Any such policy statement can be put into a system model.

A body of dynamic theory and principles of structure is emerging that allows us to organize and understand complex systems.* For example, the feedback loop becomes the basic building block of systems. Within the feedback loop there are two and only two kinds of variables. One is the level variable produced by integration, the other is the policy statement or rate variable which governs the changes in a system. The level variables are changed only by the rates of flow. The rate variables depend only on the levels. Any path through a system network encounters alternating level and rate variables. These and many other principles of structure are universal in the entire sweep of systems that change through time. Furthermore, the structure of a system determines its possible modes of behavior. Identical structures recur as one moves between apparently dissimilar fields. These identical structures behave in identical ways wherever they are found.

The same principles of structure and the same relationships between structure and behavior apply to a simple swinging pendulum, a chemical plant, the processes of management, internal medicine, economics, power politics, and psychiatry. A universal approach to time-varying systems is emerging which seems capable of dealing with systems of any complexity. We observe that students, as they master the principles and practice of dynamic analysis, develop a

*Jay W. Forrester, *Principles of Systems*, preliminary printing of first ten chapters, Wright-Allen Press, Inc., Room 516, 238 Main Street, Cambridge, Massachusetts 02142.

remarkable mobility between fields of endeavor. The same person can clarify the dynamics of how a transistor functions, organize the processes of a public health epidemic, design new management policies to avoid stagnation in product growth, discover the sensitive factors in ecological change, and show how government policies affect the growth and decline of a city.

Some diagrams showing urban behavior will illustrate these ideas. Figure 1 shows the central structure of an urban area. The nine rectangles represent the selected level variables. The 22 valve symbols represent the rates of flow that cause the nine system levels to change. Engineers often refer to these level variables as the state variables of a system. The distinction between level and rate variables is also familiar to anyone who examines financial statements. Balance sheet variables are always separated from variables on the profit-and-loss statement. They are separate because they are conceptually quite different. The balance sheet variables are system levels. They are created by accumulating financial flows. The profit-and-loss variables are system rates. This sharp distinction is found in all systems.

In the simplified urban system of Figure 1, nine levels are grouped into three subsystems. Across the top the industrial sector contains commercial buildings in three categories distinguished primarily by age. Across the center are residential buildings in three categories, also distinguished by age and condition. Across the bottom are three economic categories of population. Because of their complexity, the information linkages connecting the system levels to the system rates are not shown on this figure. In this figure one can begin to detect the reasons for urban decline. The age of a building tends to determine the character of its occupants. A new commercial building is occupied by a healthy, successful commercial organization that uses relatively more managers and skilled workers than those who are unskilled. As the building ages, it tends to house a progressively less successful enterprise with lower employment skills. In addition to the changing employment mix as the industrial building ages, there is a tendency for total employment per unit of floor space to decline. On the other hand, as residential buildings age there is a tendency for occupancy to increase as well as to shift to a lower economic category of population. One perceives then a condition where the aging of buildings in an urban area simultaneously reduces the opportunities for employment and increases the population. The average income and standard of living decline.

Figure 2 shows the same nine system levels and one of the 22 flow rates. The dotted lines are the information linkages from the system levels to control the one flow rate, here the arrival of underemployed population into the urban area. The various levels of the system combine to create a composite "attractiveness" which determines the inflow rate to the area. If the area is more attractive than those from

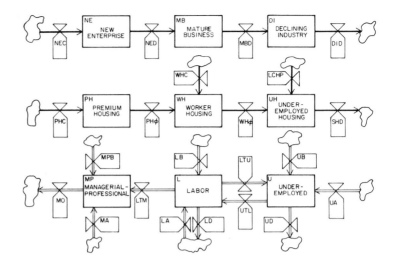

Figure 1
Urban structure. All illustrations in this
chapter are from Jay. W. Forrester,
Urban Dynamics, MIT Press, Cambridge,
Mass., 1969.

Figure 2
Information links to the underemployed-
arrival rate.

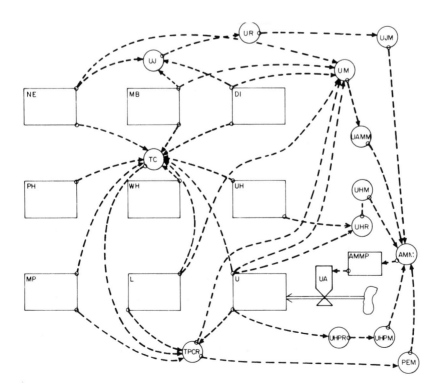

which people might come, a net inward population flow occurs. If the area is less attractive, an outward flow dominates. Five components of attractiveness are shown in Figure 2. In the upper right corner UJM is the underemployed/job multiplier which relates the population to the available jobs and represents the income-earning attractiveness of the area. The circle UAMM generates the attractiveness created by upward economic mobility. In other words, an area with high upward economic mobility is more attractive than one offering no hope of advancement. The circle UHM relates the underemployed population to the available housing. The area becomes more attractive as housing becomes more available. UHPM represents the attractiveness of a low-cost-housing program if such exists. And in the lower right corner PEM is the influence on attractiveness of the public expenditure per capita. As per capita expenditure rises, it means better public services, better schools, and higher welfare budgets.

The concept of attractiveness is fundamental to the population flows. All of the characteristics of an area that make it attractive, these five and many more, combine to influence migration. An attractive area draws people. But almost every component of attractiveness is driven down by an increase in population. If there is an excess of housing, the area is attractive, but a rising population crowds the housing. If there is an excess of jobs, the area is attractive, but the incoming flow of people fills those jobs. In other words, migration continues until the attractiveness of the area falls and becomes equal to all other places from which people might come.

An important idea follows from examining these components of attractiveness. In a condition of population equilibrium, all areas must be equally attractive to any given population class, otherwise net migration would occur. If one component of attractiveness is increased in an area, other components must necessarily fall to establish a new equilibrium. Compensating changes in the components of attractiveness explain many past failures in our cities wherein we attempted to improve one aspect of the city only to discover that other aspects have become worse.

In making a laboratory model of a social system one should not attempt straightaway to solve a problem. Instead one should generate a model which will create the trouble symptoms. Only if one fully understands the processes whereby difficulties are created can he hope to correct the causes. This means that we want a model of an urban area which can start with empty land, grow a city, and show the processes whereby economic health falters into stagnation and decay.

As another guide to modeling, one should start, not by building a model of a particular situation, but instead should model the general class of systems under study. This may seem surprising, but the general model is simpler and initially is more informative than a model of a special case. Here we wish to model the general process of urban growth and stagnation. It should be a model which, with proper changes in parameters, is good for New York, Calcutta, a gold rush camp, or West Berlin. These all seem to have very different characteristics but they have certain elements in common which describe their urban processes. There are fewer concepts which are common to all than are to be found in any one. The general model can strip away the multitude of detail which confuses any one special situation. The general model identifies the central processes and is a statement of the theory for the entire class of systems.

Figure 3 shows the behavior of the laboratory model of an urban area. It presents the nine level variables over 250 years. The first 100 years is a period of exponential growth but then the land area becomes filled, growth ceases, and the aging process begins. At year 100 (i.e., near the end of the growth phase), the labor population is almost double the underemployed population. This is a healthy mix which is well matched to the job distribution in the area and which gives a high upward economic mobility to the underemployed population. But by year 150, the labor population has fallen and the underemployed population has risen until these two groups are almost equal. Business activity has declined and the area has taken on the characteristics of a depressed city. This has occurred because of the way that the industry, housing, and populations in Figure 1 have interacted with each other.

Figure 4 shows other variables during the same 250 years. Notice especially the underemployed/job ratio and the underemployed/housing ratio. During most of the first 100 years of growth these two ratios were almost constant. The underemployed/housing ratio was high (above the center of the figure) meaning that the population is large compared to the housing. In other words, during the first 100 years there was a housing shortage for the underemployed population. On the other hand, the underemployed/job ratio was low, meaning that the population was below the job opportunities, jobs were readily available, economic opportunity was good, and upward economic mobility was high. During this early period of growth and high economic activity, the underemployed population was being effectively adjusted in relation to other activity by balancing good economic opportunity against a housing shortage.

But between 90 and 140 years, notice the sharp reversal of the curves for underemployed/job ratio and underemployed/housing ratio. Within this 50-year span, the underemployed have increased while available jobs decreased; the result is a precipitous rise in unemployment. But in this same period, the housing that is aging and becoming available to the underemployed is rising even more rapidly than the underemployed population. Jobs have become scarce while housing has become surplus. The model is behaving the way our cities do.

Many people seem not to realize that the depressed areas of our cities are areas of excess housing. The economy of the area is not able to maintain all of the available housing. Because of low incomes, people crowd into some dwelling units while other buildings are abandoned, stand idle, and decay.

Recall the earlier comments about compensating movements in the components of attractiveness. Here, as housing becomes more available, jobs become more scarce. The stagnating urban area has become a social trap. Excess housing beckons people and causes inward migration until the rising population drives down the standard of living far enough to stop the population inflow. Anything which tends to raise the standard of living is defeated by a rise of population into the empty housing.

Figure 5 shows the development for 50 years beginning with the conditions found at the end of Figure 3. At time 0, a low-cost-housing program is introduced which each year builds low-cost housing for 2.5 percent of the underemployed population. Observe what happens. Underemployed housing, which is being actively constructed, rises 45 percent, but premium housing falls 35 percent, and worker housing falls 30 percent. New enterprise declines 50 percent and mature business declines 45 percent, all in the 50-year period. Economic conditions become sufficiently worse that even the underemployed population, which rises initially, eventually falls to only slightly less than its beginning value. These changes are a result of the low-cost-housing program.

In Figure 6, the corresponding underemployed/job ratio has risen 30 percent (indicating substantially higher unemployment), while the underemployed/housing ratio has fallen 30 percent (indicating a still higher excess of housing). Again, the two components of attractiveness compensate for one another with better housing and a falling standard of living. In the long run, the low-cost-housing program has not served the interests of the low-income residents. Instead, it has intensified the social trapping characteristic of the area. Over the period, the tax levies rise 35 percent. The area has become worse from almost all viewpoints.

In this same manner job training programs, job creation programs, and financial subsidies were examined. All lie between ineffective and harmful. The low-cost-housing program was the most powerful in depressing the condition of a stagnant urban area.

The depressed areas of our cities seem to be characterized by excess

Figure 3
Growth and stagnation.

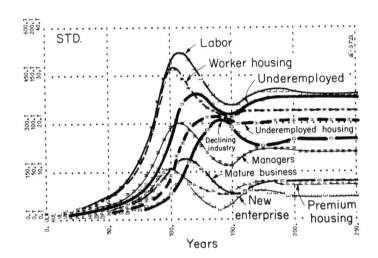

Figure 4
Compensating changes in housing and
unemployment.

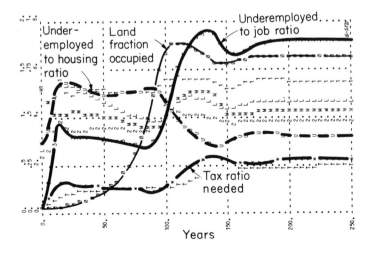

Figure 5
Decline of the urban area caused by low-cost-housing construction each year for 2.5 percent of the underemployed.

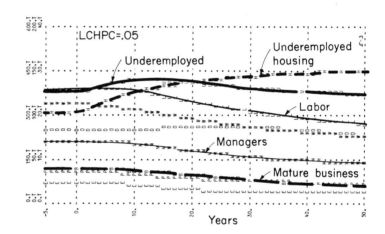

Figure 6
Rising unemployment and falling occupancy of housing.

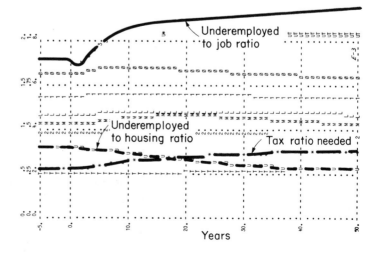

housing compared to jobs and by excessive concentration of low-income population. These conditions, created by aging industrial and dwelling buildings, interact to drive out the upper-income population and business activity, and to reduce the tax base. Once the decline starts, it tends to accelerate. Unless one can devise urban management policies that produce continuous renewal, difficulties are inherent.

Figure 7 shows an urban condition that begins with stagnation and then changes toward revival. Here 5 percent of the slum housing is removed each year and the incentives for new enterprise construction are increased somewhat. The result is a cascading of mutual interactions which raise the economic activity of the area, increase upward economic mobility for the underemployed population, and shift the population internally from the underemployed to the labor class. This is done without driving the existing low-income population out of the area. Underemployed housing is reduced. Initially this reduction comes largely from the empty housing. The resulting housing shortage restrains the population inflow which would otherwise defeat the revival of the area.

Figure 8 shows the same 50-year span as in the preceding figure. Here again, employment and housing move in opposite directions. The underemployed/job ratio falls which means more jobs and lower unemployment. On the other hand, the underemployed/housing ratio rises which means a tighter housing situation. If the economic circumstances are to be improved, we must accept some compensating change in other components of attractiveness. Here it is the increased tightness of housing which allows job opportunities to increase faster than population until a good economic balance is reached. I stress economic revival as the first stage of rebuilding a depressed area because it appears that an economic base must precede social and cultural development.

It is simply not possible to increase all of the attractiveness components of an area simultaneously. Attractiveness is here defined in a very broad sense. For example, legal restrictions like an immigration barrier into a country can produce enough "unattractiveness" to inward migration so that other components might be maintained at a high level. But wherever one component of attractiveness is high others will be found low.

Engineers, especially, should consider the compensating changes that will occur in the attractiveness components of an area because engineers tend to deal with economic considerations and technology. Economic and technical factors are more concrete than the intangible "quality of life" variables. The economic and technical aspects of a city are the ones we most easily see how to improve. Our technological society tends, therefore, to observe, react to, and improve

Figure 7
Revival caused by removal of 5 percent of
underemployed housing each year and
encouraging business construction to
generate jobs.

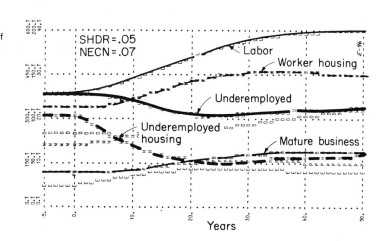

Figure 8
Falling unemployment and rise in housing
occupancy.

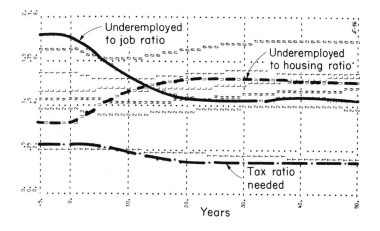

the economic and technical aspects of a city. Such improvements increase the technical and economic components of urban attractiveness. But as a result, population density rises until the urban area once again reaches attractiveness equilibrium with its environment. The burden of forced reduction in other components of attractiveness falls on the quality of life variables—crowding, pollution, and psychological stress. These less tangible variables have been weak, hard to measure, and have been defenseless against the persuasiveness and the certainty of improvement shown by the technical and economic considerations. But we are entering a time when a reversal will occur between the formerly weak and strong variables. For a substantial fraction of our population, the standard of living is already high enough so that more gain in the economic and technical areas will come at too high a price in the quality-of-life components of our environment. The engineer, if he continues to serve society, must balance a greater number of social needs against one another. At one time his task was simply to balance financial cost against economic performance of his technology. Now the product and also the medium of payment are both expanding. Social value and quality of life become part of the product. Psychological stress, ugliness, and crowding become part of the cost. Engineers who fail to recognize this broadened role will be vilified and castigated by a society which perceives them as narrow and insensitive to the demands of the times.

When a system misbehaves, we should ask ourselves what policies within that system cause the undesirable characteristics. If we examine the laws under which a city operates, we see a structure of regulations which could hardly be better designed to create stagnation and decline. The aging and decay of buildings is central to the urban decline process, yet we see throughout our tax laws and regulations numerous incentives to keep old buildings in place. As the value of a building decreases, so do the assessed taxes. The reduced expense makes it possible to retain the old building longer. For income tax purposes under some circumstances the value of a building can be depreciated several times. This produces incentives to keep an old building in place. Here is not the place for detail, but it seems clear that a different set of tax laws and city regulations could be devised to produce the individual incentives necessary for continuous renewal. As an example, I recently saw a suggestion that each building have a mandatory trust fund into which the owner must pay a levy each year. At any time, whoever owns the building can draw out the money in the trust fund if he demolishes the building and clears the land. This, you see, would create an earlier incentive for replacement. Property tax levies and income tax accounting could both be changed to produce pressures in the same direction.

Our studies of managerial, urban, and other social systems have uncovered many general characteristics of complex systems to which we must be alert if we are to avoid continuing to create detrimental modes of behavior.

First, complex systems are counterintuitive. They behave in ways that are opposite to what most people expect. They are counter-intuitive because our experience and intuition have been developed almost entirely from contact with simple systems. But in many ways, the behavior of simple systems is exactly opposite that of complex systems. Therefore, our experience misleads us into drawing the wrong conclusions about complex social systems.

Second, complex systems are strongly resistant to most policy changes. A new policy tends to warp the system so that slightly changed levels present new information to the policy points in the system. The new information, as processed through the new poli-cies, tends to give the old results. There are reasons inherent in the theory of complex systems why so many of our attempts at cor-recting a city, a company, or an economy are destined to fail.

But, third, the converse is also true. There are points in systems from which favorable influence will radiate. Often these points are dif-ficult to perceive. Often the action required is the opposite to that which might be expected. But when these points are found, they tend to radiate new information streams in such a way that the new circumstances, when processed through the old attitudes and poli-cies, produce a new result.

Fourth, complex systems tend to counteract most active programs aimed at alleviating symptoms. For example, Chapter 4 of *Urban Dynamics* shows how a job training program can increase the num-ber of underemployed in a city. When outside action tries to alter the condition of a system, the system relaxes its own internal pro-cesses aimed at the same result and throws the burden ever more onto the outside force which is attempting to produce a correction. The internal need for action is reduced and the external supplier of action must work ever harder.

Fifth, in complex systems the short-term response to a policy change is apt to be in the opposite direction from the long-term effect. This is especially treacherous. A policy change which improves matters in the short run lays a foundation for degradation in the long run. The short tenure of men in political office favors decisions which produce results quickly. These are often the very actions that eventu-ally drive the system to ever-worsening performance. Short-run versus long-run reversal processes are all around us. If an agricultural country is to industrialize, it must accumulate railroads, factories, and steel mills. This capital accumulation can only be done by for-going consumption and reducing the standard of living at first, in order that the standard of living may rise at a later time. If a company faces declining earnings because its products are obsolete, it must invest more heavily in product research and incur even deeper short-term losses if it is to recover in the more distant future to a profitable product stream. A student forgoes short-term earning opportunities by attending college in order to increase his longer-term earning capability. This reversal between the short run and the long run occurs repeatedly.

Sixth, a system contains internal dynamic mechanisms that *produce* the observed undesirable behavior. If we ignore the fundamental causes and simply try to overwhelm the symptoms, we pit two great sets of forces against one another. In general, our social systems have evolved to a very stable configuration. If the system is trouble-some, we should expect that the causes of the trouble are deeply embedded. The causes will outlast our persistence in overwhelming the symptoms. Furthermore, the internal pressures usually rise to counteract a corrective force from the outside. We can expend all our energy to no avail in trying to compensate for the troubles un-less we discover the basic causes and redesign the system so that it spontaneously moves to a new mode of behavior.

As the last of these characteristics of complex systems, we must recognize that a certain ensemble of conditions goes with each pos-sible mode of a system. More specifically, each mode of a system is accompanied by a set of pressures characteristic of that mode. We can not sustain a particular mode unless we are willing to accept the corresponding pressures. For example, contrast the depressed mode of a city in Figures 5 and 6 with the revived mode in Figures 7 and 8. The depressed mode is one characterized by the pressures that come from decaying buildings, low incomes, and social disorientation. But the revived mode also contains pressures. The revived mode is sus-tained by the housing shortage and the legal and tax pressures that generate a steady demolition and replacement of old buildings. But everyone in the system will want to alleviate the pressures. Active industry will want more employees; residents will want more floor space; and outsiders will want housing so they can move to the attractive job opportunities. Rents will be high. These pressures are easy to relieve by increasing the fraction of the land area permissible for housing, by keeping old buildings in place longer, and by allowing taller apartment buildings. But such moves will start the area back toward the depressed mode. We must decide the kind of system we want with knowledge of and acceptance of the accompanying pres-sures. Instead, much of our social legislation of the last several de-cades has consisted of trying to relieve one set of pressures after another. The result is a system mode characterized by inflexibility, conformity, crowding, frustration, supremacy of the organization over the individual, and a choking of the environment. And the result-ing pressures, acting through the counterintuitive and short- versus long-term reversal characteristics of complex systems, may well move us further in the same direction.

I am suggesting that the time is approaching when we can design social systems to obtain far better behavior. Different policies could change our urban areas from ones which are designed to deteriorate into ones which are designed for self-renewal. One can foresee a time when we will understand far better the relationships between monetary policy, interest rates, unemployment, and foreign exchange. Already such studies have thrown new light on the processes of corporate growth, on the reasons for product stagnation and loss of market share, and on the growth and decline of cities.

But to design new policies for social systems requires a level of skill which is rare. The kind of system modeling and policy design which I have been describing requires a professional training at least as extensive as that in any of the established professions. The proper training requires theory, laboratory, case studies, apprenticeship, and experience born of practice.

6
Industrialized Building: The European Experience

Valdimír Červenka

When compared with the average situation in Europe, the industrial production of prefabricated building components in Czechoslovakia is relatively highly developed. At the beginning of my lecture, therefore, I should like to elucidate some of the causes of this situation. To achieve this purpose it will be necessary for me to mention some characteristic features of the building industry and the generally valid conditions of its development.

The lag of the building industry behind the development of the majority of industrial branches has as its objective cause the specific characteristics of its final product. In comparison with the products of other industries, every building or structure is actually unique, as it is influenced by its site. For this reason, the development of the methods of industrial mass production was much more difficult in the building industry than in all other branches of industry. The process of standardization, too, is far more complicated and is participated in by a much larger number of parties than is the case of other branches of industry. The buildings and structures are bulky and heavy products, a fact which by itself is the cause of many hindrances to the development of industrial methods, as the transport and the handling equipment — as well as both of these operations themselves — more costly. For this reason, capital investments in the building industry have a far longer period of returnability and, generally speaking, are less profitable than in the majority of other industries. The sum of all these, as well as other factors, has resulted in technical backwardness of the building industry. In the general trend of economic development, the industry got into the situation where its high labor requirements were often used to advantage in the partial elimination of unemployment. This circumstance too often led to a negative attitude with regard to the use of machinery and industrial, as opposed to craft-fabrication.

With the gradual development of national economy, the difference between the standard of industry in general, and that of the building industry, specifically, increases. At the same time, however, the requirements imposed upon the capacity of the building industry increase. As soon as the reserves of manpower have been exhausted, the industrialization of building becomes an economic necessity because, otherwise, the backwardness of the building industry would retard further development of the whole national economy.

The development of industrial methods of construction requires, however, certain prerequisites. In the first place, it is necessary to guarantee the constant and continuous sales of the products of the building industry and the constant technical characteristics of buildings for a certain period, to ensure that the capital invested in the

Presented to the 1969 session. Valdimír Červenka is Director, Research Institute for Building and Architecture, Republic of Czechoslovakia.

production plant and machinery be economically utilized. As a rule, it is necessary that the creation of these prerequisites be fostered by direct participation of state authorities. The targets of the building industry ensure the growth of other sectors of the national economy, thus influencing simultaneously the development of the individual regional units, municipalities, districts and counties. Direct co-operation of central government with local government authorities is one of the conditions of this process.

What was the situation in Czechoslovakia? The stagnation of construction during the war years and vast war damage resulted in high requirements imposed upon the volume of construction, while the development of important industrial branches controlled by economic plans exhausted, in a relatively short period, the available reserves of manpower.

The balances of short-term and long-term plans of development of the national economy revealed the necessity of a considerable increase of the capacities of the building industry. The shortage of labor simultaneously showed that the necessary prerequisite for the attainment of planned economic targets is a systematic increase of the productivity of the building industry and the elimination of its technical and organizational lag behind all other industrial branches.

The plans for technical development of the building industry became parts of the plans for capital construction. The long-term plans for the development of the national economy became the basis of the calculations of the required growth of the building industry, justifying simultaneously the correctness and the necessity of investments required for the industrialization of construction.

It is understandable that the increased attention afforded to the industrial development of the building industry also gave rise to other measures, such as the fostering of the standardization of products and production methods. Particular attention was also afforded to the application of modular coordination and the development of application of standard, so-called "typified," designs. The purpose of these measures was to contribute to the improvement of the quality of buildings and to create the necessary prerequisites for economical industrialized production.

In the actual building production, stress was placed on the improvement of the methods of planning on the sites and in building corporations. Very valuable in this respect was the wide-scale application of the flowline method of construction which considerably rationalizes the whole process of construction, rendering it more economical and creating the necessary prerequisites for industrial mass production, both in the works and on the sites. More recently, the ever-increasing use of mathematical methods and computers has been assisting in the preparation, planning, and control of construction.

I have only briefly summarized the conditions which were commonly accepted for the industrialization of construction in Czechoslovakia. In particular cases there were certain deviations in the development of the individual regions due to the local conditions. It is only natural that particularly the standard of the economic and technical development of our country exerts a considerable influence on the development of both the extent and the technological quality of industrial methods of construction. Therefore, even though the method and the aims of the development of industrial methods of construction may be analogous, the contemporary state and the results in different parts of the country may be different.

It was the industrial production of reinforced concrete building components that underwent the greatest development, this being due to the fact that the raw materials required are generally available everywhere and that the technology of their production in the factory is very similar to the methods applied on the site.

In Czechoslovakia, the industrial production of reinforced concrete building components increased 5 to 7 times between 1955 and 1964, attaining a volume of more than 2.7 million cubic meters of precast concrete per year. The volume of production per 1,000 inhabitants, was 193 cubic meters. The consumption of precast concrete building components per one worker was 6 to 9 cubic meters. Recently also, the importance of metal and plastic components has been growing steadily; for instance, in the components of sanitary and kitchen cores, the production of which reaches 50,000 units a year. This means that more than half of the yearly production of dwellings incorporated sanitary cores which were produced in a factory and not on the site.

The development of the production of prefabricated building components also influences the construction methods. This is manifested most distinctly in housing construction. Thus, for example, the quota of apartments assembled of prefabricated large-size panels or blocks in the state and cooperative construction in 1960 was 30 percent, while in 1965 this quota rose to more than 70 percent. The state-controlled and cooperative construction represent about three quarters of the whole volume of housing construction.

The contribution of industrial methods manifests itself particularly by the reduction of on-site labor requirements and consequently by an increase of the productivity of on-site labor (see Table 1). This effect is increased also by the considerable reduction of the influence of the weather on the process of construction and the elimination of the seasonal character of building production. The shifting of some build-

Table 1   Time of construction of buildings with an average volume of 9,500 cubic meters.

Technology	Useful Area of Flat (Square meters)	Number of Construction Days per Flat	Percent
Bricks and Cement Blocks (TO2B)	54.4	11.3	100
Completely Assembled (TO6B)	61.0	6.5	58

ing operations into industrial works affords a considerable number of workers in the building industry similar working conditions as exist in other industrial branches. This reduces the fluctuation of the workers in the building industry and contributes indirectly to the increase of the productivity of labor in the building industry. Also, the required number of skilled craftsmen, such as carpenters, steel-workers, etc., is reduced throughout the building industry.

The cost of construction in different parts of the country varies considerably. In places where industrial mass production has been introduced to an adequate extent, and where its technological and organizational principles are adhered to, it is more successful than conventional construction methods. According to analyses of several thousands of dwelling units carried out in Czechoslovakia, the assembly of buildings from factory-made components ensures the reduction of labor requirements by about 40 percent on the site, and by about 20 percent in the whole production process, including the production of components. Also, the construction time is reduced by about 40 percent in comparison with conventional construction methods. On the other hand, the costs of transport, for an average distance of the works from the site of the order of 30 to 50 km, are 8 to 18 percent higher than in the case of conventional construction. However, as the costs of transport do not exceed 10 percent of overall costs of construction, this increase of costs represents a relatively small item.

Overall reduction of the costs of construction in financial units— some 10 to 15 percent—is not so important as the economy expressed in physical units. This small reduction in construction costs is due to the fact that industrial methods are not yet used in the whole production process. Analyses carried out in connection with precasting-plant construction has revealed that industrial production of building components offers considerable possibilities of further progress in the improvement of the quality and economy of products. Considerable improvement can be also achieved by the consistent application of the present-day level of mechanization and organization in the whole process of the production and the assembly of prefabricated components. The introduction of automation and the application of electronic computers for the preparation and the control of industrial building production can result in a considerable improvement of the present-day results.

When appraising the results atained, we can boldly say that the construction of a new industry, namely, that concerned with the industrialized production of building components, has created prerequisites and shown the way toward a positive solution of quantitative problems of the building industry. The standardization of products, connected with their industrial production, together with methods of designing based on standard (typified) designs, contributed to an improvement of the technical and functional standards of construction on a national scale.

The speedy development of this new branch of industry necessarily brought with it difficulties and shortcomings. In some cases, it was impossible to produce a sufficient quantity of new materials or train the required numbers of workers and technicians in the new production methods. It is understandable that in some places the quality of products and buildings was below average.

The application of industrial methods of construction also influenced the methods and techniques of architectural design. The schematic utilization of the method of designing based on the use of standard (typified) designs exerted, in some cases of mass construction, unfavorable influence on the appearance of housing projects. The objection usually raised against industrialized buildings is the lack of flexibility to various functional and town-planning requirements and a certain monotony of appearance.

Mass production of building components has already reached a point necessitating revaluation of certain principles of design and construction, if further development is to be attained. Some principles of the design of building components that, so far, have fostered the development of industrial methods, become a hindrance to further development when a certain standard of development has been reached. To quote an example: so far, the factory-made components for the assembly of buildings have been connected with a certain series of typified designs, or a certain structural system. Consequently, they could not be used for any other structural system or for another series of typified designs and could not, therefore, ever satisfy the new functional requirements and various layouts of newer, more comprehensive town-planning and architectural designs. Consequently, the typified designs led to smaller runs than would have been the case if their scope of application covered a wider assortment of buildings. At present, the system of typification and standardization of factory-made components and of the buildings assembled of them is being revised with the purpose of attaining such a system of building components as to enable their mutual

exchangeability and application to a larger number of buildings differing mutually, not only with regard to function, but also
to structure. If this endeavor is successful, it will be possible to increase the series of components produced and to use production
plants of a higher productivity and economy (Figures 1, 2).

One of the prerequisites for the attainment of this aim is a detailed
knowledge of the requirements of the users of the buildings. Such
investigations and evaluations are becoming the basis of the planning
of industrial mass production and for the construction of new production plants. Systematic investigations of the future requirements
assist also in the solution of one of the fundamental prerequisites
of industrial mass production, namely, the continuity of sales both
with regard to quantity and in respect to technical quality. It is from
this very viewpoint that the investigations of future consumption
are more important for the building industry than for other sectors
of the national economy and that they are becoming a standard part
of the planning of technical development and the investments connected with it.

Another important problem which is under consideration at present
is the improvement of the plant for mass production of building
components with the purpose of attaining the state when the production of components in large series would simultaneously afford
sufficient freedom for the production of a larger assortment of products. It is necessary to create such conditions which would make
it possible to satisfy, to a considerably greater extent than ever
before, the various requirements based on the functional and architectural design of buildings.

The examples of highly developed industrial branches show that progressive technology, based on the application of automation and
computers, makes it possible to satisfy to an ever-increasing extent
the requirements imposed by the users on the selection and the
quality of products without reducing the economy of production. The
application of these methods to the building industry will assist the
latter in the solution of many outstanding problems. When pursuing
this aim, however, it is necessary to base one's considerations, in the
majority of cases, on the prerequisite that the industrial product in
question is the building component and not the building. With this
in mind, it is necessary to develop the methods of the standardization
of components as well as the technology of their production and the
required plant. One of the preconditions is the ability of the production plant to adapt to the varying requirements of the user.

Another serious problem which is being solved at present regards
the level of concentration of precasting plants. According to experience hitherto acquired, the production costs drop with the increase
of the capacity of production. On the basis of investigations carried

Figure 1
A pure skeleton frame. This and the next figure illustrate the great variety and flexibility available to Czechoslovakian planners.

Figure 2
Pure load-bearing cross-walls. Czechoslovakian designers can choose from a wide variety of systems bounded by this and the pure skeleton frame shown in the preceding figure.

out in a considerable number of precasting plants in Czechoslovakia, the increase of the annual volume of production from 7,000 cubic meters to 70,000 cubic meters of precast concrete reduces the labor requirements by about 35 percent, the production costs by almost 40 percent, and the initial (investment) costs by more than 30 percent. The increase of the volume of production, however, is connected with the active radius of the plant, thus influencing the production costs. Apart from that, however, the action radius of the plant is linked also to the density of construction. In regions with more intensive construction, the precasting plants can have greater capacity and, consequently, are able to operate more economically. Generally speaking, the increase of transport costs due to the increase of the capacity of the works must be less than the economic gains due to the bigger production volume.

The greater the volume of production concentrated in one plant, the more efficient a production plant can be installed, and vice versa: a more efficient production plant increases the optimum volume of production in the plant. For a certain density of construction in the given territory and for a certain level of production equipment, it is always possible to deduce the optimum size of the works. According to the studies carried out by the Research Institute of Mechanization of the Production of Building Components, the optimum annual capacity of a plant producing precast reinforced concrete is approximately 125,000 cubic meters for an average transport distance of 30 to 40 km (about 25 miles).

At present, studies are being carried out with the purpose of verifying the possibilities of further development of the building industry by supplementing production that is presently based on reinforced concrete with the introduction of building components utilizing metals or plastics.

In conclusion, I should like to mention that the industrial production of building components is becoming an important industrial branch with development problems of its own. Simultaneously, it imposes new requirements on the development and production of machinery as well as factories for the production of building components. The quality and the standard of productivity of these machines will influence, in a decisive manner, the standard, the productivity, and the quality of the whole building industry.

The fulfillment of the great requirements imposed by society on the construction of dwellings, schools, hospitals, the reconstruction of towns, and the growth of industry, depends to a considerable extent precisely on the successful development of the process of industrialization of construction. In comparison with other industrial branches, these requirements are the more exacting because the building industry influences, more than other sectors of the national economy, the environment in which people have to live; thus participating to an ever-increasing extent in the growth of the standard of living and the cultural standard of human society.

Finally, a comparison should be made of the contemporaneous state of factory production of building components and the erection of buildings from these components in the United States and in the USSR, showing the differences and their causes and, if possible, deducing from this comparison some conclusions for further progress. The principal difference between the United States and, not only Czechoslovakia, but also the majority of European countries, lies in the fact that the United States developed a factory production of building products mostly intended for a multiplicity of the types of buildings and not for any closed system, while in Europe, in general, the prevailing majority of factory-made components form parts of certain closed systems. In the United States, the so-called "lightweight" components, made of metals, plastics, mineral wool, etc., represent a considerably greater portion of industrial production of building materials than in Europe. In the actual technology of construction, this state of affairs results in the fact that in the United States there is a relatively low quota of prefabricated buildings (if we do not take into account the timber houses), but a high standard of utilization of factory-made components for finishing operations applied to the finishing of on-site concrete load-bearing structures.

The industry of the United States took a longer road to the industrialization of construction, which is also more difficult. However, from the economic point of view, this way is more advantageous, as it is connected with lower risks. The experience amassed in the majority of European countries has shown that the development of industrial production of reinforced-concrete components for fully precast buildings can be safely ensured only with a certain amount of assistance from the government, whether it takes the form of large building contracts covering a longer period of time, or that of financial guarantees, etc. It is necessary to create such prerequisites in order to guarantee the contractors (the building corporations) that the investments of capital into highly exacting plants for the industrial production of building components are as advantageous as in other branches of the national economy. The current conditions on the building market do not afford such guarantees because, compared with other industries, the building industry suffers considerably greater fluctuations of highs and lows and more frequent changes from one type of construction to another. This is also the reason why the majority of factories of building components in the United States are provided with plants of lower technological standards and are, also, of lower organizational standard than other highly developed branches of industry. It can be generally said that the majority of these factories uses the same mechanisms and analogous methods

of work as are used on the sites, as investing capital into the plant
of a higher standard is connected with disproportionate risk.

Personally, I believe that the aiming of the building industry of the
United States on the production of flexible components which can be
used in the buildings of various types (and not intended for closed
systems) is a positive feature which should be further fostered.
Similarly, it is also necessary to foster the production of components
of metals, plastics, and other lightweight materials. Both of these
tendencies fully conform with the progressive trends of industrialization of construction.

There is a considerable gap in the building industry of the United
States, as compared with that of Europe, in the production of reinforced concrete components for fully precast buildings. However,
I do not believe that the solution of this problem would necessarily
lie in the way of closed systems. It would be correct to produce, in
this field, too, the components applicable to various types of buildings, but in such assortment so as to make it possible to erect whole
buildings. Even in the United States, the development of this type
of industrial production would require probably some sort of state
guarantee. I believe that these measures will have to be taken into
consideration as soon as it has been decided to deal with the housing
for the poor on a major scale, and when the state is interested in
the amount of construction costs. Among other things, this trend
will be necessitated by the ever-increasing wages of on-site labor
as compared with the wages in the factories.

7
The Industrialized Evolution

Laurence S. Cutler

An incredible interest in industrialization and prefabrication in the building industry has been sparked by the recent programs sponsored by the federal government and, specifically, HUD's Operation Breakthrough and the Housing and Urban Development Act of 1968. Building conferences, new courses in architectural and engineering schools, publications, and an emerging new professional, the building systems specialist, are all products of this explosive period of technological development and evaluation.

Throughout all this fashionable turmoil, the Czechoslovaks have continued to be among the foremost practitioners of industrialization in the world. Most notably, they have entered into the only known large-scale experimental construction program utilizing building systems; this program is in operation in a district known as Invalidovna in Prague. The Czechs have also used systems design for a new town, Etarea, a satellite to Prague.

The Prague Building Trust

The main strength of the Czech approach to building systems lies in the Prague Building Trust, the Stavebni Zavody Praha (in short, the SZP), a conglomeration of building construction firms providing research, design, engineering, manufacturing of components, and construction capabilities to both public and private agencies throughout the country. In the United States, we do not have an organization in any way similar to this nor do we have any similar facility for information dissemination; nor do we have testing facilities for providing government approvals, such as the agrément system in France or the NBA appraisal certificate in Great Britain. The SZP does not act as an approval agency nor does it need to, since the total efforts of Czech building construction are integrated and ordered by a single organization through a continuing evolution of research of the TO building system, which originated in 1940.

The SZP comprises eight enterprises and employs, in all, about 30,000 persons. In the course of the 1960s, SZP has built some ten large housing districts with complex facilities and over 50,000 dwelling units. The present yearly production capabilities represent over 5,000 dwelling units, and, until the recent political developments, it was expected that this would be increased in the near future.

In Czechoslovakia, the history of prefabrication goes back to the town of Zlin in 1940, when only a few precast concrete elements were manufactured, such as lintels, panels, and slabs; these were integrated with more traditional building construction. This idea of manufacturing prefabricated elements is as old as the building industry itself. Its realization, however, has gone through a varying course of development in the past, and it is only now that it seems

Presented to the 1969 session. Laurence S. Cutler is Assistant Professor of Architecture, Massachusetts Institute of Technology, and Principal, ECODESIGN, Inc.

likely that large-scale housing developments, not only in places such as Invalidovna, but throughout the world, will be constructed with prefabricated and industrialized techniques.

World War II, of course, retarded the utilization and further extension of the Czech experience, although the first units constructed were quite successful. Consequently, it has only been since the end of the War that the growth of prefabrication, both in Czechoslovakia and throughout most of Europe, has occurred.

The general advantages offered by industrialization are as follows:
1. Shortened construction time
2. Lower production cost
3. Factory and/or on-site methods of production
4. Limiting the scope of site preparation
5. All-weather construction
6. Economical utilization of labor
7. Substantial increase of mechanization in the construction process
8. Lowering the need for skilled laborers

Mrkvan and Hrncirik and Industrialization

During the conference, Ing. Pavel Mrkvan and Ing. Milan Hrncirik presented excellent papers in which they spoke of the latest developments in prefabrication in Czechoslovakia. Furthermore, they described a short history of standardization of building elements and the role it has played in determining the architecture of Czechoslovakia, as well as the phenomenal scale of usage of systems building in that country. This account of the industrialization of the Czech housing industry is, perhaps, not significant nor meaningful to the average American, but it is technically incredible to our producers, especially since the top multifamily housing producer in the United States does only a volume of 10,000 dwellings per year, with the number two and number three producers following with 4,000 units and 2,386 units per year, respectively.*

Architectural Expression

The early architectonic expression of the TO8B system was as unimaginative as any of the Eastern Block countries' architecture. However, in the recent past, Czechoslovakian architects and planners made some determined moves to halt the severe drift to monotony. The grave danger of the society being completely taken over by technology reared its ugly (ugly!) head, and the architects realized it; they understood the technology and its implications and they guided it into a creative search for flexibility and new design freedom. The manifestation of this freedom is fully demonstrated in the new town design for Etarea, yet the psychological release proved to be too much for the inhibited Czech designers. They overarticulated buildings, flinging them around the site with an overabundance of soccer fields and other social amenities long ignored by previous

---

*See *Professional Builder*, July 1969.

planners and designers. However, they did prove two things: (1) the design strength of the Czech people, and (2) the inherent design flexibilities of their building system (Figure 1).

Standardization

To cope with the great variety of designed building elements and the many consultant and building organizations within the SZP, one method has been to issue various publications and catalogues of the precast elements, standard structural and prototypical plan layout alternatives, the complex technological production regulations, and transport and assembly details. It is interesting to note that even when the architecture was little more than shelter—in 1956, for instance—no less than 750 types of concrete prefabricated elements had been standardized and incorporated into the production program and documented for general SZP usage. Needless to say, by United States standards, these elements, prepared for what we consider to be "closed systems," effectuated very stark, boxlike, and repetitive structures, inflexible in appearance, and (to use a trite expression) a certain sterile quality evolved. This is especially noted in terms of the large-scale and urban design aspects of these systems housing projects.

However, many of these elements are still being produced, and some have been in use for over 20 years without changes, but they have now been augmented by a new philosophy. This new philosophy is technically interesting in that it juxtaposes the original large precast panel system with a small, lighter weight concrete frame and allows the utilization of an infinite range of components and a broader architectural and planning expression. The inherent flexibilities of the composite structure permit the same freedoms as in traditional construction, and the package itself is an "open kit" of elements readily able to work anywhere and in any architectural idiom.

Systems Classifications

We find that building systems, in general, fall into the following categories: monolithic box units, frames, panels, and special construction techniques. The TO8B system, a composite of the panel and frame, is unique, having its first large-scale application soon to be realized in the new town for 135,000 people at Etarea. At present, no less than 85 percent of all multistory dwelling unit construction in Czechoslovakia is built with all—assembly systems techniques. In the course of the recent developments with TO8B, designers have strived to substitute the early and relatively heavy single-purpose structures by lighter elements, giving sufficient freedom for all alternative interior arrangements and enabling the attainment of an impressive architectonic expression of complete volumes.

The Czech system has gone through the pioneer period of the G40, the systems G57 and TO6B, and finally has developed the last of the series, the TO8B system, meeting the highest requirements for production, construction, and design freedom. In Prague alone, over

Figure 1
View of the TO8B system showing four-
story walk-up units used with high-
density twenty-two-story high-rise buildings for the new town of Etarea. All
illustrations in this chapter courtesy
of Stavebni Zavody Praha.

5,000 dwellings have been constructed in the last year by the TO8B system; 10,000 are presently under construction; and, another 15,000 are in the working drawings stage. In the last five years, dwellings which have been constructed by this method represent an average of 12.3 dwelling units per 1,000 inhabitants. These preceding figures are mentioned to illustrate the track record and experience of our East European colleagues. We in the United States are just beginning to realize the necessity for aggregation of market. We are investigating the total European experience so that when we begin, we can pick up at the eighth generation rather than "start all over again."

Therefore, it was truly fascinating to hear Ing. Mrkvan enumerate the newest developments of the TO8B system, summing them up in the following points: combination of transversal and longitudinal systems, use of supplementary load-bearing system (columns and steel skeleton), not set up of joints of floor and wall elements, introduction of supplementary span lengths, general elimination of door openings in panels, and a new type of assembly core units (P system). An open assembly, the system comprises the separating of the load-bearing structure from the facade elements and permits the maximum of facade treatments, both in materials and in modulation.

The TO8B System Itself

The basis of the TO8B system is in its structural design, a panel structure with transverse load-bearing walls. The axis distance of the walls is 600 centimeters, and the height for each story is usually 280 centimeters, with the depth of the dwelling units in multiples of $n \times 120$ centimeters (Figure 2). The minimum usual depth is approximately 9.60 meters (about 27 feet). A listing of the basic building elements of the system is as follows:

1. Reinforced concrete wall panels of full or hollow cross-section
2. Prestressed reinforced concrete hollow floor panels
3. Stairway panel and some supplementary elements

The sizes of all elements have been determined in conformity with the parameters for design within the system, including:

1. Minimum number of panels
2. Maximum combination versatility
3. Consistent modular coordination
4. Wide balance of building elements
5. Acoustic properties

The largest and heaviest of the building elements of the TO8B building system weigh approximately four tons. The static parameters of these building elements have been determined through a number of test structures and the long-term production runs already mentioned.

Component Elements: Bathroom Core

Sanitary installation and kitchen furnishings in the TO8B dwellings may be built-in either in prefabricated form or as separate items. The

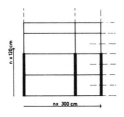

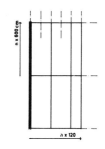

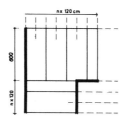

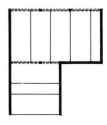

Figure 2
Diagrams illustrating various span conditions and showing the supplementary
column and panel supports.

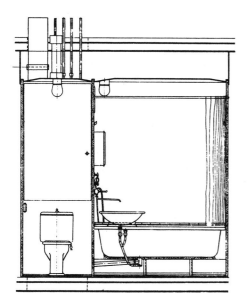

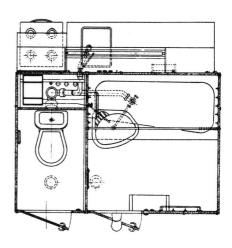

Figure 3
Section and plan drawings of the bath-
room-kitchen core unit with hot and cold
water, gas piping, and sewage lines, as
well as ventilation elements.

B3 installation unit is a typical example of the prefabricated alternative.

The covering structure of the unit determines the space of the bathroom, with w.c., and it comprises two spatial members, i.e., boxes, assembled from light sandwich-type partitions. The spatial members (bathroom, w.c.) have their own floor and soffit, thus creating an enclosed cell. The internal furnishings include bath tub, wash basin, w.c., and supplements. The w.c. box contains an installation shaft, including appropriate vertical and horizontal installation piping (hot and cold water, gas piping and sewerage) and the ventilation system (vertical ventilation precast elements). The core comprises internal electrical distribution lines and contains built-in lamps and an infra-red heater for bathroom heating (Figure 3).

The Present Structure

The calculation of static values for the structure have been determined according to extreme moments and the dimensioning utilized has been based on the principles of the theory of plasticity. All load-bearing elements are connected and joined by reinforcing and joined grooves between cavities and fully grouted with concrete. Consequently, the structural system, though presently used for low-rise housing walk-up dwelling units, is capable of construction up to twenty stories. It should be pointed out that this method of connection and structural design is totally different from the so-called dry-joint construction utilized in the project at Ronan Point in England, which failed due to a gas explosion and progressive collapse. The TO8B system comprises a fully monolithic structure and upon completion is comparable to a totally poured-in-place reinforced concrete building.

Specific Applications: Invalidovna

Experimental construction in the Invalidovna district in Prague has served as a verification of the basic economic and social assumptions for the introduction of an all-assembled building system with large floor spans, under the conditions and requirements of a large urban unit.

The project has also served as a verification of the advantages of dimensional unification of elements for housing and civic buildings. This continuous unification has been derived from a module of 60 cm for the main building structure and a module of 30 cm for the finishing elements.

Hollow structures have been used for floors and walls. The basic size of the floor panel has been set at 240×600 cm and that of walls at 480×250 cm. The thickness of all structures has been unified to the composition size of 20 cm.

For circumferential walls, sandwich-type end panels and suspended parapet panels have been introduced.

Figure 4
Invalidovna district under construction,
demonstrating the variety of generic
building types possible with TO8B, but
also explicitly indicating the starkness
of appearance.

Figure 5
The model of Etarea, a satellite community to Prague to be constructed
totally with the versatile Czech building
system TO8B. This model is testimony to
the fact that overarticulation can be as
neutral as the starkness seen in the
preceding picture of Invalidovna.

Apart from constructional, dispositional, production as well as technological viewpoints, this experiment has also served to prove the aesthetic possibilities of the proposed system in creating whole urbanistic units, clusters and groupings.

When designing the material composition of the district, advantageous use has been made of the various lengths and depths of buildings; heights are 1, 2, 5, 8, and 10 to 14 stories. The project comprises houses of the garden-type, row-type, walk-up, and high-rise buildings.

Two facade treatments are demonstrated here. One is characterized by continuous belts of parapets and windows with color textures, while the other is formed by exposed loggias and aggregate.

The structural system of the experimental project at Invalidovna has fully proven itself and it has been used as the primary basis for the further development of the TO8B system (Figure 4).

Etarea

The rapid growth of modern cities presents the urban designer with a number of pressing questions.

The Etarea project is a study aimed at fulfilling the function of basic research in the field of new-town construction; its location in a clean site has offered the chance to verify fully the ideas contained in the project. The authors have endeavored to create a healthy, functioning urbanistic organism, giving the inhabitants sufficient space for a fuller and richer life. This conception is in conformity with the role Etarea plays as a self-supporting link in a whole chain of similar satellite units, mutually connected by a common economic interest, that is, Prague. Situated some 20 km from Prague, in its final stage Etarea will provide housing for 135,000 inhabitants (Figure 5). The scale and scope of this project demonstrates not only urban design concepts, but the vast efficiencies and benefits of industrialization.

Finally, it must be clearly understood by Americans that the technological aspects of most building systems should be put to the service and needs of the users. It goes without saying that the systems themselves need not be restrictive in their use; this is certainly proven in the example illustrated by the Invalidovna project and, hopefully, in the Etarea project. The sole parameters for design in these two cases have been dictated by a social milieu and a political directive emphasizing large-scale production rather than an expression of the way people should and want to live within their built environment.

8
System Housing:
The Shelter Industry
Shapes Up

Robert E. Platts

I want to talk about housing production—*mass* housing production, for masses of people. I want to review the few unabashed successes and the raw potentials in "total system" housing production—"total system" here meaning the application of single-management, factory-through-field manufacturing muscle to the whole product, whether a house or a 40-story apartment tower.

We can best illustrate the force of such industrialization by looking at the handful of recent successes in Northern Europe—particularly Scandinavia, where many of the artificial constraints to building have been removed.* Then we can note the parallel moves and potentials in North America where the constraints and fragmentation are still alive but are weakening.

For once we should dwell upon the best part of the picture, just to feel the potentials, the incentives leading us to large-scale production systems. Not that the job ahead is easy, not that any kind of a "breakthrough" is possible; but simply that despite the constraints and fragmentation, the systems production tool can yield better discipline, quality, speed and productivity in producing shelter, and can yield cost reductions of 6 to 12 percent in the short run and perhaps 30 to 35 percent in the long run. If tied in properly to serious deployment of land assembly, block financing, overall planning with user-needs analysis, then industrialized building methods can yield a lot . . . Not a breakthrough, but a steady advance that our industry must make.

Northern Europe

Let me emphasize a few points that you can watch for in the factory-field "tour" that follows, to appreciate what real mass production of housing is all about.

Production requires market scale and continuity: particularly in Holland and Scandinavia, the housing client is often a large, independent society or cooperative that buys a large number of dwelling units (up to 20,000 a year for one such group) for its members. The state, in turn, puts housing on a pedestal, arranging for block financing (stipulating a certain efficiency level) and subsidizing through special interest rates. The effect is a market continuity and reliability to which a large producer can respond.

Production requires producers: The successful total-system ventures in Northern Europe are generally the creations of heavy engineering contractors, not of the normal builders or architects and seldom of materials groups alone. Such large contracting concerns can and do

Presented to the 1969 session. Robert E. Platts is President, Scanada Consultants Limited.
*Robert E. Platts, *System Production of Housing in Northern Europe*, report NRC 10873, National Research Council of Canada, Ottawa, September, 1969.

contribute the management, capital, planning and technical inputs required for the mammoth job of housing production.

Production requires labor: Particularly in Scandinavia, comprehensive industrial-type unions can cover the building scene, factory and field, with nothing to gain (and much to lose) from fighting for narrow protection of craft interests. Labor sits with management in achieving the remarkable new level in system building's safety aspects, scheduling control, incentive schemes, and general benefits through all seasons of the year 'round operations.

Production requires standardization of parts: Again, notably in Scandinavia, the states introduced national and international modular dimensioning families, uniform performance-type codes—again encouraging growth response by international vertically-integrated building producers and component suppliers.

The leading systems are "mixed" systems: closed and open, heavy and light. As will be shown, the best of the precast concrete multifamily projects, for example, feature half the job in "nonconcrete": The interior partitions, cabinet-wall units, closet-walls, sometimes bathrooms, and the entire curtain wall envelope are in modular, prefabricated, prefinished wood or light sandwich components slipped into the precise precast structure. Such components are reliably supplied by national-scale manufacturers who have evolved from (and may still be) producers of equally-complete small houses featuring similar interiors.

These leading systems have evolved in the most design-conscious countries on this earth—notably Denmark, Sweden, and Finland. And, yet, in North America, the design professions haven't been pushing, to put it kindly. Our history, training and "mystique" makes us somewhat anti–mass production. We think of each building as a special can-do feat. We proclaim its unique problems, its remarkable depth of foundation, its thousands of tons of steel and concrete, its architectural "integrity." Do we put equal emphasis on the building as a total product? On product design, producibility, simplicity, repetition, on higher productivity, on production flow management, to meet our shelter needs? We don't, but we must. These are *manufacturing* terms, and that's what's ahead of us. As in the leading cases in Northern Europe, building here must become a decent *product industry.* The crux of it all is housing for people.

Factory through Field

To begin our tour at the most successful edge of the picture, *large panel* precast multifamily housing ventures: Figure 1 shows the highly regarded Wates *site plant* at work in London, putting up high-rise apartment towers. Such a mobile plant can be moved to several large projects in its lifetime, and can work well in mild climates.

More recently, the movement has gone into central or regional factories for best control and productivity. The Puolimatka factory in Forssa, Finland, uses Schock-Beton compaction for beautifully detailed large-panels in precast concrete (Figure 2). All leaders have become this complete: they provide all the floors, all the cross-walls, and sometimes the exterior walls (not so often now). They provide the elevator shafts in precast (concrete), the stairway, the stairs, the landings, the refuse chutes, the ducts, the core walls, the service walls and, sometimes, the foundations—all of them in precast concrete. They provide something like one-third of the total building job out of the concrete factory. As manufacturing industries go the capital is low—about three million dollars in a plant like this, including road and site equipment, to produce 1,000 dwelling units per year per shift. To repeat the obvious, it does demand responsible, continuous volume in production and marketing, not all that easy to achieve in countries like the United States and Canada.

The trend in central precast plants is definitely toward the vertical battery type of production. We favor it in Canada because it is so much more compact and so much more heatable in our cold climate. It only takes up one-twelfth of the area of the flat precasting efforts. A leader is the Skarne system from Sweden (Figure 3). The vertical battery production gives you dead-flat, smooth surfaces on both sides of the cast panel, and it also gives you very easy striking of the molds so that you can design your concrete much more efficiently to suit the final structural needs.

"Roughing-in" the electricals into the mold as shown in Figure 4 ties up one expensive mold. The better thinking in this, of course, from any kind of production-engineering point of view, (i.e, any kind of *cost* point of view) is to do all this kind of work on subassembly tables, just like the feeder lines into an automobile line, so that the prime molds themselves aren't tied up. And the man here is an electrician, whereas he should be an assembly laborer.

Figure 5 illustrates the type of thinking now extending to the field. Everything is properly finished, catalogued, stored, selected for each large job, and moved. These panels now go from the trailer to the final position in the building without ever touching the ground. I'm talking really about a construction picture that's entirely alien to our North American practices. And this: here is a building site, not a printed circuit (Figure 6). This again is the Skarne system, and primarily what you see here are precast elements and large service subassemblies. Note the district heating subassemblies. Also of great interest: the base here is the new consolidated pad approach that the Swedes have developed, adapted from highway construction using blast rock directly.

In these systems the on-site work is made to move like an assembly

Figure 1
Wates site plant at work. All illustrations in this chapter courtesy of National Research Council, Ottawa, Canada.

Figure 2
Puolimatka factory, Forssa, Finland.

Figure 3
Precast panels at the Skarne plant.

Figure 4
Roughing in the electricals.

Figure 5
Panels being prepared for shipment.

Figure 6
Skarne System, showing precast elements and service subassemblies.

line. Cranes guided by means of closed-circuit TV perform up to 150 lifts a day on a regular basis: large panels, containers of partitions, cabinets, bathroom units and service subassemblies. One crane and crew erects up to $2\frac{1}{2}$ dwelling units a day.

The same sort of approach is shown in Figure 7: This is the Wates system again, in London. The changing face: In the background, the traditional Georgian housing and all the chimney pots; in the foreground, the system building going up, two floors a week complete. I think this is now at the eighteenth floor. They're instituting a slight change, so again the work-study people are on the job. One point to think about: In most of Northern Europe, including the United Kingdom, high-rise blocks are no longer being built for family accommodation—they are not livable enough for families.

The classic impression of a complete precast system tower block (Figure 8): Note the panel now swinging into place, an elevator shaft section with doors mounted and ready. This elegantly simple adaptation of an outstanding low-rise system has given us quite a shock. Several months after I snooped all over it (admiringly, and seeing nothing wrong) the completed building shed one entire corner, top to bottom, following a gas explosion on the eighteenth floor. By hindsight we can see a hinge-like detail that almost promotes such progressive collapse, and we can implement simple changes in detail and panel arrangement to prevent it. Unfortunately, in the United Kingdom a vicious pendulum-swing has resulted, quite naturally, I suppose, with new pressure-vessel-like requirements for tedious and expensive steel lacing of such structures, unrealistically restrictive. Getting away from the structure, the wall of Figure 9 shows the right kind of detailing, technically elegant. It's the Larsen and Neilson system from Denmark: now-typical Nordic detailing, the so-called "open rain screen" principle. It's the vented one that tends to do away with the need for magic polymer sealants on any height of building. The insulation in the sandwich panel construction extending right to the edge. There's no wrap-around, there's no heat transmission or heat bridging paths, and there's no constraints built up at the edges to cause cracks. This Scandinavian loose leaf approach in concrete sandwich construction has now become the rule in northern Europe, and it's attracting proper attention in Canada and the United States. More details on all these points are given in the NRC publication referred to at the outset.

Lessons from "Light and Dry"

Now, the next few points seems to be a complete digression away from the successful multifamily systems, but they aren't. The long and painful history of "light and dry" prefabrication has finally resulted in advances in interior systems that in turn have brought the precast "total systems" picture to its best.

We can look back 40 years and even 100 years at that long-enduring,

Figure 7
Wates system, London.

Figure 8
Precast system tower block.

Figure 9
Larsen and Neilson system, Denmark.

Figure 10
Harlow New Town, England.

Figure 11
Steel and lightweight-concrete structure,
stressed-wood infill (Maidenhead,
England).

never fully successful dream, "open system" building. This tends
to be a beloved creature among architects, built on the hope that
modular magic will allow a designer to bring together parts from
many suppliers to produce any shape of building for any client. This
hope has usually been linked with "light-and-dry" modular systems,
such as this one, 5M housing in Harlow New Town, England (Figure
10). It's a derivative of the famous CLASP school system and it brings
the same advantages: Speed and cost savings in the shell alone
(which is only one-third of a building job in cost). It uses light plywood box beam sections and steel stanchions, crisply detailed.
Laminated gypsum party walls fill in between dwellings. Everything
is made for man-handling in this system, and up to the point of the
shell close-in, it goes very precisely, very quickly, quite well. But
then, in common with so many of the light and dry systems until
recently, the rationale stops there, the bulk of the work—two-thirds
of the housing construction work, that is to say the servicing and the
interiors complete—is still done the old way.

There's a kicker in most of these light and dry developments that
are still being pushed everywhere: During the Crimean War in the
1850s Florence Nightingale ordered and installed prefabricated
field hospitals quite similar to what you have just seen—but somewhat more advanced in terms of completeness and perhaps overall
success in serving people. An invidious comparison?

Even when more complete, the framed systems tend to suffer from
tedious, repetitive "cover up" steps. Note Cubitts very precise and
modular, four-story (balcony access) steel and lightweight concrete
structure with stressed skin wood and partition panel infill—going
ahead in another borough north of London, with the quaint old Anglo-
Saxon name of Maidenhead (Figure 11). Following fast close-in, and
partitioning, you're still faced with the old problem of light and dry,
the many "make-good" steps getting from the rough shells to the
finished thing that people want to live in. The party wall in light concrete slabs illustrates this (Figure 12). Cubitts also work very
successfully with the Balency precast system as illustrated later
(Thamesmead).

The change toward far more complete light systems is demonstrated
best by Elementhus in Sweden, an 18-year-old system, using small
trees in the northern woods in Sweden (Figure 13). It uses everything, including the shavings, processed through a continuous radio-
frequency glue laminator line that was the first of its kind in the
world and is still unique. It produces 20-centimeter by 20-centi-
meter, (8-inch by 8-inch) module units of more-or-less stressed skin
or box construction forming all the floors, all the walls and partitions,
the ceiling and sometimes the roof going together precisely. (This
word keeps coming up over and over again, because this is what's

Figure 12
Light concrete-slab party wall (Maiden-head, England).

Figure 13
Elementhus project, Sweden.

so alien to our own concepts of putting together buildings in a hurry.
And these do go together in a hurry.)

Again, to a rather complete light and dry system south of Stockholm,
in the new town of Salemstaden. This is "Siporex" housing (Figure
14) in a very light, uniform gas concrete prefinished with a mineral-
filled acrylic finish. Row housing—very high quality units, beautiful
hardware, finishing and cabinetry throughout—all going together
with strictly butt-to-butt precision-fitting joints, no telerance allowed,
not cut, no fit, no expansion joints, no slop, and it works. I was there
during the early stages and the place was crawling with work-study
people in the usual Swedish manner, but it was already going very
smoothly—despite the work-study people.

Another interesting facet here. The roof sections go into place with
a rough hardboard soffit, and the wiring is distributed under that
(Figure 15). I couldn't really get a photo of the main point: Two very
relaxed Swedes come in with shopping bag under one arm. They
proceed to do the complete ceilings in two houses a day, everything,
simply by reaching into their shopping bag and unfolding precut and
pre-edged film ceilings of a white opaque polyvinyl chloride, which
stretches into place to form each room's ceiling, secured at the peri-
meter alone in special trim. The plastic skin stretches in drum-skin
fashion to form the ceiling itself.

This emphasis on interior systems has paid off for several of the leading small-house prefabricators in Northern Europe, as is well demonstrated in this interior view (Figure 16). The key thing is that everything
your eyes see was brought to the site this way. Every surface arrived
prefinished, including all the walls, the ceilings, the partitions and
even the handsome knockdown cabinetry in either baked enamel or
vinyl finishes. This is the standard quality approach now that you
find throughout Germany, Holland, and Scandinavia. Everything slips
into place with a few millimeters tolerance: no cutting, no fitting, no
gaps, no stuffing, no grouting, no "make-good." And it works fast.
Modular cabinet-wall units themselves serve as slip-in, movable
partitions. This particular example (Figure 17) was produced by the
Okal Kreibaum system in Germany. It uses an extruded tubular
particleboard to form the core material for various sandwich panel
configurations, put together with whole wall skins of hardboard on
stainless steel belt presses, forming handsome houses indeed.

**Back to Complete
Multifamily Systems**

These light, modular prefinished interior systems (and exterior curtain walls) were evolved first for small housing enterprises, but now
have been extended across Northern Europe into multifamily housing, even of up to 21, 25 stories high. Concurrently, part of the
evolution that has come along with it is the evolution away from
small pigeonhole types of large-panel precast concrete dwellings,
into more *open dwelling* forms. This again is the Skarne system

Figure 14
Siporex housing being assembled
(Salemstaden, Sweden).

Figure 17
Manufacture of cabinet-wall material
for use in the Okal Kreibaum system
(Germany).

Figure 15
Wiring in the Siporex system (Salemstaden, Sweden).

Figure 16
Prefinished interior components used in
Europe.

Figure 18
Interior, Skarne system.

(Figure 18). Everything you see came precast or prefabricated. The floor will go down in a vinyl-on-felt to cover the whole thing. The partitions will go into place in a very precise snap-in fit, after all the flooring is down of course. You can see that the ceiling is already painted on the open-room approach with a gloss paint over the kitchen and a flat paint everywhere else; the partitions will slip into place (Figure 19) now meeting the cabinet wall and closet wall units and also the precast structural columns, and meeting them all within a few millimeters, less than an eighth of an inch in tolerance in any direction. The partitions here are a vinyl on gypsum, glued to form a dead-flat stress-skin panel; very flat, very stiff, glued to a wood grid in this case, I believe. Rigid vinyl snap-in trim closes the wiring chase at the top.

And all this isn't luxury housing or somebody's stunt. This is high-volume people's housing, and very high quality work. It's yielding quality apartments in under 500 man-hours, including factory and field, as against the 1,100 man-hours we take for lesser quality apartments in North America. The multifamily buildings in precast concrete have recently taken the same light, prefinished approach in complete exterior walls. And this brings up another point in the success of system production of buildings for people, and that's the whole question of building codes. Wood curtain walls can be used in Finland, Denmark, Norway or in the United Kingdom. In Europe, Canadian lumber is used for complete wood frame curtain walls, used on high rise precast buildings in a manner that our North American building codes won't allow (Figure 20 and 21, a Wates Building). We can't use our own material the way it is being used in Europe and technically and economically these curtain walls are elegant indeed. The fire codes in London are rational enough to accept wood-framed window walls. This is the type of uniform, national and even international, performance-based building codes that we have to have. I don't see how we in North America can continue to argue this point if we are actually concerned about building buildings.

The point on rational fire codes is illustrated by material usage beyond wood frame: This is the beautifully precise SF1 steel and precast concrete structure with fiberglass plastic wall system, again going up in London, 22 stories. (Figure 22). The surface that you see is a molded fiberglass plastic, backed by a foam concrete poured into the plastic pan.

Services and Boxes

As befitting the more flexible design/production/use philosophy noted above for interior systems, there is also a growing trend away from "frozen" cast-in-panel services (Figure 23) toward a "plug-in-take-out" flexibility of services installation, maintenance and change. Core walls (Figure 24), vertical chase units, tubular voids in the cross-walls, false closets, panel joints, baseboard ring mains and chases over or under the movable partitions—all are used to attain such

Figure 19
Slip-in partitions, Skarne system.

Figure 20
Wood-frame curtain wall (Europe).

Figure 21
A Wates building incorporating wood-frame curtain walls.

Figure 22
Fiberglass-plastic wall system (London).

Figure 23
Cast-in-panel service system.

Figure 24
Case-wall system.

flexibility in the leading examples of precast systems. This approach does not require floating floors or suspended ceilings—features that reduce the overall "factory content" and productivity. It does require acceptance of shallow electrical boxes and infrequent anchorage of cables, such as in the electrical codes abroad.

There are still continuing efforts in Europe, perhaps not so much as in North America, towards the so-called box systems or cube systems or "modules." There are a dozen words for it. The Europeans have gone through the mill, especially in Russia and Israel, on these approaches. They've generally backed away to simply making the intrinsically costlier bathroom and kitchen units (Figure 25) in box form, because these better justify the shipping of so much air, so much awkward handling. The Danes are reverting back to doing the same thing in basically wood construction, using the Danish fire-treated compact wood and plywood, primarily to get the weight back down to match the rest of the large-panel concrete components. In England, vacuum-formed acrylic experimental units, and in Canada, fiberglass-plastic production units, allow much greater scope in the long run than do the wood or typical precast concrete box units; they provide single process one-piece production of all the fixtures as well as the room itself. Since in traditional Canadian housing practice the plumbing work is now completed on-site in about 17 man-hours, any box-unit bathroom effort should include the fixtures in the one process if it is to yield worthwhile gains.

Especially in medium- and high-rise housing, the complete box-module systems (going beyond kitchen and bath units alone) are restrictive in layout and tend to fight the trend towards free and changeable interiors. Further, the box units can be cumbersome in production and handling and wasteful in the resulting doubling of walls and floors. But these latter drawbacks are circumvented by the recent ventures into "checkerboard" stacked concrete units utilizing sophisticated on-site factories. Recent work is beginning to convince us that straightforward mass housing of this type can yield potential cost savings of over 20 percent compared to the best of conventional in situ concrete apartments, whereas the best large-panel precast systems are hard pressed to save over 12 percent. In low-rise housing, light box module systems are also developing similar savings as discussed later.

Here's a sectional or module house now in full production (Figure 26). It's a beautiful job of sectional housing by the Polar Company, using rather heavily engineered wood stress-skin units—three units actually, to form one dwelling. Each front window shows you the width of one unit. Then the further shorter section off to the left houses the sauna, which every house in Finland has to have. The unit is called the Polar Kansantalo: "people's house." It's a good deal similar to the Alcan work in Canada. The crisp Scandinavian design

Figure 25
European modular kitchen unit.

Figure 26
Modular house (Polar Company, Finland).

means that it's ready as is for two-story row housing in repeated stacked modules, and that's how it's now being used in Finland.

The Full Range

Again to illustrate the healthy mix that's working well in recent years, this is a large-panel precast system—one of the best known (Figure 27). It's the Jespersen system from Denmark. Here it's been used by John Laing Construction Ltd. and is forming complete walk-up housing in Livingston New Town, Scotland. It illustrates two things. One is the fact that the better large-panel precast concrete systems use a great deal of material that isn't concrete. The entire curtain wall system and much of the interiors are in prefinished wood-frame panels. Second, it illustrates the kind of livable housing forms that can get quite delightful in the United Kingdom and Finland, particularly in medium density housing, with every householder still having a place for the bicycles and baby carriages right beside the front door, even though the front door is a long way from the grass. The terminology is also delightful. The English call this, if I remember rightly, balcony-terrace-access-over-and-under-split-scissors-maisonettes. I may have it wrong, but the result is right, the livability is right for in-city schemes. The production is complicated by on-site insulating and waterproofing of terraces—simplifications will be shown later on.

The current scheme of Thamesmead in London must stand as the greatest exposition yet of this "terrace in the sky" approach—a low-rise, high-density downtown solution (Figures 28, 29). Cubitts is producing this scheme using the Balency system. This kind of thinking fits logically into the evolving multilevel city-core approach, in which traffic movement and parking is relegated to the depths, shops and light industry are next, below ground, and schools, housing, terraces, playgrounds are up above ground in the sun and air. Both the United Kingdom and Denmark have such planning underway.

From the production and technical-performance point of view the terraced balcony-access housing just shown suffers from significant complexities. The same livability can be gained by reverting to vertically faced gravity structures with similar but independent panel structures forming a stacked-terrace subsystem, greatly simplifying everything. (Figure 30). The stacked terrace is thermally separated from the building structure, which it simply twins, and water runoff, flashing and walking surfaces, etc. are no problem since the terraces are not over living space. The example shown features two-story apartment units leading from internal pedestrian streets, each two-story unit having one deep balcony or terrace. Again, the protection against the vertical spread of fire offered by the deep precast terraces allows the use of light, inexpensive curtain walls, say in steel or wood frames.

Figure 27
Large-panel system (Livingston New
Town, Scotland, built by John Laing
Construction Ltd., using the Danish
Jespersen system).

Figure 28
Thamesmead, London. Balency system.

Figure 29
Thamesmead, London. Balency system.

Figure 30
Stacked-terrace subsystem.

The whole question of a building's shape and geometry has become
a major and painful one if only because system building can yield
wild shapes more easily than can traditional multistory building practice. Large-panel structures and especially box structures can be
stacked in flying cantilevered configurations that can delight the
designer. There is a woeful amount of sophomoric exuberance that
ignores the *intrinsic* cost-raising effects of free form, non-compact
shapes; and Canada has been the worst offender. First, as the surface-
to-volume ratio goes up, so does the capital cost, heating and cooling costs, and maintenance costs. Second, if the access paths
deviate from straight lines, vertical and horizontal (whether the
traffic is people, services or wastes), the costs are driven higher
again. This is instrinsic, square-one stuff, quite independent of production volume or technology. Some of our system building exercises
stand as gigantic radiators heating the northern skies. In choosing
complex shapes we should at least know their extra cost, and they
are calculable.

Productivity and Costs

An indicator of the efficiency attained in a product industry is the
direct labor content—not the whole story, but a good indicator.
Taking the dwelling unit as the end product, and taking all the labor
functions traditionally associated with the "builder," the graph (Figure
31) shows the direct labor content for a few truly successful house-
production-systems, as a proportion of the final cost in place.

The labor measure here is for all labor beyond the *material* manufacture stage, including all trusses, walls, partitions, floors, finishing
(factory and field), and also millwork and cabinetry installation, but
not their manufacture or fabrication. As far as possible, all systems
were thus assessed on a comparable basis. With work in hand on all
these generic systems, we were able to take a measure first of wood
frame project-site housing in Canada and the Northern United States:
direct labor content, 22 to 25 percent. Then to large-scale serial
production of apartments in Holland, beautifully organized heated
flying-form in situ concrete "pidgeon hole" structure, extensive use
of service subassemblies and prefabricated partitions, etc: direct
labor content, about 15 percent. Next, to the leading "total system"
precast work in Sweden, with extensive use of service subassemblies
and cores, and prefinished interior systems: direct labor content,
about 10 percent. Finally to fairly comparable measures of mobile-
home factory labor in the midwestern United States: direct labor
content improved down to 8 percent and even 5 percent.

The interesting thing about such a production across the spectrum
of systems, filling in the types not on the graph, is that at any degree
of prefabrication a heavy high-rise system entails roughly the same
man-hours—usually a little more—as a light frame house. For
example, the project site wood frame house takes about 1000 man-
hours or a little less, including line supervision and off-site adminis-

tration, while well-organized concrete flat-plate apartments (in situ) take about 1100 or less man-hours per dwelling unit. Similarly a large-panel precast apartment (the Swedish example) can be completed in only 500 man-hours or less, factory and field, and so can a "closed-panel and core" wood frame house system.

The next graph (Figure 32) shows the rough measure of the range of "prefabrication" applied to a wood frame bungalow, three bedroom, 1100 sq. ft., with all man-hours included *except* basement and grade work. (The graph applies very closely to recent steel-frame housing too.) The "shop content" goes up from near zero ("traditional" housebuilding, if it still exists somewhere) to over 90 percent, while the overall direct labor (factory and field) comes down from around 700 man-hours to under 300, above foundations. But the investment in plant climbs to over $2 million to achieve this. The net gain in moving across the graph to the most advanced "box" system works out to about 6 percent to 12 percent in costs, given a reasonably constant material quality and type, and equal wages factory and field. Precast apartment systems at best achieve the same gains, and add another few percent saving by reduced capital charges due to faster completions.

That booming "constraint-free" example of mass housing industrialization, the mobile home, can move the man-hours down to about 200 for a two section "house," and gains further cost reductions because of simple "applications engineering" over many years resulting in *material* economies. This is all-important. It is not a permanent house, but its measure as a production tool (the total box approach) is this: its retail price has stayed constant or decreased slightly as sizes have increased, since 1947, while the construction cost index has more than doubled. The inferences for true mass housing of any quality are well appreciated, if not yet well established. Finland's "Kansantalo" is moving in very good company, and it's all just beginning in the low-rise field.

Working from mobile home experience, we can infer fairly reliably that stacked, light box modules can yield savings beyond 12 percent in permanent low-rise multifamily housing. Certain code restrictions not affecting quality must be changed, but surely the building industry is adult enough to effect such changes. Going into medium- and high-rise housing, we have noted before that the recent logical moves toward checkerboard stacking, relocatable plant, and smart design can offer potential savings of over 20 percent over traditional apartments, although this must yet be proven. However, where we want considerable flexibility for wide income ranges, the best work in medium and high rise still lies in that breed we can call "precise large-panel precast / box cores / light prefinished infill and interiors."

The whole challenging business is in a state of flux, with housing

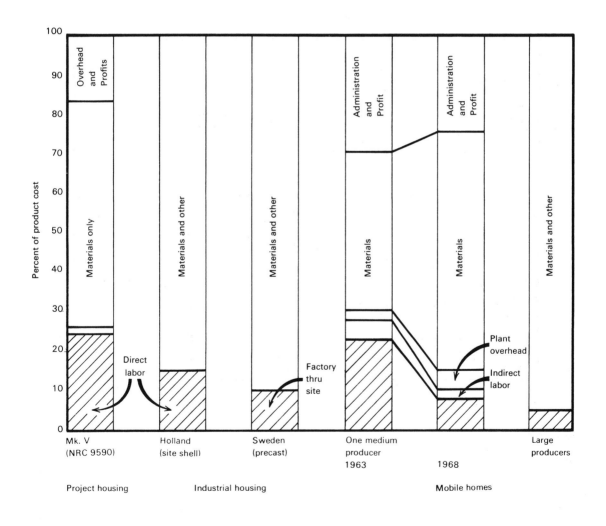

Figure 31
Direct-labor content of successful house-
production systems.

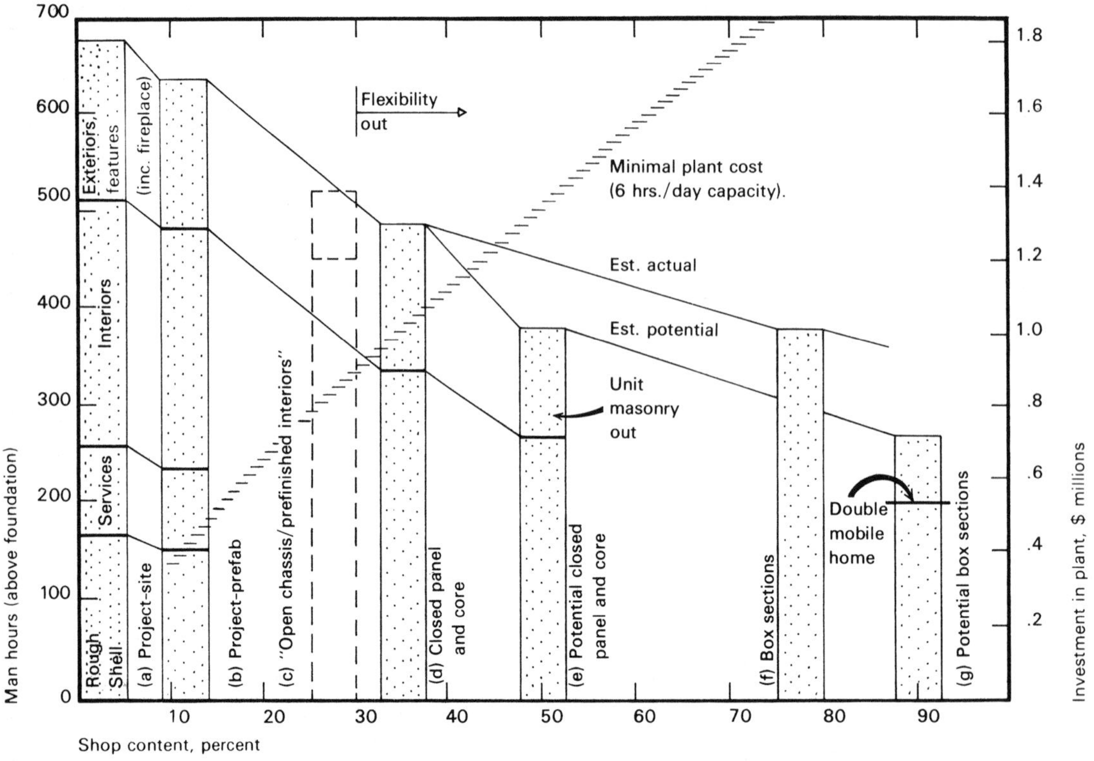

Figure 32
Division of man-hours between shop and
on-site work.

sorely needed but not yet tied to *sustained* high volume procurement. In these troubled but exciting times the better end of the shelter industry must applaud the modest beginnings such as "Breakthrough." We must encourage any mechanisms for massive research and development, large-scale sustained housing production—and basic efforts into better community design using the evolving production tools.

9
A Philosophy for Industrialization

David M. Pellish

In presenting a philosophy for industrialization, I shall briefly discuss the following: (1) The state-of-the-art of housing technology; (2) The prerequisites for industrialization; (3) Required institutional changes for advancing industrialization; (4) Some suggested approaches for the federal government; and (5) Some programs now being developed by the New York State Urban Development Corporation to take advantage of innovations in industrialized building.

To lay the groundwork for this discussion, it is necessary to review some points. The term "housing technology" will refer to the entire process employed in planning, producing, and managing the housing delivery system. It does not refer only to exotic hardware systems of miraculous widgets or to the latest wave of new building systems. Sophisticated management techniques applied to conventional construction are also considered a significant aspect of housing technology.

The nation's pressing need to sharply increase its housing inventory, particularly homes for lower-income families, has focused attention on the potential of housing technology. Industrialization of homebuilding has been proposed by many as the most effective approach to achieving that objective.

Disregarding current claims and international publicity, one must recognize the fundamental basis of industrialization: its full potential can be attained only through high-volume production. Constructing a prototype with an industrialized building system merely proves that it can stand up against the elements. It is the dress rehearsal before the formal debut. The objective must be production—not experimentation.

Those promoting housing industrialization follow two different approaches. On the one hand, some believe that industrialization will best be achieved through large companies and new total building systems. Convinced that the fragmented nature of the building industry is inhibiting progress, they would rather rely upon the large companies regardless of their current ability to produce homes. If such companies produced the necessary technology to reach the moon, are they not also capable of providing the necessary know-how for producing housing? With abundant technical and management resources, their proponents feel they could transform homebuilding into an industry that is more in tune with the twentieth century.

Another school of thought, which I am inclined to follow, is more pragmatic than the first. It prefers to concentrate on those industrialized building techniques that are now available. Rather than con-

Presented to the 1970 session. David M. Pellish is Housing Technology Officer, New York State Urban Development Corporation.

centrate on a few long-term experimental programs with large companies which may or may not prove successful, it would emphasize further improvement of the building industry's present capabilities. The objective of this approach would be to create a more receptive climate for all types of innovations, produced by companies of all sizes, and applicable throughout the building industry.

Although both approaches have a common objective, i.e., to advance industrialization, there is a basic difference in philosophy and timing. The first takes a somewhat cautious attitude towards industrialization. It proceeds on a systematic basis from one level of commitments to another, in a manner similar to federal contracting for aerospace and defense programs. HUD's Operation Breakthrough is a good example of this approach. By focusing on a few selected companies and their proposed building systems, chances are that some of them will provide unprecedented showcases for industrialization in this country. Unfortunately, there still is no clear indication of HUD's commitment to provide for the first full production run of any system. The second approach assumed a more optimistic, philosophical attitude. It states that the nation's housing problems can, and must, be dealt with now with innovations that are already on hand. Pointing to authorization granted to the Secretary of Housing in Section 108 of the 1968 Housing Act, proponents of this school of thought contend it is possible to proceed immediately with government programs for industrialization.

Of course, the targets are lower and less dramatic with Section 108. Congress referred to only five new building systems—not 22. But the authorization provides for production runs of 1,000 units a year for five years.

The distinction between the two approaches revolves about one critical question: Are current industrialized building systems to be considered ready for experimental models—or for full production? We know that, aside from producing thousands of mobile homes and some low-rise housing modules, the American homebuilding industry has had little experience with industrialization. Nevertheless, I believe it would be interesting to determine whether we in the United States aren't taking a rather parochial view in this field. There is sufficient evidence to indicate that far-reaching advances in housing technology have already been attained in other countries.

State-of-the-Art of Housing Technology

During the past decade, countries throughout Europe responded to urgent housing needs in war-ravaged cities by making it possible for industrialized building systems to be employed. Confronted with severe labor shortages, they developed new institutions to facilitate the introduction of innovations. The result was that scores of new construction methods and materials emerged from the European building industry.

To illustrate advances already made in Europe, let us examine experiences in the United Kingdom, where half of all housing constructed receives government assistance. In response to the government's encouragement, over 40 percent of publicly assisted housing was constructed with industrialized building techniques.

Preassembled utility walls and prefabricated building components were developed and incorporated in all types of housing. The construction of high-rise multifamily housing with precast concrete components has been employed in thousands of dwelling units. The use of colored exposed aggregate and other surface treatments on exterior concrete panels have made it possible to avoid monotony with these mass-produced elements.

On-site precast concrete plants for large projects have minimized problems normally associated with transporting components. Since the Ronan Point disaster, new building standards for joints between precast concrete floors and walls have been developed to improve structural continuity between these elements.

Unfortunately, as a result of our own institutional constraints, some materials and assemblies that are widely used in the United Kingdom cannot be easily transferred to the United States. For example, plastic tubes for electric wiring and plastic pipes for draining wastes are incorporated in precast concrete panels in the United Kingdom. Nevertheless, American code standards and local building practices usually prohibit the use of plastics in such applications—even in conventional construction.

These examples were intended to merely illustrate the point that many technological innovations have been developed and used outside the United States. The know-how and experiences with such advanced techniques are already available. The problem that confronts us is not developing new innovations. Our greatest challenge is: "How can we let these innovations happen here now?"

The Prerequisites for Industrialization

Rather than dissipate our energies on searches for technological novelties, we should concentrate on developing a framework conductive to industrialization which would be comparable to those established in Europe during the past decade. To do that, we should focus attention on the two major prerequisites for industrialization. First, continuous production of standardized elements must be assured. Second, a steady supply of vital elements essential to housing construction must be provided.

If we do not consider these basic considerations, future cost-saving innovations will follow the same route to oblivion as their predecessors. The history of housing innovations in the United States is strewn with failures, because their proponents either did not fully comprehend the prerequisites for industrialization or underestimated their impact on the innovation's future.

Production Continuity

The primary objective of industrialization is to reduce unit costs through continuous production of standardized elements. It is insufficient to merely prove that a product can be manufactured on the assembly line. Ford's Model T demonstrated industrialization's benefits because it lowered costs to the average family's level through assembly-line production of thousands of cars—not just through the building of a few prototypes.

The development of industrialized homebuilding methods requires the same consideration. Cost-savings through industrialization can only be demonstrated when mass-produced standardized elements are repeated in hundreds of similar structures. The primary objective of government-sponsored programs involving industrialization should, therefore, be concerned with incorporating innovations in regular production runs.

Getting an innovation into production, however, is only the first hurdle. Inevitably, unexpected bugs are bound to emerge in the first phase. Management and labor must also learn to become proficient in their respective tasks. The true test of the innovation will come after that initial learning period.

The most meaningful target for introducing industrialized building techniques is rarely mentioned in current discussions on housing technology. Winning acceptance of a new concept—or gaining approval of the prototype—are merely preliminary events. They are initial skirmishes before the main battle for a place in home-building. However, that battle often ends in failure for too many experiments with housing industrialization.

The primary objective of housing industrialization programs is to achieve and maintain *continuity of production*—not just production of the first units. Realistic cost savings will emerge when the production line can be sustained for long periods. Only then will management and labor reach high levels of productivity. Only then will the high-risk investments required of industry begin to pay off.

There has been much talk about aggregating the markets required to assure continuous production. Recent pronouncements from Washington indicate that this task will be left to the innovators. After the prototypes are built with government assistance, it will be up to private entrepreneurs to develop their own markets and production goals. That final phase contains the greatest hazards to an industrialization program.

Contrary to popular thinking, those in industrialized housing are confronted with many more problems than the typical developer and homebuilder.   In addition to the many uncertainties and obstacles that any innovator must overcome, they must provide for continuous production. It isn't sufficient to simply identify markets with a potential demand for their innovations. When that assembly line grinds to a halt, the company's existence is threatened if it cannot defray the continuing costs of plant and equipment.

Unlike the conventional homebuilder, who builds 5 to 25 units per year, industrialized housing companies must produce hundreds of units annually to obtain real cost savings. I believe it is unrealistic to expect private entrepreneurs to cope with the overwhelming difficulties of maintaining high production without the assistance of public agencies.

Government programs designed to stimulate advanced housing technology must also develop new approaches for resolving the many problems that have plagued the housing industry. If we accept the principle that continuity of production must be obtained to provide cost savings through industrialization, there must be a steady flow in the supply of land, money, labor and materials, and technical information. To a great extent, these factors are more significant than the new construction techniques to be employed. Supply breakdowns in any one of these areas threaten production and will spell inevitable failure for the industrialized housing systems.

Steady Flow of Supply Elements
Land Supply

When each industrialized dwelling unit rolls off the assembly line, there must be a land site ready to receive it. Unlike other industries, housing cannot be stored on shelves in a warehouse. The costs and space required for each unit are too great to permit extensive stockpiling.

Present practices employed by homebuilders for assembling and preparing land are grossly inadequate for industrialized housing. Land use regulations, for example, severely limit the supply of housing sites. The typical homebuilder copes with the restricted land supply and high costs for available lots by "leapfrogging" from one community to another. His low production volume permits him to adjust to the vicissitudes of local zoning. On the other hand, industrialized housing does not enjoy this advantage. In order to survive, it must have a continuous supply of sites—at reasonable cost.

The authority to promulgate and administer zoning ordinances and subdivision regulations resides in the police powers granted by state governments to local communities. Until now, the federal government has taken little interest in this area, except to promote technical improvements in local regulations. There have been recent suggestions that the federal government preempt restrictive land regulations. This observer believes that such moves will gain little headway against the opposing forces defending local home rule.

Nevertheless, it is extremely critical to resolve the fundamental problem of restrictive regulations if the land supply is to be increased to meet our housing goals. Fundamental changes must be undertaken to remove the abuses of constitutional authority that permit middle-class families to obtain new homes but prohibit housing for lower-income families in the same communities.

The United States Supreme Court must now review the constitutional issues involved in local land regulations. The question to be resolved is whether these regulations deny equal opportunity to lower-income and minority families to use the available land supply in and around our cities.

It is conceivable that the long-awaited decision by the Supreme Court will have as much impact on easing the flow of land for housing as the historic decisions to end segregated schools. The objectives are quite similar. Rather than nibble away at local discriminatory patterns, it is necessary to attack these issues at their roots. Local laws which abuse our democratic principles must be struck down and denied their present aura of legitimacy.

Money Supply

The current low level of housing production is directly attributable to high interest rates and the lack of mortgage funds. If the nation's housing needs are to be filled, and if continuous high-volume production is to be maintained, new ways must be developed to assure a steady flow of money to finance housing.

At present, money flows to those sectors of the economy offering the highest rate of return. Housing is the first to feel the impact of our fluctuating economic patterns. Resulting high interest rates raise housing costs beyond the reach of lower-income families.

We cannot expect unlimited public subsidies to absorb excessive interest rates for the large volume of needed housing. There may never be sufficient public funds for that purpose. Nevertheless, the steady flow of money—at reasonable cost—must be assured.

One direct approach to this problem is to provide for a flow of money that would be insulated from the fluctuations of the general economy. Regardless of the attractions of other economic sectors, money for mortgages and construction loans can, and should, be assured by government fiat. I have proposed that all institutions accumulating the public's savings be required to direct a nominal portion of their annual investments to lower-income housing.

Some sectors of the financial community, such as savings and loan associations, invest most of their available funds in housing—but not necessarily lower-income housing. On the other hand, a group of public-spirited life insurance companies did set aside special funds amounting to one billion dollars for investment in urban ghettos. My proposal would spread the responsibility by making such worthwhile steps mandatory for all financial institutions.

Thus, all banks, life insurance companies, and pension funds would be required by federal law to invest a minimum of 5 percent of their annual investment portfolio in housing programs for low-income housing. The risks would be minimal because government assistance programs already stand behind this type of housing.

Supply of Labor and Materials

To meet the nation's housing goals, over 2.6 million housing units must be constructed annually for at least the next ten years. The closest the building industry ever came to that level was in 1950, when about two million units were built.

During the past decade, when the housing industry was producing at about one-half of the desired rate, shortages in labor and materials were commonplace. In view of these recent experiences, there is strong reason to believe that more serious shortages will arise when production approaches the country's housing targets.

An adequate supply of materials needed for large-volume production cannot be taken for granted. For example, the building industry always assumed that lumber would be available—until grave shortages arose about one and one-half years ago. In desperation, builders and the lumber industry strongly demanded that trees in the nation's forest preserves be cut down to supply their pressing needs.

Employment in the building industry has traditionally followed erratic patterns. Severe labor shortages emerge from time to time. Then, again, a drop in construction employment by about 30 percent between August and February is expected in normal years. Little wonder, therefore, that the supply of labor is always a matter of grave concern in the building industry.

A steady, dependable supply of labor and materials is essential for high-volume housing production. The building industry should not have to raid the nation's reserves or resort to pirating labor from other industries when expected shortages develop.

Sophisticated planning systems must be developed to anticipate potential shortages and to prepare for alternative sources of supply. It takes three to five years to train apprentices. The present hit-or-miss approach to construction planning programs makes it difficult, or impossible, to anticipate labor shortages that far in advance.

Advanced information systems developed and maintained by government and industry could fill such gaps.

Supply of Information

The fragmented nature of the building industry and the many uncertainties confronting all sectors of this industry now inhibit progress in housing technology. Architects, engineers, homebuilders, and producers—to name a few—make daily decisions without benefit of vital technical information. The result is their judgments tend to be conservative in order to minimize losses in this risky business.

Industrialized building systems depend upon increased acceptance and use of technological innovations. But there is no dependable system for informing all decision-makers in this industry that a proposed innovation is technically valid. In fact, innovators have no reliable system to inform each other about current technical advances in the state of the art.

There have been recent efforts in the federal government, particularly in HUD and the Department of Commerce, to organize information systems. Unfortunately, such endeavors have received low priorities in their respective departments. Until there is a long-term commitment by a public or private agency to provide an appropriate information system, that is supported by sufficient funding and adequately staffed with competent technicians, we must expect technological advances in industrialization to continue to be inhibited.

Required Institutional Changes

If the products of housing industrialization are to be universally accepted, radical changes must be made in the present chaotic system that controls the introduction of innovations. Building industry spokesmen inveigh against this system by focusing attention on building codes. I submit that this is a simplistic approach to complex problems.

Those who seek acceptance of innovations are faced with a wide array of obstacles. Code approval by the building inspector is really the end of the line. The inspector relies upon code requirements established by standards-making organizations, such as the model code groups, trade associations, and other technical bodies.

But code standards usually lag considerably behind technological advances. More important, these code standards represent only one facet of an evaluation process that often requires new test methods and criteria.

Unfortunately, there is no authoritative framework for evaluating innovations which may be referred to by those developing new building methods and materials, as well as those approving their use. The standards that are used for testing materials, for enforcing building codes, and for evaluating innovations are now developed and administered by dozens of different groups in government and industry that have little, if any, communication with one another.

It has been claimed that the model code groups provide uniformity for local building codes. Even if we assumed that the four model codes were exactly alike, we would find that they have insufficient impact on local code administration.

A survey conducted by the Census Bureau for the Douglas Commission found that a majority of the more than 3,200 local building codes were based on the model codes. Nevertheless, only 15 percent of those communities amended their codes in line with the updating procedures of the model code groups.

It is irrelevant to consider the origin of building codes unless they are constantly updated. In this era of rapidly changing technology, obsolete standards are the greatest obstacles to the introduction of innovations.

Recent developments in Europe have demonstrated a more effective system for establishing technical standards and for evaluating building innovations. Faced with urgent housing needs and critical labor shortages, they turned to industrialized building methods. However, conservative traditions imposed constraints that inhibited the introduction of new technology.

The agrément system was developed by the French to overcome the traditional reluctance to approve innovations. An agency in the French national government was authorized to evaluate new methods and materials and to grant approval certificates to those that met nationally accepted standards. This provided local code officials, builders, professionals, banks and insurance companies with vital information concerning the validity of proposed innovations.

The French system was adopted by other nations and formed the basis for international arrangements under the agrément union. It even attracted technicians from behind the Iron Curtain, who were also interested in benefiting from this system.

One weakness that emerged is of particular significance to the United States. Operating under the usual bureaucratic tempo, it took too long for technical evaluations to be completed. Private industry felt that much time could be saved if the work was conducted outside of government.

To provide a similar mechanism which would facilitate the introduction of building innovations in the United States, I developed the concept of the National Institute of Building Sciences (NIBS) when I served with the National Commission on Urban Problems, headed by Senator Douglas. The proposal was intended to establish a new framework—outside of government—for existing organizations and institutions that are now involved in standards-making and product evaluation.

The primary objective of NIBS is to create an umbrella for all technical activities relating to testing and materials, code standards, product acceptance, research and development, and the exchange of information in all these fields. The fundamental concept is that all of these activities are interconnected. Rather than concentrate on one facet—as those who promote a national building code would have us do—it is necessary to create a single, well-coordinated framework, to facilitate the introduction and use of technological innovations.

Under this proposal, the National Academies of Sciences and Engineering would be requested to establish guidelines so that no interest group would dominate the proceedings. A permanent technical secretariat would be appointed to see that all work was carried out expeditiously. Recognized coordinating organizations, such as ASTM and ANSI, would be requested to assist in the administration of NIBS. All work would be carried out by a series of national and regional technical committees, with each devoted to a particular technical specialty (Figure 1).

The proposal was included in the report of the Douglas Commission. The concept was endorsed by the Kaiser Committee and, more recently, by the Panel on Housing Technology of the Commerce Department's Technical Advisory Board. The American Institute of Architects and the Council of Housing Producers, representing the largest homebuilders, also gave it their support.

In 1969, Senator Javits and Congressman Moorhead introduced bills in Congress to establish NIBS. A total of eight senators and 30 representatives were co-sponsors of these bills. It is significant that they represented both political parties and all sections of the country.

Despite these encouraging signs, however, the movement to obtain major institutional changes through the proposed legislation received a sharp setback in its initial round in Congress. Unqualified acceptance of NIBS, as it was originally conceived, was considered to be a secondary issue. We had hoped for full public discussion of all problems, followed by a commitment from government and industry to develop the new approaches required to facilitate the introduction of innovations.

Unfortunately, the bills did not receive sufficient support within the congressional committees to which they were assigned. Nor was there any major discussion of this issue on the floor of Congress

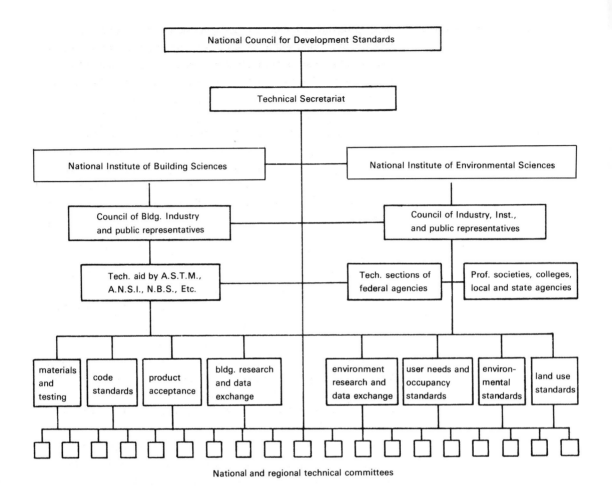

National Council for Development Standards

Technical Secretariat

National Institute of Building Sciences

National Institute of Environmental Sciences

Council of Bldg. Industry and public representatives

Council of Industry, Inst., and public representatives

Tech. aid by A.S.T.M., A.N.S.I., N.B.S., Etc.

Tech. sections of federal agencies

Prof. societies, colleges, local and state agencies

materials and testing

code standards

product acceptance

bldg. research and data exchange

environment research and data exchange

user needs and occupancy standards

environmental standards

land use standards

National and regional technical committees

Figure 1
Organization of a national council for
development standards and related
groups as proposed by the National
Academies of Science and Engineering.

when housing legislation was being considered that year. At this moment, it is irrelevant to review the merits and weaknesses of that specific effort. I suggest that this proposed approach will not fade away. The problems that remain to plague innovators in the building industry will thrust it into the public forum once again.

Suggested Approaches for the Federal Government

If the nation's housing crisis is to be resolved, a new type of leadership must be provided by the federal government. No other entity in government or industry has as much impact on homebuilding as HUD. No other agency or private group has comparable authority or potential resources for overcoming the many obstacles and uncertainties that plague this industry.

As I see it, the critical problem that has not yet been solved is finding the appropriate division of responsibilities between the different levels of government and private industry. In the final analysis, it is up to industry to build the necessary homes. It cannot do the job, though, without governmental assistance.

The trouble with government has been that sometimes it tries to do too much, and at other times it doesn't do enough. The many government regulations that confuse builders and delay projects are either taken for granted or cursed as the price for dealing with government.

It isn't merely a question of bureaucratic red tape. The question should be: What can agencies at all levels of government do—besides protecting public health and safety—to expedite the delivery of housing where it is most needed?

The federal government can contribute much to this task. It must first take a much more comprehensive view of its own position vis-à-vis the homebuilding process. By judiciously using its many assistance programs to obtain defined national goals, HUD could make profound changes in the present chaotic system. Let us examine how this would affect the future of industrialized housing.

It must be recognized that a vast amount of knowledge and experience with industrialized housing systems has already been accumulated in Europe. We can proceed immediately to use the most advanced European building systems, as well as some advanced techniques that were developed in the United States.

Rather than concentrate resources and manpower on experimental programs to construct prototypes, HUD could move now into a program of full production. Section 108 of the 1968 Housing Act authorized the Secretary of HUD to make the necessary commitments to five industrialized building systems for five years. That is sufficient to demonstrate the effects of a full production program now—and to establish the credibility of these innovations in the American home-building system.

To ensure the success of this new approach, HUD must take the leadership in providing for a continuous supply of the critical elements described above, i.e. land, money, labor and materials, and vital technical information. Of course, HUD has little authority to effect the necessary changes in each of these areas. However, the Secretary of Housing and his staff could provide the initiative for mobilizing the necessary forces to achieve those goals.

To cite one example, I believe the time has arrived for HUD to step into the zoning question in much the same way as HEW and the Justice Department have moved to force localities to end discrimination in voting and education. It isn't merely a problem of finding land for federally-subsidized, low-income housing. Discriminatory ordinances also affect middle-income families who are denied multi-family apartments in the suburbs.

The constitutional basis for restrictive zoning must now be reviewed. The Secretary of Housing should provide moral leadership in this issue—all the way up to the Supreme Court. Of course, the forces for maintaining the status quo represent a very formidable phalanx opposing progress. I submit that federal housing officials now have sufficient mandates in the offices they hold to justify all activities required to pursue this objective.

Notwithstanding my suggestions for *increased* federal involvement in assuring a steady flow of those supply elements that are vital to homebuilding, particularly industrialized housing construction, I believe there are other areas that require *reduced* intervention by government. To cite one example, the evaluation of technological innovations should be conducted by qualified experts under conditions that are isolated from government—and from vested private interests as well.

When the proposal to establish a National Institute of Building Sciences was being considered by Congress, HUD requested amendments that would assign primary responsibility for evaluating building innovations to the Secretary of Housing. This was, of course, the antithesis of the declared principle of NIBS—that it become a nongovernmental institution. The lack of skilled technicians on HUD's staff and the urgent need to concentrate on moving housing programs expeditiously are sufficient arguments against this proposal to expand authority into this area.

New York State Urban Development Corporation

I stated earlier that there must be a new distribution of responsibilities among government agencies with respect to housing construction programs. Having described proposed approaches for federal agencies, I must hasten to add that state and local governments also have significant roles to play in this field.

Under our system of government, those agencies that are closest to our urban communities still have functions that cannot be assumed by the federal government. It is they who are best able to respond to local needs and their particular characteristics, which vary from one end of the country to another.

The federal government has traditionally provided the initiative and financial resources for housing, but local communities and states have been responsible for implementing those programs. Rarely has a federal agency actually gone into the business of building housing.

There are many who claim that local governments have been unable or unwilling to carry out their responsibilities in housing development. Recent developments in New York State will illustrate the positive contributions that local governments can make in advancing the state of the art and in providing urgently needed housing.

In 1968, the Urban Development Corporation was established by the State Legislature with the primary mission of assisting local governments in providing housing for low- and moderate-income families. It was granted extraordinary powers, including authority to condemn and acquire property, to override local codes and ordinances and to float its own bonds. Under Ed Logue's leadership, UDC's housing programs mushroomed in this brief period to about 35,000 units (as of the date of this conference).

To check spiraling construction costs, a special program for new technology has been developed in UDC. Its basic philosophy conforms with the principles I referred to earlier with respect to industrialized building systems. In contrast to other programs on the national scene, we have undertaken a more pragmatic approach.

Our goal is to provide a maximum volume of housing *now*—with cost-saving innovations. We cannot afford to wait for the completion of experimental prototypes, and have, therefore, concentrated on promoting the use of available technological innovations in our housing construction program immediately.

Rather than concentrate all attention on new hardware, we are also promoting the development and use of innovations throughout the construction process. Rather than focus on large companies responsible for delivering a total housing package, we are attempting to plug new products and materials into our housing projects throughout New York State.

Our consultants, the Tishman Research Corporation of New York and

Goody/Clancy Associates of Boston, have developed a unique system for evaluating innovations, called the Cost Analog System. Using their techniques, we have been able to sift through dozens of proposed innovations in order to determine their cost effectiveness.

In the first phase of our technology program, the following innovations were designated by the Cost Analog System: staggered steel truss; filigree wide-slab floor (or Omnia); metal-edge gypsum plank; romex wiring; high-bond mortar single-wythe wall; factory-fabricated plumbing wall; combined vent-drain system; dry shaft wall; instant painting; and ceramic tile panels.

By incorporating these innovations in appropriate combinations in our projects, we anticipate up to 11 percent savings in construction costs and up to 36 percent savings in construction time. We are now working with UDC's consulting architects and engineers, seeking to incorporate, wherever possible, this first generation of innovations in projects that are now on the drafting boards.

The second phase of our work has concentrated on the structural systems using precast concrete components, including those that have been widely used throughout Europe. Some of them will be singled out for possible use in our projects in the very near future.

Our Technology Office also plans to undertake long-range programs to determine how technical and design standards that have traditionally inhibited new developments can be improved. On the basis of earlier studies, we have been able to focus on those areas of construction that provide the maximum opportunities for cost savings. For example, we have determined that innovations affecting the structure, interior partitions and surfaces, and the mechanical systems have top priority.

Our primary objective is to create appropriate conditions to facilitate the introduction and use of cost-saving innovations. Recognizing that many innovations can only prove their cost-saving potential through high-volume production, we are attempting to provide a large-scale assured market for those that pass our Cost Analog System.

We know that UDC, operating alone, cannot create the necessary conditions for advancing housing technology. Therefore, we are working with other state and local agencies to create a more receptive environment for innovations. Cooperation from members of the building industry and construction labor unions are equally important. The response to our program from those quarters has been very encouraging.

Conclusion

The history of housing construction is replete with examples of noble experiments. In some instances, they were successfully incorporated in homebuilding. However, more often, they were set aside among other dreams on bookshelves. Those of us who wish to help solve the housing crisis through technology must be constantly reminded of two considerations: (1) the housing crisis confronting our cities must be solved now; and (2) a favorable climate for new housing technology will only be obtained when innovations can demonstrate their cost-saving contributions.

I submit that these two objectives can be met at this very moment. We know that some advances in technology are already available—without further experimenting. Our success in the initial phases can lay the foundations for further advances in the future. Let us get on with the job now.

10
European Panel Systems

Guy G. Rothenstein

Before delving into the subject, I would like to state that I have reservations about such absolute categorizations as panel systems, module systems, etc., inasmuch as it may lead to rigid and dogmatic concepts which are incompatible with the systems concept of solving problems. More important than panels or modules is the degree of systematization of a building system, and if we are out to solve building problems, and, more particularly, housing problems, we cannot settle for less than *total building systems*.

Total building systems are made up of "hardware" and "software." Once the technology controlling the hardware aspects has been perfected, the major thrust in building systems is the constant evolution of the software aspects. Inasmuch as some of the European systems have solved the hardware aspects to a large degree, emphasis of the more sophisticated European systems is now in the area of software solutions. But before I discuss the software aspects in detail, let us have a look at the hardware of those systems making extensive use of panels.

The main reasons for the use of panels are flexibility, relative lightness, the possibility of mechanizing the production with relatively inexpensive machinery using a minimum of factory space, simple storage, shipping, and erection, and proven economy. In comparing a space made up of panels with a space enclosed by a module, it can be said that six panels correspond to approximately $1\frac{1}{2}$ modules, while six sides of enclosed space usually form only one module.

However, as implied before, the true building system cannot be dogmatic, and the Balency large-panel system has made it a practice for many years to combine panels with modules whenever such a solution has economical advantages.

Production Equipment

The production equipment used by different European systems for the production of panels varies in design, but not in basic principle. There are vertical machines producing solid reinforced panels with all incorporations. Sandwich panels of exterior walls including exterior finish and insulation are usually produced in horizontal machines which can be raised toward the vertical for demolding. Mechanical blocks containing plumbing, ventilating and electrical work are usually produced with special machines and other machines or molds are used to produce stairs, balconies, etc.

Factories

The factories of European systems vary greatly from sophisticated central plants such as the Balency system's MBM plant in Milan, to temporary on-site plants used in other English and French systems.

Presented to the 1970 session. Guy G. Rothenstein is Vice-President, Balency-MBM-US Corporation.

One aspect which affects the design of factories is the handling of the components during manufacture. The most sophisticated plants use in-plant bridge cranes to service the casting machines and have openable roof sections over the finishing areas to permit the yard tower crane to reach in and lift out the daily production for storage in the yards. Simpler factories have sliding roof sections over each casting machine, and the yard tower crane is used for both servicing the machines as well as storing the production in the yard. An important aspect of the central plants are the social facilities which become feasible through continuous industrialized production. These include excellent sanitary facilities, lunch rooms, and continuous training courses permitting the employment of unskilled workers, who are trained for specific tasks rather than for a complete trade.

The decisions on what type of factory to use should be based on the market, amortization time, cost of money, amount of money available, cost of labor, and other factors affecting the cost of the product. In general it can be stated that where a continuous market exists central factories permit us to obtain the lowest possible cost of the product. This should be particularly true in the United States, where on-site labor rates are in general substantially higher than off-site factory rates.

Transportation and Erection

Central factories require a transportation system forming a continuous link between factory and production sites. In general, special trailers permitting vertical transport of panels are being used. Generally, economic radii are equal to the distance a truck can travel from the factory to the site and return in one day.

The erection is usually fully programmed and proceeds in accordance with schedules prepared during the design phase of a development. The more sophisticated European systems produce about 75 percent of the building with the system and even portions of the work done on the erection site are fully industrialized.

So much for the hardware aspects.

As I pointed out before, the software really makes the system, and among the software items one towers over all others, and that is *management*. It may be said that the systems hardware merely sets the stage for the deployment of industrial management techniques using scientific methods. I will here present a series of charts demonstrating how management works in: (1) A theoretical nonbuilding closed system, and an open system (Figure 1); (2) A closed building system (Figure 2); (3) A traditional building system (Figure 3); (4) an open building system (Figure 4); and (5) A partially open special program system (Figure 5).

European systems using predominantly panels are generally closed

Figure 1
Closed and open systems; the relationship between consumers and products.
All illustrations in this chapter courtesy of Balency-MBM-US Corporation.

Figure 2
Closed building system.

Figure 3
Traditional building.

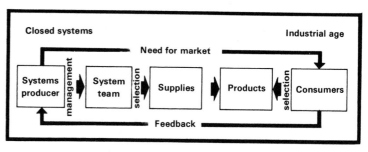

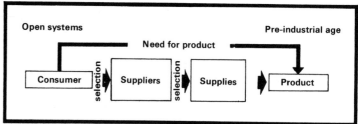

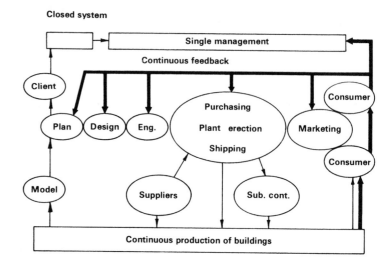

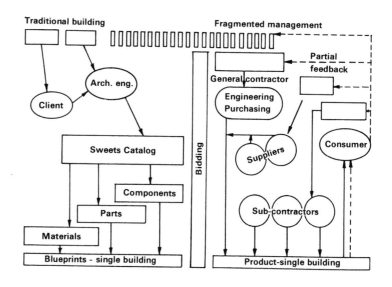

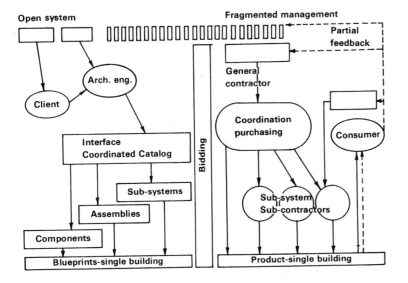

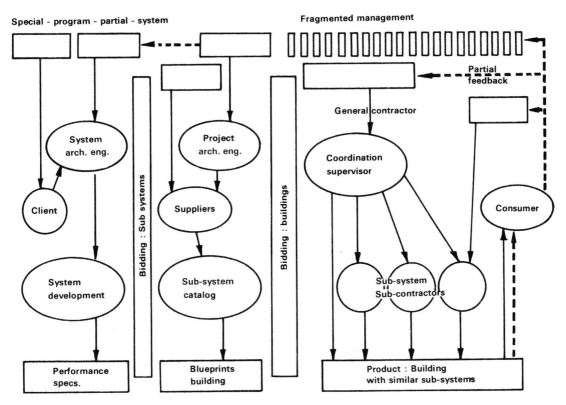

Figure 4
Open building system.

Figure 5
Special-program partial system.

Figure 6
Thamesmead, London. A "new-town in-town" consisting of low-rise walk-up units and high-rise tower-slab structures, all constructed from a single panel system.

Figure 7
Thamesmead, London. Architectural treatment of the low-rise walk-up units includes poured-in-place ramps and richly articulated facade balconies.

Figure 8
Thamesmead, London. Access ramp to the low-rise units dramatically slips past the cantilevered balconies constructed of precast panels.

systems, and yet they vary greatly in the type of management and the degree of management's involvement in the total process of producing buildings

Total management involvement is still very rare inasmuch as most European systems do not have control of the market. Exceptions to this are the Balency-system operation in France involved with marketing several thousand single-family homes per year, and the Milan operation—which has recently launched a very successful marketing program of high-rise condominium apartments. It may be said that controlling the marketing aspects provides that continuity which is the basis of any industrial activity, and it closes the link of feedback of consumer reaction that is lacking in operations limited in serving others who do the marketing of the product.

Some of the European systems are controlled by consulting engineers, who are obviously more involved with the hardware aspects of systems. Other systems act as licensors without operating plants of their own, and one of the British systems generally acts as supplier to general contractors.

Looking at the systems future in the United States, it appears that total management involvement will be natural. We have many large-scale builder-developer organizations very strong in marketing who can move into systems building merely by becoming involved with a working building system. Examples for these are the Rouse-Wates Company, and our own team of the Henry C. Beck Company, Raymond D. Nasher, and Balency-MBM.

System building will undoubtedly accelerate the trend towards large independent producers, and I believe that the day is not far away when we will have in housing production manufacturers as strong and clever in design and marketing as the automobile industry has now. I am looking forward to this day because fewer and larger housing producers may become politically important factors and may help in establishing the nation's priorities quite differently than they are at present. I believe that the closed systems are the best vehicle to move in this direction.

Illustrated here are photographs of the typical Balency product covering anything from single-family homes to complete new towns such as Thamesmead, presently being developed by the Greater London Council using our system (Figures 6–8). Last year, we produced approximately 2,000 single-family homes in our 16 factories in France. This makes us the second largest home producer in that country.

Last, but not least, I would like to speak about the economics of building systems predominantly using panels. With volume and continuity, there are definite savings in our European operations. We anticipate higher savings in the United States because of the relatively higher costs of labor in the United States and because our systems savings are almost entirely produced by labor savings, with savings in time running second. It may be of interest to note that in Italy during the period of constantly rising building and labor costs, the Balency system operation of MBM in Milan experienced first a spectacular lowering of its cost and then a levelling off extending over several years, which provided a hedge against inflation.

11
The Third Era of System Building

Ezra D. Ehrenkrantz

To my mind, these sessions have reinforced the fact that we are embarking on what one might call the beginning of the third era of system building. Elementary systems of proportion served as the basis upon which a great deal of the major architectural work of ancient through renaissance times was coordinated. The second era began when the building industry first began to emphasize the use of building materials in Elizabethan England. The main stream of stone construction gave way to clay, and we find man's ability to handle products (e.g., the use of the 9-inch by $4\frac{1}{2}$-inch brick, based on the span of a man's hand) beginning to play a major role in structuring the construction industry.

During the Elizabethan period, we also find the beginnings of diversity in sizes which had no relation to one another. The fireplaces in the Elizabethan houses were two bricklengths, 9 inches each, and 18 inches total. This resulted in cordwood being cut to 16-inch dimensions to fit into the fireplace. When the wood frame tradition came in, wood was cut from 16-inch cordwood, and the 16-inch tradition began to grow, as opposed to the 9-inch brick and 18-inch masonry tradition. The two traditions vied with one another, and to this very day we still have tile sizes related to the 9-inch and $4\frac{1}{2}$-inch dimensions, while most of our sheet products are related to the original 16-inch dimensions of cordwood. As new products of larger scale have been developed, the 16-inch dimensional increment has been unilaterally enforced with little regard for the handling or use of the item. For example, 32 inches is slightly more than is necessary for an inside door and slightly less than an outside door; 48 inches is a little too big for a man to hold effectively on an actual building site, and 64 inches is impossible for a single person to handle. Eventually, we found that we had very little choice among products based upon their relation to people's sizes or to the eventual use and handling of the product at the building sites.

Today, we are faced with another problem. The skin of buildings is not nearly as expensive as the services within a building. We have become more concerned with the sophistication of electrical, mechanical and plumbing services. The structure or the enclosure only presents an armature which holds or through which passes the more expensive portions of the total building. As such, dimensional coordination based on old proportional systems alone, or modular coordination based on additive principles of enclosure elements is no longer applicable. This is particularly true with respect to enclosure elements in that we no longer have the common brick as a basis of our everyday construction; in the past, as long as a window or a door was sized to a brick multiple, it would fit. Today we are talking about a variety of planning grids, a variety of modules and large-sized pro-

Presented to the 1969 session. Ezra D. Ehrenkrantz is President, Building Systems Development, Inc.

ducts. The basis of their relationship to one another must be much more sophisticated, because we are no longer fitting something of 12 brick widths into a brick wall. Rather, what we are trying to do is match up something of 9 brick widths to another of 12, and this calls for a complete different basis of coordination. We are at a point, today, where coordination of the old type, based on the dimensions of skins, results in buildings designed in a vernacular. This is akin to the way in which a child begins to speak. By saying the same syllable over and over again he uses only a single dimension as the basis of coordination. More sophisticated dimensional disciplines for relating products to one another are not yet available.

If we are going to look at any kind of development which is going to handle more sophisticated building requirements, we have to be able to have large products work together with one another to accommodate small differences that may relate, for example, to joining different column or wall thicknesses, or to a variety of surface requirements. These cannot be handled quite so easily in a simplistic manner. In this respect, I think the challenge is out to us now; if we want to have an approach to construction which offers a considerable number of options for design of our buildings, we must have a system by which we can coordinate those products in the exterior and with the rest of the fabric of the building so that all the products in the building work together. This must be dealt with in a much more sophisticated manner than has been necessary heretofore, and this is the beginning of the third era of system building (Figures 1–5).

As we begin to talk about systems, we find that there are a great number of different definitions. In fact, it is almost impossible to get a single definition because, very simply, "every man's system is another man's component." No matter what we are working on, we are dealing with something which is to someone else just a portion of the problem. Nevertheless, I shall attempt to discuss the systems approach to building as I view it and as has been developed in work in our office (Building Systems Development Inc.). Our basic problem is to design buildings which meet a given set of user requirements. These relate to the needs of the people who will be using the building or to the people who represent those users or to a combination of the two. Furthermore, our job is to relate the requirements to the available resources so that we get a cost-effective opportunity to meet those requirements. The resources of land, finance, management, technology, and labor must be related in a reasonable manner so that we have the opportunity to do the best job for the client.

This process becomes extremely interesting when one considers that if any one of the resources is missing, one does not have a chance to do the job, like a small security council with each resource having the right of veto. Unfortunately, in our professional activities, we dwell too frequently on technology, by itself, and this does not

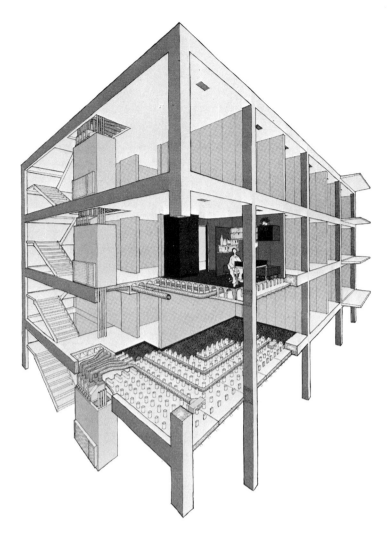

Figure 1
URBS components. A perspective cut-
away view of a dormitory residence
utilizing the URBS integrated mechanical
and structural system. Note the flexibility in interior wall panel layouts, balcony locations, and, of course, the
omnipresent mechanical network, willing
and able to locate itself on command
with total freedom. Courtesy of Building
Systems Development Incorporated.

Figure 2
Floor slab, prepared with L-shaped reinforcing bars, located according to modular planning, facilitating installation of
flexible mechanical ducts. Courtesy of
Building Systems Development Incorporated.

Figure 3
Installation of flexible duct with "mechanical chairs" to assure proper installation of components and subsystems.
Courtesy of Ron Partridge.

Figure 4
Concrete slab is poured over the mechanical systems after steel-reinforcing is placed on the modular grid. Courtesy of Ron Partridge.

Figure 5
Plumbing stacks slip into position and
like the other subsystems are placed
with little chance for error, thanks to
the modular design. Courtesy of Building
Systems Development Incorporated.

provide opportunity to solve our problems. If we take an approach towards a new technology in terms of costs alone, when the costs are slightly higher we may throw the technology out. In one instance, we analyzed the cash-flow requirements for building one thousand units a year based on a six-month completion time as against a three-month completion time, starting one-twelfth of the units (83) monthly. This was done in a steady-state situation; escalation costs were not considered. The cash flow requirements were reduced 350 percent by a 50 percent decrease in production time.

It becomes rather obvious that one would be willing to pay some extra money for technology which enabled one to build twice as fast. Conversely, we look at new ideas which affect the way in which products are put into the building and the way in which the workman must work at the building site. We may have an extremely interesting idea that should be effective in terms of cost, or that may be effective in terms of theory, but the end result will be less efficiency and higher cost if we cannot integrate the process of installing the products. One must begin to take a look at all the facets of how a building goes together. One must relate land density requirements to the cost of money itself. Requirements for money, interim financing, and for operating and maintenance costs over time enter into our decision making. We have to have a management capable of assimilating this information and making the appropriate decisions as well as organizing the entire process to get the job done. We need those appropriate technologies to do the job, but we cannot think of technology alone. I think that one of the reasons that people say we have all the technology we need is that people working in technology have done so without regard to the total context. So we have more ideas on the table than we can use, but this does not mean that we have the appropriate ideas to fit with the other resources to do the job. It is in this regard that we must consider new ideas of technology with respect to their relation to all of the other resources with which they must be used. Much of what has gone on in the architectural and engineering professions for the design of buildings has related to the handling of technology and the way in which technologies are introduced in the buildings. We frequently have little opportunity to effect decisions on land usage, financing, and the management of the entire process. For this reason, we often work within a context that does not give us an opportunity to get to the root of the problem or to have a chance to solve some of the basic requirements. If we take a good look at this particular point, we are working with a technological resource in the subsystem of a total systems process.

On any job, one has to design a building with a budget. There may be requirements for a certain number of square feet and other requirements relating to the quality of the environment in terms of acoustic, thermal, and luminous standards, the quality of the finishes, etc.

If the dollars are too few, you need either less square footage or a lower quality of finished environment. This is always based on a given context for previous resources. A change in the interest rate changes the construction time. A change in the land density—or zoning, which permits a higher land density—may change the way in which the construction laborers work. One must always recognize that this tradeoff must be made within a given context. Frequently, we do not have the opportunity to investigate the context, nor in the normal programming process do we have the opportunity to make the trade-offs at the right time. If we take the design process as it usually works, a client has an image of what is needed and may or may not engage someone to assist in programming.

Medical and educational facilities frequently enlist someone to do this job, and it is usually done without regard to cost. Programmers, therefore, are all too frequently in a university environment and use the university as an example. Each professor tries to build the empire he foresees as available to him when he gets all the grants that are expected. We all know that these are usually 50 percent less than what is anticipated. But nevertheless, a program is established which is rather large and unrealistic, and is usually given to the architect who then has the task, in each of the subsequent design stages, of cutting back the program in order to meet the budget. The architect typically goes through a cyclical situation, not in terms of trying to find out what is necessarily the best way in which to build the building, but in terms of where to put the pressure on the best opportunity to cut back. If the opportunities are not sufficient, he has a good mechanism to take care of this. He goes over the budget in the bid and then, during rebidding, cuts out things wholesale. All of this takes a good bit of time. We go through a process of developing un-realistic building designs, knowing that we must eventually cut back on the budget.

Unfortunately, another process is now coming into fairly consider-able use, related to what one would consider package building or pre-engineered designs, wherein the client has only two choices: to buy or not to buy. People who market a package building will do so, not on the basis of trying to find out the nature of all the problems, but rather in presenting a solution with a price, performance, and time. If the nature of the needs can be related at all to the cost, per-formance, and time, in order to save time and get a predictable job, the client usually will go in this direction. All classes of building are disappearing—literally disappearing—from the individual design situation because the architect is unable to give the basic information in terms of time, cost, and performance at the beginning of the de-sign process. Therefore, we are in a weak position, with respect to clients who need things done quickly, and who need them done with-in a very specific budget. We have a problem wherein the architect's major way of doing business is becoming outmoded by the extent and the rapidity with which our needs are arising. The way in which the package builder's response is now being made is not necessarily related to the nature of the needs, but is made truly to meet the requirements of time and cost. For example, a developer who has built five separate projects may sell the sixth by taking his client around, whether it be a housing agent, agency, or other group, and shows them the last five, literally asking "How do you want the building to be arranged this time?"

One cannot change this direction if one does not have the capacity to meet the urgency of the requirements with the ability to accurately predict time and cost as well. The new profession of management contracting is responding to this need. A major effort is being made to provide better predictability for the traditional design process. By adding a contractor to the design team, there is an opportunity for greater efficiency.

There is a great deal of evolution of new methods of doing business but unfortunately, I believe, we are not moving as rapidly as is necessary in order to do the job. Until we can begin the process with sufficient information so that professionals can say at the beginning of a job, "We have an opportunity to meet your requirements for time, cost and performance, in the same way that the package builder can do so today," we are going to lose out to the pressures which are being brought to bear on the industry. I believe that it is possible to develop that type of information, but it will take considerable efforts to do so. The following example may indicate how such information can be gathered and organized.

The number of areas relating to environment, i.e., acoustic, luminous, and thermal requirements, square footage, qualities of finish, flexibility of space, etc., and the thresholds of performance required in each case, results in a large number of options to be considered for a given job. In a student housing project for the University of California, an analysis of ten residence halls which were recently constructed showed that in most subsystem areas (structure, interior partitions, air conditioning, etc.), at least a 2 to 1 variation appeared in cost. The total price was the same—same client, same set of requirements and criteria; but the way in which the monies were distributed varied greatly. There were no criteria established for determining where the money should be spent. If one looked at the compatible low costs in each area, it would have been possible to put up a residence hall for 30 percent below the norm.

If, for example, one wants interior partitions which will perform acoustic separation at a level STC (sound transmission class) 40, the cost is about $2.20 per sq. ft; at STC 45, it is $3.50; at STC 50, it is $7.50 per sq. ft. Now, when an educator says that he needs a soundproof room, it becomes very easy to ask at what level and what is he willing to give up for the different levels of performance. Unless we can make appropriate tradeoffs between these factors before we begin to design the building, we are making unprogrammed tradeoffs after we have committed designs to paper. This is precisely the wrong time.

What one must do is subject the user to a series of discussions where one challenges every aspect of the building in order to know where to allocate funds. One may find new kinds of profiles for where the monies are or should be allocated. With this discretion, in working with any community group, there are thresholds of performance which must be determined professionally. We must relate to real user requirements, and should not go below them. We must permit— and, indeed, it is mandatory with respect to the design process— those who will be users to play a role in determining where discretionary funds will be used. A level of performance must be contained within the programming process before we begin to design a building. We must have the information to do this and this must be done at the very beginning of a systems approach to building. We must then have the capability of working with our clients, or those who represent our clients, to make appropriate tradeoffs. With information on cost and performance, we have some hope of meeting the needs and relating to the aspirations of those whom we would house.

I believe more and more—and I think the young people across the country in colleges and universities are expressing part of our problem—that our mission today in designing facilities must be based, not on how we can awe our clients, but rather on how we can facilitate creative release on the part of the user. People are asking to be involved within the process, not necessarily in terms of design per se, but in terms of their ability to put their own mark on the building over time. Therefore, I think one of the things that we must be able to do in meeting the basic user requirements is to develop facilities that provide a keyboard for the user. We must also be thinking about building systems which provide a keyboard for the architect, recognizing that in his design of the building, he determines what keyboard there is for the user. We must provide the appropriate services and artifacts; we must provide the opportunity for change— flexibility over time—as the requirements of the user are changing over time, and the user, too, is changing over time. In short, we must meet a great variety of different life patterns.

The following are a few very simple examples of studies related to user requirements. In doing work for student housing, we analyzed a great number of different residence halls. We found the majority of them designed as double rooms along double-loaded corridors. All furniture and appurtenances were affixed to the wall. In some cases, the only things which could be moved were the student's bed and desk chair. People designing the facilities did not realize that there was an alternative, perhaps more desirable, location for the bed. Since it was movable, it was often placed in front of the door so you'd have to walk up and over it every time you entered or exited the room. And to show their individuality, naturally all the students moved their bed to that location. These double rooms were designed, and are continually being designed, without taking into account that 80 percent of the time most students study out of their rooms. These students have grown up in an era when groups within the family are arrayed in front of the television set and in order to concentrate one has to remove oneself to one's own room. And so, they study alone. When we went to the university, many of us here, the double room was not so difficult to work in. Our studying was done in the bosom of the family with the radio going for background noise and working at the kitchen table. Noise disturbance was possible while visual disturbance affects concentration in a completely different way.

So we find that patterns of living which were acceptable 20 years ago are not acceptable today. We have requirements in housing for below-market interest rate programs wherein, for example, allowance is made for small galley-type kitchens. Perhaps a little smaller and less luxuriously appointed than a middle-income family has, but of the same type. Fifty percent of the families who qualify for below-market interest rate are single-parent families, and so the mother who works all day and who does not have contact with her children comes home to a kitchen which further isolates her from her children to prepare her meals, serve, do the cleaning up, and prepare sandwiches for the next day's school lunches.

I think that we do not have proper attitudes, proper studies, or basis of information available so that we can legitimately respond to the need of the people who live in and use our buildings. If this is the case, we have no comeback to the package builder. We are not able to deliver the quality of the building, with respect to the life that will take place within it, and we certainly are not able to offer the predictability of time and cost as the package builder does. In order to have any reason for being, we have to master basic information study techniques so that we know what it is we are going to provide in our buildings for the needs of the user. Until this is done, we have a very weak case, indeed.

We find today that much of what has been developed outside of the profession is done on marketing principles. This is something that is hard to contest, but we must develop the tools to do so. We must find a way to manipulate, not only the relationship between dollars, square footage and the quality of the environment, but to manipulate the context within which we work. We have a basic problem within our cities which requires all kinds of new methods of organization. We are not in the mess that exists today because we want to be, because we do not have intelligent people, because we do not have technology, or because we don't have the will to change the situation; we are there basically because we are working within an organizational context which all too frequently makes it impossible to solve the problems. For this reason, as we take a look at any kind of systems approach to building, we must play our part in decisions made by government, and by others who affect the building process. If the appropriate market does not exist, in order to be able to change the nature of the technology that one will use, we must develop methods of restructuring the nature of our client. In some cases, perhaps, we must create new clients in order to be able to serve them well.

One of the major things, I think, which causes us to be concerned with innovation in terms of the building industry is change. The area in which we have done the least work is in designing buildings which will be useful over time to a changing range of user requirements. We can no longer predict the style of life or the way in which people will live and work within our buildings. The rate of change in environmental needs is exemplified by people in the medical field who predict that present new facilities will be obsolete in three years. These changes are extremely relevant in building types where operating costs are very high in relation to building costs. We particularly need a basis of information so that building can work in a manner analogous to a dance sequence going through a series of different steps in order to meet changing needs at different points in time. If we develop the capacity to design individual buildings to meet individual user programs with the same capacity for predicting cost, time and performance as exists with pre-engineered buildings, I think we will have a tool with which we can work. It is obvious, as you take a look at the nature of our cities and the nature of our building industry, that the former approach does not exist and that problems are not being solved.

If we look to the resources available, we find bonds failing for highways, educational and health facilities, at an ever-increasing rate. The attitudes within society are explained by William Baumol, Professor of Economics at Princeton, who has indicated that the building industry acts as a service industry in terms of its efficiency while society expects it to act as a product industry. Take a look at what has happened in the automotive industry, which has increased production by, perhaps, 15 times since the end of World War II. Walter Reuther knew this; the auto workers wages reflect this. On the other hand, we take a look at a true service industry: education. We find that a teacher has 30 students today, as she did in 1890. Teachers' wages have never been at the same level as the auto workers', but even at only half the rate of increase, there is obviously an increase in the cost of the service. Baumol maintains society can afford it because the only reason that the cost of services is going up is due to the efficiency of other sectors within society. But we do not recognize it nor are we willing to pay for it even in the service areas. So when we take a look at the building industry, which we expect will act as a production industry, and find that its productivity has gone up at a rate of one percent per year, we see why problems exist. Earlier, Professor Dietz mentioned something about the growth of the building industry. I have the latest figures given by Mr. Christie of McGraw-Hill. From 1965 to 1968, money spent on construction went up from 72 to 85 billion dollars; of this 18 percent increase, $14\frac{1}{2}$ percent was due to escalation. Very little increase in volume, just higher costs. If building costs escalate at their current level, the majority of people will not be able to afford housing without major government subsidy. If 75 percent of our below-market interest rate houses are handled by mobile homes, we see what the nature of the building industry will be like if we do not find an approach that results in the economical construction of other, hopefully more acceptable, kinds of housing.

In our own work, we are attempting to attack this problem, but I do not think that we have been able to develop sufficient information in a way to make a significant impact. This is not yet possible. However, in a number of cases, I think we are providing some information and some of the formats for developing an information base for a truly systematic approach to building.

I think the key is the ability to develop an approach which would enable us to use mass-produced, standardized products which we can compose freely and economically. I think this is a major direction in which we have to go. It can only come, however, from developing information and a management system which is going to enable us to produce predictably and on time. If we do not do this, our right to survival as professionals who provide clients with appropriate physical facilities will not be sustained. I think this is a battle that we must fight and that we must win.

12
The Mobile-Home Industry: A Case Study in Industrialization

Arthur D. Bernhardt

Introduction: The Mobile-Home Industry and the Industrialization of the Housing Sector

The findings of a myriad of recent studies and conferences on the housing crisis can be summarized simply: Our housing production and delivery system must provide:

1. More housing. The annual production rate must be increased by more than 100 percent.
2. Better housing. The responsiveness of the production and delivery process to the psychological and physical needs of the user must be greatly increased.
3. Cheaper housing. Occupancy costs per square foot of usable floor space must be substantially reduced.

The housing industry does not now have the capacity and efficiency necessary to provide better and cheaper housing. The federal government seems committed to helping industry to meet these national needs. Two basic strategies are available: (1) channel enough real resources into the housing industry so that it can provide enough adequate housing with its present efficiency level; (2) provide a setting for the housing industry to substantially increase its efficiency and responsiveness to user needs.

Only by diversion of resources from other high national priorities can the first strategy succeed. Since appropriations for other priority areas, such as health, education, welfare, and environmental quality will in any event remain below the desired level of funding, it is necessary to minimize the need for diversion of resources.

The task of minimizing the need for resource diversion is identical with the second strategy of maximizing the efficiency of our housing production and delivery system; that is, maximizing the productivity of the material and labor inputs.

From a political perspective, the strategy of efficiency maximization again appears to be the most feasible solution. This is because a given amount of resources will probably have a greater positive effect on the supply of housing if used to increase efficiency than if used to subsidize the housing production and delivery system at the present efficiency level either directly, by subsidizing the production and delivery process, or indirectly, by subsidizing low-income consumers.

All segments of the housing industry are highly aggressive, competitive, and innovative. This applies to the on-site residential building as well as to the mobile-home and manufactured-home industries. During the last five or ten years the industry has adopted many of the advanced organizational and managerial techniques developed in other industries. Today, an avant-garde breed of managers run the larger corporations in the industry as they would run a

Presented to the 1970 session Arthur D. Bernhardt is Assistant Professor, Department of Architecture, Massachusetts Institute of Technology.

corporation in any other industry, recruiting professional talent in fields such as systems analysis and industrial engineering from mass-production-oriented and other advanced industries. The housing industry has begun to think about potential scale economies under assumed annual production rates per plant of 10,000, 20,000, or 50,000 units.

Within the housing industry there is both the motivation and capability for radical innovation. Innovation by invasion is clearly not necessary.

Yet, the industry's potential is still inhibited by a number of external constraints. These constraints, largely a consequence of public policy, include the erratically fluctuating impact of fiscal and monetary policies, the fragmentation of demand, zoning constraints, differential building codes, restrictive union practices, lack of a viable system of nationwide standardization or modular and dimensional coordination, a practical nonexistence of building research, and lack of a system of dissemination of information. These obstacles constitute a hostile environment for industry-initiated innovation and prevent the industry from fully exploiting its substantial potential for more efficient operation. The result is that all attempts at innovation in the housing production and delivery system—whether initiated by government or industry, whether undertaken in the Americas, Europe, or Japan—have been confined to more rationalization of the historically formed craft- and location-oriented organization and production concepts in building without questioning these crucial traditional concepts underlying the structure and operation of the housing production and delivery system. This approach holds a very limited potential for improving the efficiency of the system.

With the elimination of the most critical constraints, however, the housing industry could achieve a substantial increase in efficiency through substitution of the basic concepts of industrial organization and production for the traditionally formed concepts presently underlying its structure and operation. Substitution of concepts of industrial organization and production for traditionally formed concepts in building implies a comprehensive approach to the industrialization of the housing sector; extending radically beyond our present efforts at industrializing the building process. This approach implies a joint effort by the housing industry and government to provide a setting for radical innovation through the restructuring and synchronization of:

1. The operation and structure of the housing production sector—which includes the on-site residential building industry, the manufactured-home industry, and the mobile-home industry.

2. The operation and structure of the supporting sectors—such as finance, the real estate brokerage industry, and the building materials and products industries.

3. The complex political, economic and social framework, especially in an institutional sense, within which production and support functions operate—this area includes government institutions, labor organizations, nonhousing-oriented industries, and other vested interests.

Reforming these areas, for example, is a prerequisite to automation and mass production, one aspect of comprehensive industrialization. The writer's work to date, for example, indicates the existence of substantial scale economies in the manufacturing of volumetric dwelling modules, with minimum optimal plant size (fully efficient scale of operation) on the order of 60,000 to 80,000 units per year. Average costs for fully efficient operation are less than $4.00 per square foot. To exploit these scale economies fully, the industry would have to make major adjustments in the planning, production, distribution, and servicing phases. New technologies, and consequently designs, have to be developed. Manufacturing and subassembly operations with a potential for substantial scale economies may have to be performed in one central facility, while transportation costs dictate that the final assembly of the bulky product takes place in regionally dispersed facilities. The cooperation of labor has to be negotiated; training and retraining programs must be developed. The final product will be of a different design and will cost much less than the traditional home. The innovations will call for further adjustments in distributing and marketing. The larger scale of operations will enable the manufacturer to negotiate better prices with his suppliers and to shift certain operations to them. The public sector would have to assist by initially securing and ensuring the continuity of a high volume of aggregated demand. Producers have to be convinced of the potential for adequate and sustained profit if they are to embark upon the substantial investment in plant and organization which would be necessary in order for them to operate at output levels of 50,000 to 100,000 units. Promotion of consistent nationwide systems of standardization, modular and dimensional coordination, and of building and housing legislation requires governmental assistance. Reorganization, planning, coordination, and stimulation of building research and the improved dissemination of information are equally crucial and call for additional public initiative. On a broader scale, for example, policy planners will have to recognize that once the industry invests heavily in automated mass production facilities it must be protected against strong countercyclical induced demand fluctuations. Thus, forecasts of future demands for housing, manpower, materials, and financing must be improved. In general, the industry must view its efforts at reorganization as an experiment in a sensitive socioeconomic-political environment that can succeed only if it does not disturb the equilibrium of this environment.

Of course, a comprehensive industrialization of the housing sector would call for the development and adoption of corporate and public policies aiming at long-range planning, initiation, stimulation, co-ordination, and direction of this transformation process. The writer believes that such a policy is politically feasible, because of its inherent long-term character. The development of sensitive strategies and tactics can ensure that critical political hurdles will gradually be overcome. Individual programs and measures, which would be necessary in any event, would be molded as consistent intermediate steps in accordance with the long-range goal. At present the unfortunate practice is to design programs exclusively in response to the immediate needs, thus sacrificing the chance of simultaneously utilizing the step for developing the industry. The widespread hope to achieve the desired breakthrough of industrialization of building without laying the necessary structural groundwork is unrealistic. There is need for a policy which aims to accomplish the prerequisite structural change. Industrialization of building is not a technological problem; it is primarily a political and economic problem.

This paper analyzes the mobile-home industry as a case study because the development of the industry up to this point confirms the notion that the industrialization of building first requires a restructuring of the socioeconomic-political framework, and also because the industry is prototypical in many respects for the future building sector. The mobile home industry testifies that, with relatively modest initial support from the public sector, the housing industry can achieve radical change. In fact, the mobile-home industry has developed without any public assistance, striving vigorously to overcome a large number of critical constraints. The industry has, for example, virtually created its own market—the mobile-home park industry. The mobile-home industry has already demonstrated that a vigorous "systems" approach will enable the housing industry ultimately to achieve radical industrialization without government interference. The basic objective of this paper is to evaluate the potential role of the industry in stimulating the process of industrialization of the housing sector.

This paper presents first the growth record of the mobile home industry; an analysis of the structure, operation and performance of the industry follows. Finally, building upon trend analyses and projections, some statements relative to the future development of the mobile home industry and its future role within the total housing sector are attempted.

Historical Development of the Mobile-Home Industry

In 1929, the father of the mobile home industry, a Detroit manufacturer of vaccines, built a small house trailer for his private vacation use. By 1936, the company that he subsequently established had reached an annual output of 6,000 high-quality trailers, thus controlling 15 percent of the entire 1936 trailer-coach market. In the same year, trailer manufacturing was reported to be the fastest-growing industry in the United States, with more than 400 manufacturers. It was predicted that by 1956 more than half of the total population of the United States would be living in trailers.

This dramatic growth aroused the interest of the automobile industry. The Ford Motor Company and General Motors Corporation for a long time seriously considered entering the young industry, and some automobile, truck, and body companies actually did.

In 1930, 100 percent of the trailer production was for vacation use. By 1937, 50 percent of all trailer coaches were sold to vacation enthusiasts, 35 percent to retirees, and 15 percent to migratory or mobile-occupation workers. The latter two groups represented 200,000 families living permanently in trailers.

After 1940, serious problems arose as a result of the defense build-up. Officials of the federal government recognized the potentialities of mobile dwellings as an adjunct to the defense housing program. The federal government purchased 38,000 trailers during the war. Private sales were forbidden by executive order. During the war, servicemen and workers in large numbers became adapted to the use of trailers as primary housing. The industry was emerging as a supplier in the housing market.

In the immediate postwar period, following the large population movements associated with World War II and the reconversion from a war-time economy, the severe housing shortage created an abnormal mobile home market. The federal government asked manufacturers to increase the production of trailers. The number of manufacturers doubled. The country also witnessed an enormous industrial expansion during this period. The migrant army of workers needed for long-overdue heavy construction projects in remote sections of the country provided another ready market for trailers. For some of these projects, more than 10,000 trailers were moved in.

By 1950, 45 percent of sales were for primary housing, migratory workers bought 35 percent (1937: 15 percent) of the output, and retirees 15 percent (1937 : 35 percent). The vacation market represented a mere 1 percent (1937 : 50 percent). Eighty percent to 90 percent of the owners used mobile homes for year-round living. By 1953, the transformation to primary housing was complete: over 1.8 million Americans lived permanently in more than 700,000 mobile homes.

This process was emphasized in 1952, when the trailer-coach industry began to split into two distinctly separate industries. The "mobile-home industry" began to concentrate exclusively on the production of primary housing, whereas the "travel-trailer industry," later "recreational-vehicle industry," specialized in the production of vehicles for recreational use. In terms of structure, operation and markets, both industries are independent and separate to such a degree that this paper can concentrate exclusively on the mobile-home industry (see Figure 1).

According to the official definition, a mobile home is "a movable dwelling constructed to be towed on its own chassis, connected to utilities, and designed without a permanent foundation for year-round living. It can consist of one or more units that can be joined into one integral unit, horizontally or vertically. Mobile homes are towed to their sites by trucks." A travel trailer, as opposed to a mobile home, "is towed by an automobile, can be operated independently of utility connections for only a few days, is limited in width to 8 feet, in length to 32 feet, and is designed principally as a temporary vaction dwelling."

The growth record of the industry since 1950 warrants a more detailed analysis.

In 1949, after the mobile-home boom of 1947 and 1948, the stationary home builders caught up with the demand and the mobile home market showed a drop. The trailer was still too small and still without toilets. Rather alarmed, manufacturers in 1950 introduced bathrooms. These contained only shower and wash basin, yet the market responded immediately. Finally, in 1951, toilets and length were added. In 1952, by further design improvements, the industry continued its growth. A walk-through bedroom was added, and the bathroom was made a walk-through. This was about all which could be done in view of the eight-foot width limitation. And even though the industry tactically changed the name of its product from "trailer-coach" to "mobile home," it could not provide as much floor space as the public wanted, and in 1953, the market again showed signs of a drop. This stimulated the introduction of the first ten-foot-wide units, which provided the possibilities of private bedrooms and bathrooms opening to a longitudinal hall. By 1955, a boom year for all housing, the ten-wide had become accepted, and the industry passed the 100,000 unit mark; by 1956 the ten-wide was produced in large production runs. The ten-wide became a sensational sucess. But manufacturers' enthusiasm caused overproduction, and dealers over-stocked the product. In 1957 and 1958, sales declined. In response to the still unsatisfied demand for more space, a twelve-foot-wide model was introduced in 1959. But permits for transportation of twelve-wides did not come forth; instead ten-wides were made longer, which caused a 55 foot long ten-wide mass market upsurge. Yet, 1960 saw another decline, and 1961 showed a further drop. In 1962, with twelve-wide permits still rare, further length was added to ten-wides. Double-wide and more expandable units were introduced and sales started a new upswing. The trend gained momentum in 1963, when many states yielded to the twelve-wide.

Since then, the twelve-wide has become standard. Industry shipments passed the 200,000 mark in 1965, the 300,000 mark in
1968, and the 400,000 mark in 1969.

Today 12-wides, 55 feet to 65 feet long, constitute close to 90
percent of the total production. Fourteen- and 16-wides have already
been built. The average mobile home of 684 sq. ft., completely
furnished down to curtains, retails for $6,050, or $8.85/sq. ft.
Wholesale prices (F.O.B. plant) are $5 to $6 per square foot, completely furnished, or slightly less than $5, unfurnished (Figures
2–4).

**Role and Status of the Mobile-
Home Industry within the
Housing Sector**

Statistics on the mobile home industry alone do not convey the impact that can be produced by comparing the mobile home industry
to the larger housing industry.

In Figure 5, comparing mobile-home and single-family home production, the mobile home scale is set at 10 percent of the scale for conventional housing. Until about 1961, demand for mobile homes trailed that for conventional housing rather faithfully. But from 1962 on,
the mobile home share moved sharply upward. During 1961 to
1970, which were years of a declining market for conventional
single-family housing, mobile-home production rose by 300 percent.
However, the pickup since 1962 parallels gains in apartment production. Mobile homes and apartments appeal to the same age groups.

In 1960, mobile home shipments equaled 10.7 percent of conventional single family starts; in 1964 it was 20.3 percent; in 1968,
36.1 percent; and in 1969, 52 percent (Figure 6). In 1969, mobile
home shipments equaled 29 percent of total housing starts.

The mobile-home share of speculatively built single-family homes
demonstrates the significance of the mobile home even more. In
1963, the total number of mobile homes marketed equaled 26.9
percent of the single-family units built for the speculative sales
market. In 1964, this figure was 33.8 percent, and in the mid-
sixties it was 45 percent. The dealer's lot is becoming a strong
competitor to the builder's subdivision for the weekend home shoppers.

Similarly, since about 1968, mobile home output is increasingly
exceeding the output of manufactured homes (Figure 7).

In the meantime, the take-over of low-cost housing by the mobile
home industry is almost complete. Ninety-four percent of new one-
family homes, valued up to $15,000 in 1969, were mobile homes
(Figure 8).

Finally, a look at the role of the mobile home in the total housing

Figure 1
Evolution of the mobile home. *Top*, early
'40s (courtesy of Schult Mobile House
Corp.); *center*, early '50s (courtesy of
Schult Mobile House Corp.); *bottom,*
contemporary.

Figure 2
Types of mobile homes. *Top*, single-wide;
center, double-wide (courtesy of MHMA);
bottom, two-story double-wide (courtesy
of BIG Enterprises).

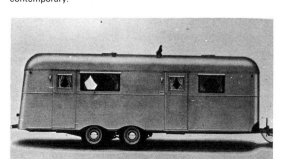

Figure 3
Industry shipments of mobile homes,
travel trailers, and recreational vehicles.
Data compiled from various sources.

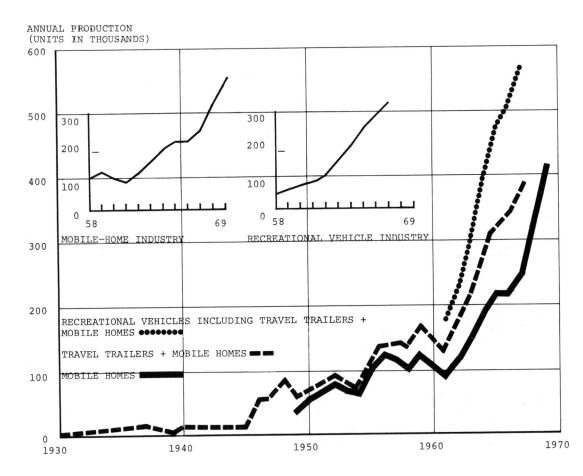

Figure 4
Annual dollar-volume of retail sales of
mobile homes and recreational vehicles.
Data from various sources.

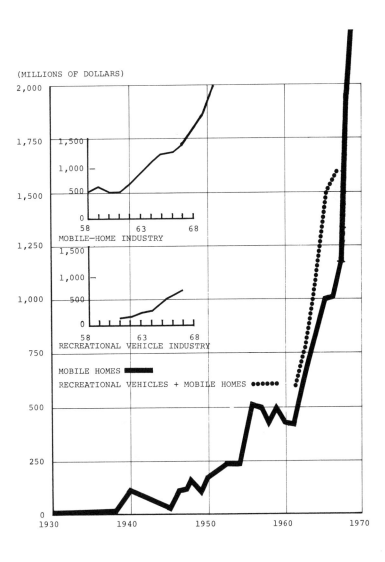

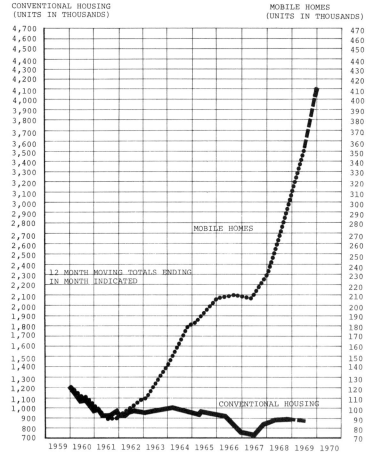

CONVENTIONAL HOUSING
(UNITS IN THOUSANDS)

MOBILE HOMES
(UNITS IN THOUSANDS)

MOBILE HOMES

12 MONTH MOVING TOTALS ENDING
IN MONTH INDICATED

CONVENTIONAL HOUSING

Figure 5
Trend-line comparison: mobile homes
produced and conventional private nonfarm single-family housing starts. Data
for mobile homes from *Mobile Home
Sales, Stocks and Shipments*, Marketing
Information Associates, Chicago; data
for conventional housing from *Construction Reports—Housing Starts*, United
States Bureau of the Census.

Figure 6
Mobile-home units shipped by manufacturers as percent of nonfarm conventional single-family starts. Graph
based upon data supplied by MHMA
and others.

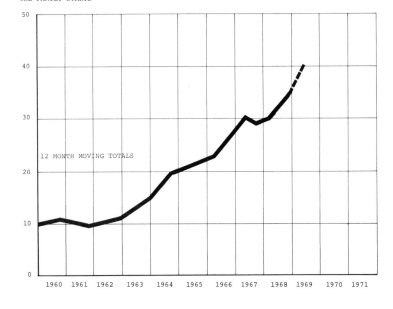

MOBILE HOMES AS %
OF CONVENTIONAL
ONE FAMILY STARTS

12 MONTH MOVING TOTALS

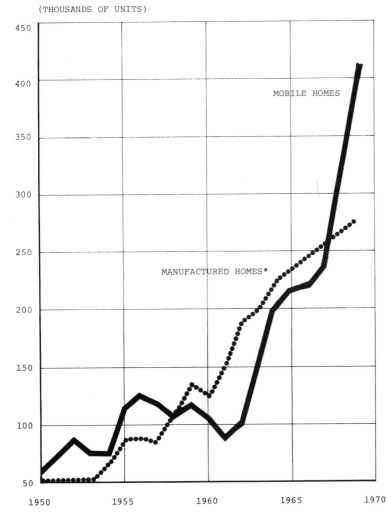

(THOUSANDS OF UNITS)

MOBILE HOMES

MANUFACTURED HOMES*

Figure 7
Mobile and manufactured homes. Based upon data supplied by Home Manufacturers Association, United States Bureau of the Census, and MHMA.

Figure 8
Sale of mobile homes compared to total housing sales. In 1969, mobile homes accounted for 94 percent of all single-family homes sold for less than $15,000. Data supplied by United States Department of Commerce Bureau of Census Data and MHMA.

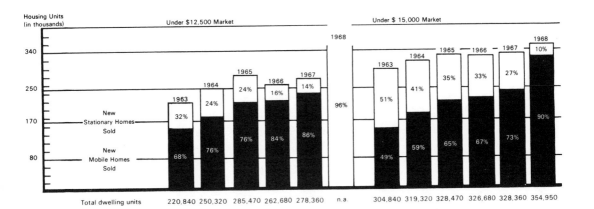

Housing Units (in thousands)

Under $12,500 Market

Under $ 15,000 Market

New Stationary Homes Sold

New Mobile Homes Sold

Total dwelling units   220,840 250,320 285,470 262,680 278,360   n.a.   304,840 319,320 328,470 326,680 328,360 354,950

supply is necessary. Since World War II, more than 3 million mobile-homes have been produced. Approximately 70 percent of these are currently in use, of which 50 percent are in mobile-home communities. By 1968 the mobile-home inventory represented 3.3 percent of the total housing stock. Today, the mobile-home inventory exceeds two million units and the mobile-home population approaches seven million (Figure 9).

Structure, Operation and Performance of the Mobile-Home Industry
Mobile-Home Manufacturing

It would clearly exceed the scope of this paper to discuss the production process in detail. Basically, the spine of every mobile home production facility is the main assembly line, with anywhere from five to more than twenty assembly stations. Basic manufacturing and subassembly operations take place on one or both sides of the main assembly line. The layout of the subassembly lines is typically perpendicular to the main assembly line. There are two basic main assembly line arrangements—the "side-by-side line" and the "straight line"—the main line stations in either case being fed by subassembly lines (Figure 10).

A series of illustrations should suffice to communicate the basic characteristics of the production process (Figures 11–13). In a well-organized plant, every twenty to forty minutes, one completely finished and furnished dwelling unit leaves the main assembly line for transportation. As should be evident from the photographs, this high degree of efficiency in production is not a result of sophisticated technology but rather of a high sophistication of the management of the production process.

Turning now to an analysis of the structure and operation of the industry, still focusing on the production phase, one finds that in 1969 there were approximately 334 firms producing 10 or more mobile homes per year in 593 plants. Though most of these were privately owned, more than 20 were publicly held.

Originally preferred plant locations were close to automotive suppliers. Manufacturers and suppliers concentrated in the so-called "prefab" belt, the Detroit, Chicago, and Northern Indiana and Ohio areas. A large labor pool with specific skills developed. The general external economies became significant.

But in the 1950s, with increasing unit dimensions, high freight rates stimulated a decentralization process. Producers expanded their operations either through acquisition of other companies or construction of branch plants in key market areas. This has made possible the design of a product for a particular market area with a resulting better market penetration, and provision of faster service to dealers. The trend continues. Company size expands more than plant size. Apparently, a medium-sized plant can still achieve efficient operation. This suggests what is in fact the case, that the presently

Figure 9
Mobile-home inventory and population
growth, 1939–1970. Data from various
sources.

Figure 10
The two types of mobile-home assembly
line.

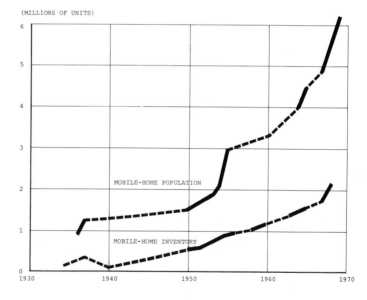

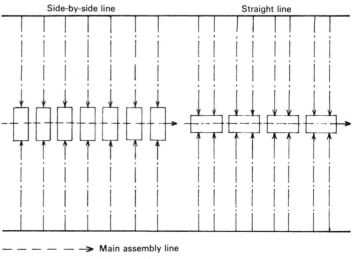

Figure 11
Subassemblies used in mobile-home
production. *From the top*: roof sections;
wall sections; floor sections; and under-
carriages.

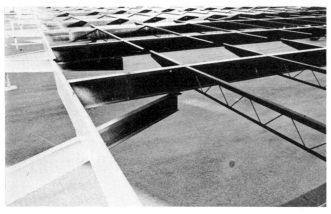

Figure 12
Mobile-home assembly line: straight-line
type.

Figure 13
Mobile-home assembly line: straight-line type.

common plant sizes are too small for achieving noteworthy scale economies.

A relatively homogeneous network of plants spread evenly over the country has developed. The original leading states, such as Indiana, Michigan, and California, have continuously produced a declining share of the national output. The share of formerly unimportant states has increased, particularly Alabama, Georgia, Kansas, North Carolina, Pennsylvania, and Texas (Figure 14).

Geographical diversification prevents manufacturers from being tied to economic fluctuations within a single area. Thus, the industry is relatively cushioned against isolated jolts in our economy.

To help analyze the industry, this paper will first consider: (1) the degree of concentration, (2) the degree of product differentiation, and (3) the industry's barriers to entry. Then the implications of these characteristics will be examined.

An industry is commonly defined as concentrated if the largest eight firms make more than 33 percent of total industry sales. Already in the early sixties, the eight largest mobile home firms accounted for about 40 percent, now for close to 50 percent (Table 1).

These concentration ratios indicate that the industry is rather concentrated, and clearly oligopolistic. Of course, this pertains only to the national market. These concentration ratios probably understate the amount of concentration in some regional markets, whereas in others the market may be atomistically competitive.

How does this degree of concentration compare with the rest of the larger housing industry?

In 1968, the top ten home manufacturers accounted for approxim-

Table 1   The Leading Ten Mobile Home Manufacturers by Unit Volume, 1969

Company	Units
1 Skyline Corp.	40,000
2 Guerdon Industries	26,000 (est.)
3 Redman Industries	24,000
4 Champion Home Builders	21,000
5 Boise Cascade	17,474
6 Fleetwood Enterprises	17,474
7 DMH Corporation	15,492
8 Commodore Corp.	13,860
9 Winston Industries	11,750
10 Zimmer Homes	9,400

SOURCE: The trade journal, *Automation in Housing*.

Figure 14
Regional mobile-home production,
1960–1967. Compiled from various
sources.

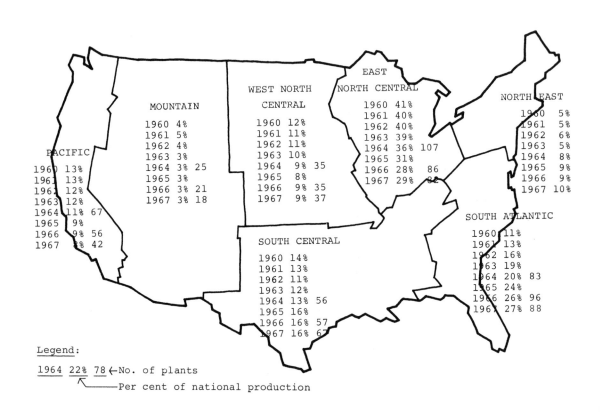

EAST
WEST NORTH   NORTH CENTRAL
CENTRAL   1960 41%
MOUNTAIN   1960 12%   1961 40%   NORTH EAST
1960 12%   1962 40%
1960 4%   1961 11%   1963 39%   1960   5%
1961 5%   1962 11%   1964 36% 107   1961   5%
1962 4%   1963 10%   1965 31%   1962   6%
PACIFIC   1963 3%   1964   9% 35   1966 28%   86   1963   5%
1960 13%   1964 3% 25   1965   8%   1967 29%   1964   8%
1961 13%   1965 3%   1966   9% 35   1965   9%
1962 12%   1966 3% 21   1967   9% 37   1966   9%
1963 12%   1967 3% 18   1967   10%
1964 11% 67
1965   9%   SOUTH ATLANTIC
1966   9% 56
1967   8% 42   SOUTH CENTRAL   1960 11%
1961 13%
1960 14%   1962 16%
1961 13%   1963 19%
1962 11%   1964 20% 83
1963 12%   1965 24%
1964 13% 56   1966 26% 96
1965 16%   1967 27% 88
1966 16% 57
1967 16% 67

Legend:

1964 22% 78 ←No. of plants
      ↖
       ——Per cent of national production

ately 12 percent of total industry sales. This industry is clearly un-concentrated.

Similarly, in 1968, the top ten merchant builders accounted for less than 10 percent of the total dollar value of merchant-built conventional nonfarm single-family starts.

And, finally, looking at the total home-building industry, excluding the mobile- and manufactured-home industries, in 1967 the top ten firms accounted for less than 2 percent of the dollar value of new residential, nonfarm housing. Thus, the mobile home industry is the only concentrated sector of the housing industry.

Turning next to product differentiation, one finds that there is practically none. Mobile homes are shopper's goods. Choice is based on quality, price, and features. Thus, there is a pressure on manu-facturers to sell at a single competitive price.

As for price policies, there appear to be no illegal methods of price coordination, such as price-fixing or pools. Like most pure oligo-polies, prices appear to be set by a price leader, but they are prob-ably close to marginal cost prices.

Turning now to the third market structure element, barriers to entry, one has to determine whether there are:
1. scale economy barriers
2. absolute cost barriers
3. product differentiation barriers, or
4. barriers to entry from vertical integration

In some industries, such as cement or rayon, new firms do not achieve the lowest possible production costs until they have grown to occupy a large portion of the national market. But, the technology presently employed by the mobile-home industry holds little poten-tial for economies of scale. Thus, there do not yet exist noteworthy scale economy barriers.

Similarly, there are no absolute cost barriers. Newly entering mobile-home firms are not confronted with absolute cost disadvantages, which would make their production cost curves lie above those of going firms. It is true that established firms possess valuable know-how. But management can be bought and there are, for example, hardly any exclusive patent rights. Mobile-home production requires a relatively small amount of equity capital. In the early fifties, with good supplier connections, it took about $10,000 to $20,000 in equity capital to start a manufacturing plant. The manufacturing process is largely assembly. This has contributed materially to mak-ing mobile home manufacturing a good "small business." But this same factor has partly discouraged "big business" from entering. As the decade progressed, more capital was required. Approximately $200,000 is necessary today, provided one has good credit and good supplier connections. This amount is still very low compared with most manufacturing fields. Thus, even now there are no absolute cost barriers.

Similarly, as discussed, there are no product differentiation barriers.

But one possibility of blockading entry, namely barriers to entry from vertical integration, may soon gain significance, even though they do not constitute an entry barrier today.

Thus, today, entry is still relatively easy. The high turnover of firms testifies to this. In 1969, an estimated 110 new manufacturers entered the industry. But it appears that during the last three years more firms went out of business than entered.

In summary, the relatively high concentration ratio, taken by itself, would clearly define the market structure as oligopolistic. But the regional marketing focus combines with lack of product differentiation and ease of entry to make competition among the manufacturers of mobile homes as keen as among prefabbers and merchant builders.

What can be concluded from this analysis?

First, the level of R&D and the rate of innovation appear to be functions of industry concentration, as well as of some other market elements. There is some evidence that higher concentration is associated with greater research intensity. This refers, specifically, to industries in which the prospects for achieving product differentiation are limited. Also, technical entry barriers, i.e., scale economy barriers and absolute cost barriers to some moderate degree, are associated with the highest levels of industrial research.

Since the mobile-home industry does not yet invest in R&D, one might conclude that more concentration and higher technical entry barriers are necessary. Trial and error is substituted for R&D. The chances for institutionalization of centralized industry R&D are poor, because the industry leaders prefer individual R&D efforts. The latter boil down to mere routine development work. The fragmentation of effort does not allow exploitation of the potential of the traditional mobile home concept, in terms of product engineering and product design, not to mention individual R & D efforts aiming at modular developments, which are quite inadequate.

Second, industries with higher seller concentration usually tend to earn higher profits than industries with lower concentration. A financial analysis of a sample of 24 major mobile-home manufacturers, merchant builders, and prefabbers, all publicly held, showed indeed that the average profit margins (net income as percent of sales) were 3.1 percent in the mobile home group, 2.3 percent for merchant builders, and 1.6 percent for prefabbers. The mobile home manufacturers, on the average, turned their assets into sales nearly four times, which compared with average assets turnover ratios of about one for the prefabbers and of well below one for the merchant builders. The average turnover of inventories was 10 times for the mobile home manufacturers, 4 times for prefabbers and 2 times for the merchant builders. Accordingly, the mobile home manufacturers earned an average of about 15 percent on their capital; merchant builders and prefabbers, less than 4 percent. Skyline Corp., for example, earned 49 percent on its capital by turning assets into sales 8 times and inventories into sales 62 times. Those are probable the best turnover ratios for the total shelter industry. Skyline has no long-term debt, so this performance enabled it to report return on stockholder equity of 49 percent.

After having discussed mobile home production by focusing on the industry as a whole, one should look more closely at characteristics and problems of the individual firms.

Turning to the scale of operation, one finds that plant capacities vary widely. The largest plants can produce up to 45 units per day. But average capacities are in the order of 5 to 8 units per day. The production breakdown for 1967 was as follows: 332 plants produced between one and 1,500 units; 24 plants produced between 1,501 and 3,000 units, 8 plants produced 3,001 or more units per year. Thus, small-scale producers are still predominant.

Seasonality is a major problem. Because of financing difficulties and shortage of space, production for inventory is a rare exception in the industry. Sales and production are still largely a matter of consumer initiative (Figure 15). In fact, the residential construction industry as a whole appears to have greater relative seasonal regularity than does mobile home production. In 1968, two-thirds of the industry's manufacturers were utilizing only 58 percent to 87 percent of their production capacity. Achieving greater seasonal regularity is a prime prerequisite for stimulating innovation in the industry.

The financing of manufacturing is another problem relevant to sources on intermediate and long-term funds. An important means of financing production is trade credit extended by suppliers. However, commercial banks and insurance companies now play a more active role in supplementing trade credit and equity capital. Until recently the equity capital in the industry was largely retained earnings. During the past few years, a number of the large firms have sold securities, mainly common stock, to the public. Current financing is less a problem because producers generally sell to dealers for cash.

Figure 15
Seasonality. Data supplied by MHMA
and Elrick & Lavidge.

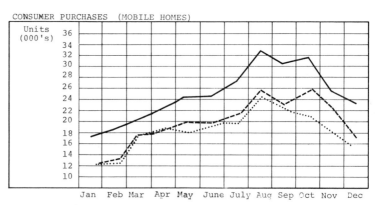

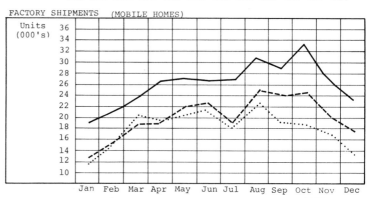

The cost structure of mobile-home manufacturers is dominated by material costs, which declined from an average of 70 percent of total costs in 1951 to an average 65 percent today. During the same period, direct labor constantly accounted for about 12 percent in the average, while average profits before taxes rose from 5 percent to nearly 7 percent.

The cost structure is a function of company size. Direct labor costs decline with increasing size, from 22 percent down to 7 percent. Profits before taxes grow as size grows, from less than 3 percent to more than 10 percent.

In terms of hourly wages, the average common production base rate approaches $3.00. But the cost of labor is rising.

Looking at labor, one finds that the industry largely uses nonunion labor who work on a piecework basis. Labor is about half organized, with about half the organized shops belonging to the United Auto Workers. Shop organization is industrial rather than craft, which eliminates trade jurisdictional disputes. Friction occurs when mobile home units are used as part of other construction. The industry then comes in conflict with the craft building unions.

Finally, regarding productivity, it seems that the widespread payment of bonus or incentive rates has had a bearing upon efficiency, in addition to the effect of mechanization. In 1950 an industry-wide average of 189 man-hours was needed to produce one unit. Today large efficient plants report below 100 man-hours.

Mobile-Home Marketing

Regional retail sales patterns show the same development over time as regional production patterns. The trend is clearly toward a more even geographical dispersal of regional shares of total mobile-home sales.

In 1950, there were four clearly leading states: Illinois, Indiana, Michigan, and Ohio—the old prefab belt. By 1967 Florida, Texas, and North Carolina had taken the top ranks, but are now closely trailed by many other states.

The major marketing problem of the industry is that the number of new units sold each year is much less than the number of new residents that must be attracted. Each year a substantial number of households leave mobile-home living, two to three times more than unit removals from the mobile-home inventory. Additions to the mobile home supply can only be generated if net increases in mobile-home population can be achieved. Thus, the primary marketing objective of the industry must be to create demand for additions to the supply. New units sales are only the end of the marketing process (Figure 16).

Figure 16
Mobile-home shipments, new owners,
and replacements. Data supplied by
MHMA.

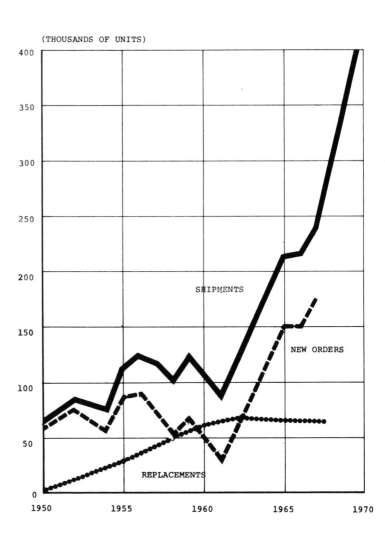

To meet this marketing challenge, the industry must try (1) to decrease the rate at which households leave, and (2) to increase the number of households that are converted. The first objective can obly be achieved by making mobile-home living more attractive. One of the industry's most severe marketing liabilities is its deficiency in providing adequate sites. Furthermore, the industry must broaden the range of housing that it makes available, on both a unit and a site basis. The second objective, to increase the number of newly entering households, primarily requires improving the general attitudes toward mobile-home living: eliminating the causes of negative attitudes and establishing a legitimate housing-oriented product image.

In light of these challenges, the actual marketing performance has been poor. Manufacturers place too little emphasis on marketing programs, and the basic marketing theory of the industry is misdirected. The wrong media and the wrong advertising appeals are used. Most advertising is narrowly class- or trade-journal oriented, thus addressing market segments which are already attracted. And if prime radio or television time is devoted to commercials, or if advertising campaigns are run in national general magazines, then the pleasures of mobile-home life are being extolled instead of the commercials being addressed to the real, the traditional housing market. The industry is still caught by the mobile-life tradition. The industry misses its real market. Since the burden of consumer advertising falls on the dealers, who have neither the funds nor the necessary problem-awareness, mobile-home advertising will continue for some time to be an intra-industry monologue.

In terms of the channels of distribution, there are no middlemen in the industry who can assume the marketing functions traditionally performed by service wholesalers. Direct contact with dealers is the channel employed by practically all manufacturers.

There are close to 8,000 mobile-home dealers—a highly unorganized sales force. Dealerships are local, independent, and relatively small, often inadequately financed, and with little selling experience. The mortality rate is high. Manufacturers do little dealer training, even though often believing that a more drastic upgrading and reorganization is called for. Dealers generally handle from four to six lines. Franchising or exclusive representation is the goal of many manufacturers, but progress toward this end is very slow. Markups are very high, ranging from 20 percent to 40 percent. About 40 percent of the dealers are operating mobile-home parks, because a chronic shortage of park space results in a loss of many "safe" sales. Usually, one year of free service is offered. Manufacturers commonly offer a 6- to 12-month warranty. About 60 percent of sales involve trade-ins.

Now, more and more dealerships are incorporating and selling stock;

professional and business men are becoming silent partners. But still, the typical dealer does not have sufficient capital to carry an inventory himself so he must seek "floor-plan" financing. Common lenders are sales-finance companies and commercial banks. The usual advance is 100 percent of the manufacturer's invoice. Interest rates on floor-plan loans are relatively low because many lenders require dealers to sell all their retail paper to the floor-planning institution.

The narrow sales orientation holds a bleak future for most dealers. They will definitely be out of the modular housing business if they do not mature into developers.

Another radical change is imperative relative to retail financing. The purchaser of a mobile home can finance it as he does an automobile. Down payment ranges from 20 percent to 30 percent. Finance companies and commercial banks finance most mobiles with up to 10-year chattel mortgages at about 7 percent to 7.5 percent add-on interest, meaning that simple interest figures to about 11 percent to 14 percent. A conventional mortgagor would pay much less in simple interest. The contrast is startling. It is not necessary to enter here into a long discussion about alternative solutions. There is only one solution: to finance mobile homes like traditional homes.

In this respect one important trend began in 1964 when some savings and loan associations offered mobile home mortgages of 15 to 20 years at simple interest rates of 6 percent to 7 percent. The new 1968 Housing Act established authority for federally-chartered savings and loan associations to finance the purchase of mobile homes.

The mobile-home industry for a long time expected that the FHA would extend mortgage insurance to mobile homes. FHA insurance for mobile homes is an urgent objective—since it would activate the low-cost potential of the mobile home. Many mobile homes have for quite some time already enjoyed FHA insurance, usually when both the land and the mobile unit are included. A large number of manufacturers are constructing their sectional units to FHA standards. Now, the FHA can insure loans on mobile homes in general. The FHA insures loans in an amount not exceeding $10,000 up to a maximum of twelve years. The interest rate varies from 7.97 percent to 10.57 percent. In this context, it should be noted that delinquency ratios for present-type mobile-home installment loans are lower than for FHA 1 to 4 family mortgages. Repossession ratios are neglegible. Many lenders consider mobile home paper a better risk than automobile paper. The returns are most favorable.

Regulation and Taxation of Mobile Homes

During the 1930s, public officials recognized that trailers were a substitute for housing. Routine application of regulation for traditional housing seemed necessary and logical, yet proved impossible, for legal and administrative reasons, and because the trailer industry stubbornly fought regulation attempts. The traditions of individualism and laissez-faire were vividly alive in the industry. The net effect of this clash of intentions and interests was the virtual absence of consistent trailer regulation and taxation. The trailer population consumed public services, thus causing a drain on community budgets. Yet they often escaped the obligation to pay, by simply enjoying the lack of a trailer tax. Also, there were small groups of unemployed or semiemployed nomads in slum-type trailers that sometimes constituted a moral and safety hazard to a community.

Even though most trailer camps were not of slum character and most trailerites did not try to evade (mostly nonexistent) taxes, in the mid-thirties a highly negative public image of the trailerite was firmly established. "If trailers ever get into mass production—God help us," warned a government official in 1936. The prejudice remains to this day.

Mobile-Home Taxation

Because the rapid development of the mobile home greatly exceeded the ability of government to cope with the resulting problems, most taxation laws were inconsistent and generally obsolete by the time they were enacted. From state to state, and for the nation as a whole, mobile-home taxation is an impenetrable jungle of inconsistencies and impracticalities, whether seen from a theoretical, legal, or administrative point of view.

The major problem is the unsettled status of an object that is not clearly real or personal property, mobile or immobile, permanent or transient. There is a wide range of taxation situations that the mobile home may involve. On a factory lot awaiting shipment, it constitutes inventory. On the highways, it is considered a vehicle. On the dealer's lot, it again becomes inventory. Later it ends up in a mobile-home park on a rented park space, in a mobile-home subdivision on a privately owned lot, or outside of a mobile-home park on isolated private property. After having passed through the first stages of the filtering process, the mobile home finds a multitude of nonresidential uses.

From a taxation standpoint, every situation may call for a different treatment. Accordingly, an amazing range of different taxes and fees has been imposed upon mobile homes. And these conceptual complexities are supplemented by another set of difficulties: the administrative problems of tax collection and revenue distribution.

A summary of present alternative methods of taxation is quite revealing. Even though the mobile home may use the highway only once, in all states it is subjected to the state motor vehicle license fee. This practice is now anachronistic; the charge is no longer equitable. Used as a dwelling, the mobile home may be taxed as realty, together with the land, or separately as personalty. Yet, it may be exempt from property taxation by payment of an "in lieu" excise, ownership, or privilege tax, or by purchase of a vehicular license. Nearly every state has statutes with different provisions. Some states have none at all. Apart from making or not making the park operator responsible (directly or indirectly) for collection of the tax imposed upon the units, in all states the mobile-home-park owner pays a real-estate tax on land and physical improvements. The tax treatment of the other aspect of a mobile-home park, namely the business of operating it, again fluctuates greatly from state to state. Since this is essentially a rental service, the park operator is subject to the business and occupational licensing fees.

And in most states different methods are applied for units on rented park spaces, for units on owned park spaces, and for units outside of parks. Furthermore, most states methods of assessment differ radically from those of assessing traditional housing. Mobile-home-park taxation, which is equally chaotic, aggravates the situation.

State and local governments attempt to raise more revenue from the mobile home population, which leads to widespread testing at state scale of potential or available fiscal devices. The variety of mobile-home taxes and fees seems to be on the increase.

Since most states tax mobile homes differently from other types of housing, the owners of permanent dwelling units suspect that the mobile-home owner is not paying his "fair share." This is because the different tax treatment of mobile-home residents makes their actual contribution to the local government budget invisible to the rest of the community. The "fair share" argument intermingles with general anti-mobile-home prejudice to make mobile-home regulation a chaos of discrimination.

Mobile-Home Regulation

Local mobile-home policy is a direct function of what the community "thinks" about the mobile home. If a dominant political, economic, or social group is hostile toward the mobile home, repressive controls will reflect this. Prejudice will merely be cloaked in legal language. Vested interests and bitter citizens push for exclusionary or repressive, and often punitive, ordinances. Regulatory powers granted to local governing bodies are often grossly abused. Mobile-home parks are zoned into city dump and cement-plant areas; they are still classified with junkyards, asphalt plants, stockyards, and used-car lots. Forced to live in areas surrounded by industries and heavy traffic, park residents find little incentive to participate in community life or to maintain the residential character of the mobile home or the mobile-home park. This in turn nourishes and confirms prejudice and bias, and a self-perpetuating vicious circle is established.

But apart from discrimination, the development of the regulatory structure has been characterized by panic action. In almost every area of mobile-home regulation, the United States is balkanized by state, municipal, and county laws which lack uniformity, consistency, and often logic.

The regulatory pyramid is a highly complex and redundant network. The state may have regulations applying universally to sanitation in all mobile-home (and/or travel-trailer) parks within its boundaries, or applying only to those outside of urban jurisdictions. Thus, the state health departments may exercise control. The county may also have jurisdiction over all such facilities within the county, or over those in incorporated areas in the county. And there may also be myriads of local units of government authorized to regulate mobile homes and parks. All may encumber themselves with duplicate administrative expense. Similarly, in zoning matters, parallel and often conflicting regulations have been prepared by municipalities on matters where the county or the state was already exercising jurisdiction. Or, in terms of county zoning, regulations are promulgated on matters already covered by state operation.

The federal government does not directly regulate mobile homes or mobile-home parks, yet it does regulate indirectly. FHA park standards in many localities have more impact than locally promulgated rules. The Small Business Administration's guidelines for loan commitments may be in conflict with local codes. Model codes by various federal agencies further add to the chaos.

And in a horizontal respect, even though many applicable standards are contained in existing local codes, often slightly varying standards are developed for separate mobile-home-park ordinances.

Finally, there is a problem of definition. Still in 1968, at least 24 state statutes made no distinction between travel trailers and mobile homes, referring simply to "trailers," which keeps the judiciary hopelessly confused. The courts are struggling through semantic labyrinths. Primarily for this reason, many serious legal problems have arisen.

The regulatory and legal framework is outmoded and inadequate. Mobile-home regulation and taxation are obviously in need of a complete overhaul. All this severely retards growth and development of the industry. Repressive or exclusionary legislation obstructs or completely prohibits the development of mobile-home parks, particularly of high-quality parks in desirable locations. Sixty percent of "safe" sales of mobile homes are lost because of lack of park space, and also because most statutes and ordinances confine mobile homes to licensed parks. This latter constraint limits the potential market for the low-cost product to those market segments which are prepared to accept the particular sociological characteristics of mobile-home-park living. Removal of this artificial barrier would enable the industry to offer a low-cost product, without any strings attached, and of a design indistinguishable from traditional housing, so that mobile homes could be allowed in normal residential districts.

Development Trends
Factors Conducive to
Industry Growth

Before attempting some speculative statements relative to the future development of the industry, it seems helpful to summarize: (1) the factors which have contributed to the growth of the industry, and (2) the critical problems the industry faces or is going to face. First, the most important factors of the growth so far:

1. The vehicular definition makes the mobile home immune to the restrictive controls that are exerted by the conservative institutional forces operative in the housing market. The mobile-home industry has been forced to operate outside the traditional housing market. Thus, e.g., it could escape building-code-imposed redundancy, could standardize and thus employ mass production. Not considered housing by labor institutions, the industry could use unskilled nonunion factory labor. As a result of vehicular financing the lending institutions did not, because of lesser risk, place the same tight institutional controls on mobile-home loans which they had placed on conventional home loans.

2. The vehicular definition results directly in lower occupancy costs. The unit, whether new or used, including furnishings and appliances, is financed in one package. There are no extra charges for points, title search, lawyer's fees, and other closing costs. After the loan is repaid, the mobile home is low-occupancy-cost housing for some 15 years.

There was formerly a considerable advantage in terms of taxation. Trade-ins can be handled as easily as auto trade-ins. Divorcing the house from the land has led to economies: the illusion of mobility excused densities which would not be tolerable for fixed housing. And the land is obtainable without purchase.

3. The major reason for the growth is that the industry sees itself as an industry and works with vigorous initiative to remove barriers to further growth, in contrast to the manufactured-home industry. The focal point of initiative is the Mobile Home Manufacturers Association (MHMA) which through long-term campaigns has overcome major obstacles. The association has concentrated primarily on the socioeconomic-political environment, particularly on problems of the postdistribution phase.

The MHMA has consistently worked to upgrade the negative trailer image, and has tactically lobbied for maintaining the vehicle definition.

In the late 1940s and 1950s, the association worked successfully to educate the financial sector to finance mobile-home retail purchases.

The successful development of a national performance-type code was a most significant achievement. Building code restrictions, often imposed upon mobile homes as an exclusionary device, would have continued to constitute a significant problem if the industry had not circumvented the menace by a drastic step.

During the 1950s the Mobile Home Manufacturer's Association initiated a long-term program of self-regulation. The objective was the development of a nationwide uniform production standard. The basic tactic was to enlist the cooperation of impartial nationally known and respected institutions, such as the American National Standards Institute. In 1969, after some 15 years, ANSI Standard "A—119.1—1969 for Mobile Homes—Body and Frame Design and Construction; Installation of Plumbing, Heating, and Electrical Systems" was published.

This program is one of the most impressive and successful ones ever launched by any trade association. The Building Officials Conference of America and the Southern Building Code Congress have adopted the Standard. The electrical section is contained in the National Electrical Code C—1. Many states have already incorporated Code A—119.1 into their laws, or have such legislation pending. The MHMA is pressing that all state legislatures incorporate these standards into their statutes. The mobile-home industry now has a nationwide uniform-performance-type code.

Building regulation of mobile homes illustrates the broad institutional implications of industrialization of building. The principle of industrialization is identical with the principle of standardization of products and centralization of operations and quality-control systems. The process of industrialization, delocalization of hitherto site-oriented operations, immediately makes established, localized control systems obsolete. This is particularly true in the case of complete assemblies which conceal from inspection most of its components and subassemblies. There is only one solution: precise definition of control objectives and performance requirements, and establishment of an impartial machinery approved by state or federal government for periodic control of the centralized production process. The Mobile Home Manufacturers Association has grasped this principle.

Probably the most important achievement, however, was that the industry virtually built its own market. The association worked vigorously for over two decades to stimulate mobile-home-park development, by interesting the financial sector in financing such developments, and by educating local-government officials in an effort to overcome the practice of discriminatory zoning. The mobile-home industry has created the mobile-home-park industry as an indispensable support function.

For the future growth of the industry, it will be decisive to what degree the industry will suceed in reinforcing the growth factors already discussed. Attempting to tap the vast urban housing market, the industry will have to sacrifice many of the advantages it derived so far from the vehicular classification of its product. But the industry can and should try to reinforce its position as the only subsector of the housing sector now capable of delivering low-cost housing. If the industry can maintain this competitive edge, its further growth seems certain. To achieve this the industry must give more support and leverage to their association and, in particular, must give more support to the longer-range planning activities of their association.

Factors Retarding Industry Growth

While reviewing the major problems which the mobile-home industry faces, one should keep in mind that despite these problems the industry has achieved a dramatic growth rate. The elimination of any one of the obstacles should greatly stimulate the development of the industry. But most of these constraints can only be overcome through consistent, joint efforts of the industry as a whole. This again points to the need for the industry to give more power to their association.

The most critical problems are:
1. The industry is still maturing, and is too unconcentrated and unstructured.
2. Most firms are undercapitalized. Current, intermediate, and long-term financing constitute problems.
3. The industry is subject to heavy seasonal fluctuations.
4. The industry suffers from a critical shortage of management, marketing, engineering, and design talent. The industry image attracts too little qualified professional talent.
5.   Except for routine development, there are practically no central or individual R&D activities.
6. There is a critical need for modular and dimensional coordination and for standardization. There is little synchronization with the supply sector.
7. Most states have not yet incorporated into law the industry's construction standard A-119.1. The industry has not yet succeeded in having its standards accepted for modular construction.
8. With the advent of modules for fixed-site housing, the industry faces conflicts with building-trade unions.
9. Equipment requirements for highway transportation differ from state to state and are redundant.
10. The industry's emphasis on immediate problems works against formulation of long-term strategies. The industry is still narrowly mobile-home oriented.

11. The industry is not yet marketing conscious. Marketing strategies are poorly funded, unsophisticated, and misdirected. The obsolete distribution system retards industry growth, and is inadequate for the move into modular developments.

12. High dealer mark-ups and high-cost retail financing absorb the production economies. With the trend toward the module, a complete overhaul of retail financing is imperative.

13. Zoning is perhaps the most critical problem. The relatively slow rate of new park development freezes the replacement rate. (Fig. 16) The urgent physical upgrading of the mobile home inventory is retarded. Lack of park space and confinement of units to parks results in a 60 percent loss of safe sales. In 1969, only an estimated 118,000 new park sites became available, as compared with an output of more than 400,000 mobile homes.

14. Mobile-home taxation is obsolete.

15. Modular developments may confront the industry with regulation problems which so far have been circumvented with the vehicular definition.

16. The industry still faces a negative-image problem. The mobile-home population still experiences discrimination and enjoys little social integration. About one-third of the mobile-home population is not satisfied with mobile-home living.

17. Government agencies, in general, still look negatively at the industry. Federal housing programs continue to use the industry only in a stop-and-go manner.

Market Growth Potential

The growth potential of the industry, particularly of its markets, can here be given only a cursory examination.

The inflation in on-site housing costs strikes particularly at two rapidly growing age groups: young married couples, the 20 to 29 age group, and retired people, the 65 to 74 age group. Both are groups of limited income. Both, thus, are prime prospects for mobile homes. Adding together probable increases to 1980 in the two groups, and considering earlier retirement and increased suitability of mobile homes for larger families, then almost double the current market potential will be available by 1980.

The middle-young adults (30 to 34 years old) also will register a prolific rate of growth. Likewise, employed people between 45 and 65 constitute a relatively untouched market.

Three other potential markets should be mentioned: (1) the second home market should be 200,000 units a year in the early seventies, of which the mobile home industry could capture 50,000 to 100,000; (2) HUD is permitting the use of mobile homes as temporary residential and nonresidential facilities for urban renewal programs; and (3) the industry could press for a federally aided program for reserve lands to be occupied temporarily by mobile homes which can give way to future subdivision—highway departments, private investors, or military services, etc., might release undeveloped land temporarily.

The big market, however, for the industry is urban housing. The industry might produce 500,000 modules per year by 1975.

Combining the growth potentials of these various markets, one has to conclude that the industry should produce one million relocatable homes per year by 1975. This capacity expansion is no problem. With one additional shift per day and with some adjustments in materials handling, the present capacity would approach one million units.

These projections have been arrived at with the notorious assumption of the industry, resulting from its mobile-home orientation: that also in the future they will have to rely on their traditional markets, and that they will continue to operate as a separate industry.

There is reason to doubt this assumption. Four major trends will be discussed which will lead to a different conclusion. One will not conclude that the projected annual output of 1.0 million units by 1975 is to be questioned, but one may find that the mobile-home industry may not be clearly identifiable any more by 1975.

Trends
Mobile-Home Parks:
Development Trends

As the first identifiable trend, the development of the mobile-home park should be traced. The old trailer camp of the thirties, characterized by unacceptable densities and hazardous sanitary conditions, has gradually developed into the present-day low-density mobile-home park which meets high health and sanitation standards, which is often luxuriously sited and landscaped, and which provides a multitude of recreational amenities and facilities. Figures 17, 18 should document that in terms of site planning, landscaping and general appearance, mobile-home parks are rapidly becoming indistinguishable from traditional residential single-family developments.

The Product of the Industry:
Development Trends

The future development of the mobile home itself constitutes the second trend. The industry plans to rename their product "relocatable home" instead of "mobile home." Figures 19, 20 are intended to illustrate how the industry is rapidly moving into development and mass production of three-dimensional "modules" of mobile-home size for fixed-site single-story, multistory, or high-rise housing. Other segments of the total shelter-producing industry conglomerate, and even outside industries, such as the container industry, are simultaneously developing such modules; mostly using the same technology, and in any event ending up with the same product in terms of appearance.

The illustrations, then, are intended to demonstrate that, in terms of its product, the mobile-home industry soon will no longer be

Figure 17
Early mobile-home parks. Courtesy of
MHMA.

Figure 18
Mobile-home parks.

Figure 19
Modules produced by mobile-home
manutacturers. Courtesy of MHMA.

Figure 20
Modules under development in the
mobile-home industry. Courtesy of
MHMA.

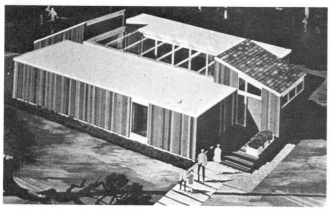

identifiable as a distinct and separate entity within, and will be absorbed as an integral part into, the total shelter-producing industry conglomerate.

Trends in Mergers and Acquisitions

As for the future position of the mobile-home industry relative to the total shelter-producing industry, the trends in mergers and acquisitions involving the mobile-home industry give important clues. One can identify some major patterns. Mergers and acquisitions take place:
1. between mobile-home manufacturers
2. between mobile-home manufacturers and home manufacturers
3. between mobile-home manufacturers and builders
4. between mobile-home manufacturers and real-estate developers
5. between mobile-home manufacturers and firms from outside industries

In recent years about 70 major mergers and acquisitions were reported involving the mobile-home industry. About 30 of these took place within the mobile-home industry itself; at least 12 involved home manufacturers; at least 5 involved builders, and about 20 involved outside firms.

Within the mobile-home industry, most of the industry leaders have grown through acquisition of other mobile-home companies.

Leading home manufacturers have acquired mobile-home companies. A mobile-home industry leader was licensed to manufacture and sell sectional homes designed by a prefab company. Some companies are producing prefabs and mobile homes.

Mobile-home industry leaders, needing building-industry know-how in connection with modular developments, intend to buy or have bought one or even some top-volume homebuilders. Top homebuilders have bought or are shopping for mobile-home manufacturers. Some of the nation's top builders have added, by internal expansion, mobile-home manufacturing to their operations.

Then there are real-estate-oriented firms. A giant investing company, with holdings in manufacturing and real-estate companies, put together a housing conglomerate by acquiring the third largest mobile-home manufacturer, the latter itself a conglomerate. Big Florida land developers have bought mobile-home manufacturers.

As for acquisition-eager outsiders, there is, of course, Boise Cascade with Divco-Wayne, or a giant cash-and-carry building materials dealer, who has acquired three mobile-home makers. Broadly based manufacturing firms have bought several mobile-home companies. Many other major nonshelter-oriented corporations are interested in similar moves.

We should note here another significant parallel trend: the mobile-home-park industry is already dominated by nonmobile-home-industry forces. About 50 percent of all new parks are being developed for either building contractors or real estate developers. This percentage is growing. Active members of NAHB (National Association of Home Builders of the United States) have forsaken homebuilding and become park developers. Major construction companies have developed parks. Major developers, investors, or insurance companies are developing 1,000-acre tracts into mobile home parks that eventually will have up to or over 10,000 residents.

And apart from mobile-home-industry involvement, builders, home manufacturers, developers, and outside companies are also merging.

There is certainly quite often the disappearance of shelter-oriented companies into major corporations where they become mere operating divisions. But it seems that mergers between firms of different segments of the total shelter industry are motivated more by functional, rather than merely financial, considerations.

Typically, the largest housing producer, Boise-Cascade, is a fully integrated building company active in practically all shelter-oriented fields.

It seems then that there is a definite trend of integration of all segments into one big shelter-producing industry. Already, the difference in operation and product between home manufacturer and home builder is small. Neither will there be a significant difference between mobile-home and home manufacturers. And the difference between the mobile-home and building industry will in fact tend to bring the two together. With the trend toward modules, the mobile-home industry and the home builders will need each other.

The trend of integration is also evident through seriously discussed merger proposals involving the associations of the different segments. Thus, there are NABM (National Association of Building Manufacturers)—MHMA (Mobile Home Manufacturers Association) merger proposals, and a NAHB—NABM merger was proposed. However, the NAHB—MHMA relationship is still a bit frosty. AIH urged all three associations to lobby as one industry.

One can already find statistical evidence for a slow progression toward one fully integrated shelter industry. The concentration in the total shelter industry rises rapidly.

In 1967 the 50 largest firms in building (and most of the largest are integrated) had sales above $10 million. In 1968 there were already 87 firms reporting sales above $10 million. In 1967, the 50 leaders in dollar volume accounted for 6.7 percent of the total value of new housing units started (including mobile homes). In 1968, it was already 11.5 percent. Looking at the top 100 firms in 1968, we find that they accounted for 18 percent of total housing starts. It is also interesting that in 1967 nearly 50 percent of the total housing starts were accounted for by 3 percent or 4 percent of all firms in the industry. Concomitant with growing concentration is a growing integration.

Regulation and Financing of Mobile Homes: Trends

Finally, it should be considered how the major problems of the mobile-home industry can be overcome. The solutions constitute in a way the fourth trend, because finally the mobile-home industry will press for elimination of growth-retarding obstacles.

Regulation and taxation of mobile homes are obsolete. There is only one solution: The mobile home should be regulated by the established regulatory systems for traditional housing.

Some more random examples that should be mentioned: As has been concluded already, mobile homes should be financed like traditional homes. Or, the high dealer markups call for elimination. In developing modular concepts, the industry is beginning to deal directly with traditional homebuilders. For modular developments this will soon be the rule. Or, in order to eliminate redundant equipment requirements imposed by highway regulation, the mobile home should be accepted by the Department of Transportation as a legitimate form of housing.

Recommendations for Public Policy

Thus, an examination of all four trends leads to one conclusion: The mobile-home industry develops and should be treated as an integral part of the total shelter-producing industry.

The alternatives are clearly defined.

Failure at the federal and state level to take into account these trends will result in inconsistent stopgap decision making. This will not slow the industry's growth, yet it will not stimulate and direct its development either. It will cement the mobile-home orientation of the industry. The mobile home and the mobile-home park are not optimal housing forms developed in response to user needs but are accidental compromises dictated largely by regulations lacking housing orientation.

The proposed alternative is to stimulate an optimal development of the industry. Such a policy could create sufficient high-quality park space supply, which in turn would increase the annual industry output by at least 30 to 40 percent, and it could encourage location of mobile homes in residential districts, which would yield a further increase in output of at least 20 percent per year. This possible expanded output could be tactically used to guarantee the industry year-round, full-capacity operation. Shielded from seasonal fluctuation, the industry would be able to and should be encouraged to invest in, R&D activities. Sensitively supported by tactical "lollipop" control, gradual improvement of the product, especially in terms of design, would be insured and the industry could be expected to produce functionally and architecturally acceptable modules with potential for urban housing. It would mean the creation of a growth industry capable of continuously producing acceptable low-cost housing for medium- and high-density urban situations.

At this point it is necessary to turn to some broader implications.

The mobile-home industry can only achieve a dramatic cost breakthrough, i.e., significant economies of scale, by synchronization with the entire building-materials and -products sector and the entire broader institutional system which, however, are geared to an inefficient, fragmented construction industry. Policies focusing solely on developing the mobile-home industry, however successful, cannot increase the economic and political force of the industry to the degree necessary to compete with the construction industry in controlling the important supporting sectors. It is a vicious circle, which seems to rule out "innovation by invasion" by the mobile-home industry.

Thus, if maximum possible cost reduction and a drastic increase in housing output are national goals, it must be recognized that comprehensive industrialization of the entire industry conglomerate, including the supporting sectors, is the necessary prerequisite.

The mobile-home industry should be treated tactically as an integral part of the entire industry conglomerate. Then its innovative characteristics can influence any program or policy relating to the entire conglomerate. This tactic uses the mobile-home industry as a nucleus of innovation. The mobile-home industry as an outside competitor would force the traditional sector to utilize its superior political and economic power to prevent the supplying and institutional sectors from supporting the rival industry. Yet, as an accepted integral component, the "atypical" mobile home industry would be valuable in pointing to deficiencies in the existing structure, thus forcing critical reexamination of traditional concepts and the traditional framework.

The Kaiser Committee suggested how their target of 26 million housing units could be achieved, should their recommended traditional approach fail. "If it fails, we would then forsee the necessity for massive federal intervention with the federal government becoming the nation's houser of last resort."

While failure is indeed possible, "massive" federal intervention is not necessary. The need is for a consistent long-range policy for the comprehensive industrialization of the building industry. Subtle "lollipop" type strategies guided by a consistent long-term policy will achieve far more than massive, panic-motivated intervention.

There can be no doubt that the building industry will enter a phase of drastic industrialization. But in the absence of constructive guidance, this process may well take an accidential and irreversible direction. Perhaps, as demonstrated by the example of the mobile-home industry, by developing in a direction which by mere accident is not blocked by institutional constraints.

In less than some 20 years the building industry must fabricate the equivalent of the entire housing stock of the United States. What we put into this effort will determine the quality of our built environment by 1990. It is a unique chance. But it is also a unique threat. Failure to control this process may well leave us by 1990 with an environment of early Levittown- or early mobile-home-park-like qualities.

13
Mechanical Systems for Industrialized Building

Norman L. Rutgers

The term "industrialized building" can be greatly misunderstood; it is intermixed with the term "prefabrication," and it is quite important that a relatively high level of prefabrication exist in order to arrive at an industrialized solution. There are several different types, or different levels, or, perhaps, degrees of industrialized building. One example of a rather highly industrialized solution is the mobile-home industry. Other examples could include Habitat which was developed for Expo '67, and, in spite of many problems and tremendous costs and all of the other negative elements of Habitat, it does exist, it was completed, and, in my estimation, it does represent a step forward in industrialization. Conrad Engineers, working in California, developed a lightweight version of the Habitat element known as the "Uniment Structure." Edward Rice, a well-known architect, worked with the group in designing the Uniment solution and one of the features of this development was a special, thin-shell concrete that would not contract as it cured and dried. This thin shell was approximately 2 inches thick and was 30 to 35 feet long and approximately 12 feet wide. The shell was completely finished at the point of manufacture and transported to the site. In the development of Uniment, a situation occurred which has happened in many of the other previous industrialized approaches. Most of the attention was focused on the structure, and the mechanical services were not considered until many of the initial design decisions were made. In effect, there was no real provision for the installation of a mechanical system on an integrated basis. I understand that additional development work has been done, and some changes have been made in this regard. The initial prototype was a five-story apartment project which worked quite satisfactorily for the geographical area in which it was erected. However, if this same solution were moved to a different climate, such as Washington, D.C., or other areas of high moisture content, some very serious problems of moisture condensation on both the inside and the outside of the building could well occur at certain times of the year. Yet, as a structural solution, it was a beautiful example of developing the techniques of handling concrete in new and innovative ways, but it did lack in the environmental control area by not being able to provide a good thermal insulation for varying locations.

As I mentioned before, the mobile-home industry has, perhaps, gone further than anyone else in the true industrialized solution. The mobile-home home manufacturer produces a total product—it is built in a factory, it is transported to the site on its own running gear, and people can move in and start living immediately. In 1969, this has answered the housing need for approximately 400,000 people. It has, perhaps, the one major drawback that, regardless of how it is built, it still looks like a mobile home with the conventional mobile-

Presented to the 1969 session. Norman L. Rutgers is Assistant to the President, Lennox Industries, Inc.

home exterior appearance. Some steps are being taken to give additional architectural treatment to change the basic appearance and also the roofline of these units. I firmly believe that this solution must arrive at a different visual identity. The element that created the shiny aluminum exterior at the time the mobile home was originally developed made real sense—but when you try to put this type of structure into a community, take the wheels off and say this is a house, the big question is, what will be its acceptance rate?

Magnolia Homes in Vicksburg is an example of a firm that is moving beyond the original mobile-home concept. They are beginning to stack these elements. They are using textured materials for exteriors, and other modifications, and changes are being developed to take this out of a rather traditional category. We have looked at a complete thermal package which does not actually go into the mobile home, but slides underneath it. This would be a complete heating and air conditioning unit and would conserve the critical space that is normally taken up by the heating equipment located internally in the traditional manner.

There is another interesting development in the industrialized package, box, or module which is being developed by the Fruehauf Corporation. The Fruehauf Corporation has built shipping containers, insulated vans, and cubicles which take roughly the same shape and size and the general form of the living unit. Fruehauf's development includes a total module which fits together into basically four sections. Two sections installed side by side produce the first floor and one of these sections is what we would call a wet unit in which all of the plumbing and other similar elements will be located. The other half is a totally dry unit and all of the mechanical systems are installed at the factory. This approach creates a whole new set of problems for our industry in responding to a factory-installed, completely manufactured product. The manufacturer's distribution, merchandising and marketing has all been geared to a traditional dealer-distribution program. Similar to the mobile-home market, the modular housing market, such as Fruehauf, requires the direct sale of the product to the manufacturer of the module. Obviously, this type of sale is not an impossible development, but it is necessary to plan and program reliable service and maintenance to be able to handle that piece of mechanical equipment after it goes out into the field and people are using it.

There is still another element of industrialization which can be called the component approach. This is a series of prefabricated elements which are cast or manufactured in a factory and then assembled on the job site. An example of this component approach might be the Neal Mitchell Framing System, which is a post and beam system with prefabricated, lightweight concrete elements and also prefabricated infill exterior walls and interior partitions. A component approach requires more on-site labor; however, the level of skills of this labor could well be below that required for the conventional housing construction. If a good job of interfacing is done at the point the product and solution is developed, then the pieces will fit on the job site with almost a snap, snap–click, click type of operation. All of this is very simple to talk about, but it is not quite so simple to accomplish without substantial technological development. One subsystem approach which is being developed at this time is the "heart package" which is perhaps a less sophisticated approach than the core unit, which was discussed by Mr. Bud Breyman of Borg-Warner. The process of developing a heart package involves a series of steps arriving at a final totally prefabricated and assembled heart-package unit. In developing this unit, various trades have to work very closely together. A plumbing tree supplier, for instance, is working alongside bathroom-fixture people, who are also coordinating with the kitchen-appliance group, and they, in turn, are working with the supplier of interior finishes and the heating, ventilating, and air-conditioning people to provide a closely related assembly that will substantially reduce on-site labor.

One example that I can cite of the reduction of on-site labor was the test installation of several housing units in Austin, Texas. In the Austin-Oaks Project, there are ten low-income housing units that were built under a grant that was probably one of Lyndon B. Johnson's last efforts to make a mark in the housing field. He authorized the funding of these ten examples and they go all the way from the Dicker Stack-Sack approach, which actually is very fundamental and uses a concrete-sand mix in sacks that are stacked up on top of each other. A rod is driven down through the stacks and the stacks are sprayed with water and, behold, you have a 1970 version of the adobe house. This is not a totally fair evaluation, inasmuch as the unit does have a finish which carries it beyond the adobe house, and it is a very inexpensive approach. In any case, at the Austin-Oaks Project a Mitchell Frame structure was also one of the ten erected and, incidentally, this was a low-income project, and it was air conditioned, which is sort of an interesting thing to think about in itself. Many of us believe that we are going to see more and more air conditioning in lower-income units. The Mitchell Frame structure was installed in one hour and fifteen minutes. The reason for this short installation time was that there were certain pre-scheduled functions that were performed in a mechanical contractor's place of business. He developed a duct system made of lightweight fiberglass board, which could be easily handled by two men in a single piece. This duct assembly went up into a predetermined ceiling area and the refrigeration connections were of a very simple snap-in type. This was a completed installation, including the outdoor condensing unit, and the two men completed the installation—as I mentioned before—in one hour and fifteen minutes. Also, this was an all-electric system with electric heating and electric cooling, which eliminated other

time-consuming elements such as the installation and connections
of flues and fuel lines.

One of the most fragmented segments of the construction industry
has probably been the concrete, precast, prestressed operators.
These individual precast companies operate independently and there
has been no real effort made to coordinate their efforts on a systems
basis. Recently, a new organization which is called Precast Systems
Incorporated was established with national headquarters in Chicago,
Illinois. This group is made up of 41 separate precasters who all sub-
scribed to a operating fund which totals $1,000,000. The express
purpose of this group is to develop an industrialized solution that can
be used interchangeably by the 41 precasters all over the United
States. Therefore, if a good building system evolves from their efforts, we now have the mechanism being generated where a precast
concrete system can be reproduced in New York, Los Angeles, Min-
neapolis, and so forth. This is the first time that this industry group
is beginning to pull together. Naturally, they have a real job ahead
of them before they really have an operating identity. However, they
will be putting in a bid for "Operation Breakthrough," which will be
primarily high-rise, although it can be used on low-rise buildings.

There are some interesting ideas in industrialized housing, and I
believe that there will be many noteworthy developments in "Operation Breakthrough" and beyond, spread out, perhaps, over the next
ten years or so. We will be seeing housing units which are functional, which are efficient, but which probably will not look like the
Cape Cod bungalow that we are used to calling a house. Although
public acceptance is tremendously important, we are approaching
cost levels which will require us to look at and consider a good housing solution which may differ substantially in appearance to that
which we are used to.

The filament winding concept of the Hercules Powder Company that
was developed and tested by the University of Michigan has produced an interesting structure. About a year ago, architect Steve
Paras, of the University of Michigan architectural faculty, actually
produced a filament-wound partial element of a housing unit.

The concept was then used to develop a proposal for military housing
for the Department of Defense. This proposal is a far cry from the
Duckers Portable Barrack (Figures 1, 2). This work was done in competition with the group that was headquartered right here at MIT
and also in competition with several other groups working throughout the country. Admittedly, this is a pretty far-out approach, and expensive machinery has to be developed, but the point is that some
of the space-age technology, some of the developments that we use
to create nose cones on rockets was transferred into a housing solution. I think that from our space group we will find an influence and

Figure 1
Duckers portable barrack and field
hospital, as advertized in the *Scientific
American*, June 26, 1886.

Figure 2
Duckers portable barrack and field
hospital. Working drawings and details
of this early example of prefabrication.
Building Systems Development Incorporated has been so enamored of the
system and its place in history that they
have used this drawing as a Christmas
card over a hundred years after it was
made.

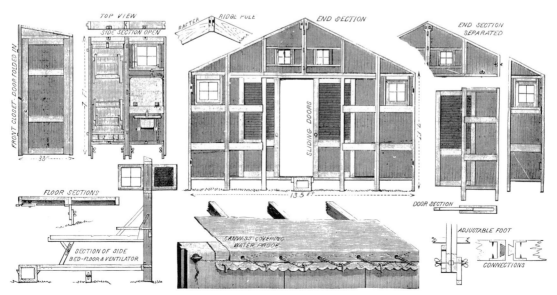

DUCKER'S PORTABLE BARRACK AND FIELD HOSPITAL.

as Bill Hooper—formerly with the Science and Technology Department of the presidential staff of the United States—has indicated, unless the construction industry responds in a meaningful way, it may not be the construction industry that houses America 50 years from now. It might well be the space-technology people or the aerospace groups. Particularly after we accomplish the things that we are starting out to do and have explored the moon and, perhaps, even gone on to Mars and a few other places, and we find it more difficult to dream up new places to travel to. Then this tremendous scientific input might find its way into the housing industry. TRW is moving into the housing market. They are developing, in addition to the exotic filament-winding concepts, sewage waste systems which are integral and which become packaged systems. There is certainly a great need for this type of human-waste disposal.

Dreaming about what is coming along in the future is fine, but I would like to talk about the present level of industrialization. As the previous speakers have said, the main emphasis on industrialization has been on the structure and this is understandable. If I were to ask you to go out and look at an industrialized solution, what would you see? The thing that you would see, obviously, would be the structure because it forms the envelope that houses all of the other components, and, yet, on the Toronto SEF School Project the structure only accounted for 11.7 percent of the total cost of the complete system. I don't think it is a question of whether the structure is more important or less important. It is a question of a total integrated relationship of all the components—the structure obviously being one of them. I readily admit that the structure is important because almost everything else is related to it, tied to it, or located within it. We need a much higher level of coordination between structural and mechanical elements. We went through an illuminating exercise at the Graduate School of Design at Harvard University about a year ago, where we had six graduate students who over a period of two weeks considered the problem of integrating mechanical functions within the structure. It was very interesting to note that this was a no-credit assignment, but it did involve some rather elaborate drawings and considerable effort. We told the students to allow their imaginations to run free, to attempt to tie the structure into the mechanical requirements and not to worry about loadings or stress or structural integrity as much as trying to make the structure perform on a dual basis—not only as the envelope of the building framework, but also to make it function as a part of the mechanical system. It is extremely interesting to see the novel ideas. Some of them, you might say, were ridiculous, but the students did respond. We need more imagination, we need more relief from conventional thinking. Someone mentioned that the Fruehauf people who, for instance, are going into the housing program, perhaps do not know all of the problems they face. I am quite sure that they don't. However, in a way, that could be a great benefit because they are not restricted by conventional thinking. Nobody told them that it couldn't be done so that they are going to go out and do it.

I'd now like to speak briefly about some of the factors that can strain greater industrialization. One of them, a very important one, is the lack of industry coordination. Before the School Construction System Development project in California, we at Lennox did not know the first thing about a structure and cared less. Frequently, we design mechanical units in total isolation of all other elements, develop a product, put it on the market and say to the architect and engineer, in effect, "We defy you to put this in the building and make it work." The mechanical unit actually bore no relationship to the building, it was just a box, a piece of mechanical gear so no one really gave the interface and coordination requirements too much thought.

Let's take interior partitions, for example. There is a great future in using the interior partition as a channel or a chase for running electrical conduit and other services on an organized basis. We might even start putting air through partitions someday to get it down to the floor level, or to get it from the floor level up to the second level.

Another serious problem is the aggregation of the market. Ezra Ehrenkrantz, in the development of the SCSD project, actually developed the market by bringing 13 school districts together and getting them to agree on a standard solution. As so many people have said before, it seems as though industry requires a carrot to reach for, and the only way in which you can stimulate industry to develop new products is to show them a reasonably sizable market. There is no point in going to all of the expense in developing an industrialized solution if we cannot look at a market that represents a large enough volume to be profitable. Systems developed in Europe have had one big benefit that we have not experienced here. Virtually all of the systems building in Europe has been done on a governmental basis and the government actually furnishes the market and the volume, while here in the United States the system must be marketed to private developers without any guarantee of the market size. I hope that we in the United States can develop sufficiently large markets without the government functioning as the major market source. Our government can be extremely helpful in other areas and I am sure that this is necessary, but I am from a reasonably small company from the middle of Iowa and up there we become quite independent—which I don't think is too different than most other manufacturers—and we much prefer to develop our markets privately rather than through federal requirements.

Another constraint to industrialization can be labor unions. We have seen some examples of significant steps taken to minimize the labor problem, that of the Stirling-Homex labor agreement and also the agreement made in Orlando, Florida, at the Disneyland project. These are all special agreements made with the labor unions for specific projects. In the area of low-income housing, we might have to go to the labor people and, in effect, say "Here is a very important social need. Let's not break down your whole labor relationship with the community and, at least, for this market—low-income housing— which we need so desperately. Let's work together and get the housing built." Naturally, this isn't going to be easy, but I do see some favorable indications. Someone had asked about the California SCSD project and how that project related to labor. One thing that allowed that project to proceed was the meetings held with labor at the very beginning of the project. Also, SCSD was built as an experimental job. If the project developers had not sat down with the labor unions, initially, before construction was started, I am sure we would have had some serious problems. Local codes also can present a problem, and there does not seem to be any such thing as standardization of codes. Each local code-writing agency seems to be an independent identity within its own community, and to get some of these people to give up their prerogatives on some sort of a standardized basis is a serious problem. However, this problem must be considered before we can really have any far-reaching industrialization of the building process.

Finally, we are not going anyplace in industrialization unless we have an effective marketing plan, and unless we can market our high-technology solutions. We still haven't accomplished any worthwhile work. Somebody has to buy the product, somebody must accept the product, and all of this means that somebody has to sell it. That brings us up to the point where we might have an equipment manufacturer look at systems and then determine what has to be changed within his own company to really get into the true systems business. It is necessary to look internally at your organization, and this starts with the very top management and continues on down through research and development, sales department, service department and even to the billing department. In most of the companies that have been involved in systems work, the ordinary salesman in that organization really does not understand the system, and the sale is normally carried on through a small number of specialists within that company. Each component manufacturer must design a merchandising and marketing program within his own organization. This amounts to a completely new dialog, a new series of terms, relationships, and responsibilities, all of which require a new approach within the company. I mentioned top management, and that level of management must realize they are dealing with a new dimension. If management does not recognize this and attempts to approach the system development in the traditional way, there can be very serious problems. The research and development department must assume new attitudes when dealing with the systems. One new element is the performance specification which must be understood and must be responded to.

Generally speaking, in our own firm we have worked in the past pretty much on material specifications with the only performance requirements as established by our own design parameters for the product. New materials must be investigated, and, in the case of Lennox Industries, we are basically a sheet-metal fabricating and manufacturing company. This has, for years, kept us at arms length to plastics, fiberglass, and so forth. We are now making humidifiers out of plastic. The reason for this is that we could not provide any metal that would withstand the most corrosive element, water, particularly when you start to evaporate water and get all of the mineral deposits collecting on the metal surfaces. So now we are in the plastics business. The manufacturer must be ready to accept a more complete responsibility for prefabricated components. We call it "single source of responsibility," and it is a fine term. In addition to supplying the total mechanical system, the manufacturer may be faced with the requirement of supplying a service and maintenance contract. I firmly believe that as total systems develop, the subject of service and maintenance will be one of the very important components to be considered. In the development of a system, it is necessary to begin to relate a mechanical component to the structure, to the lighting and ceiling, and to the partition. All of these relationships should be established before we begin to draw lines on a piece of paper or do any mock-ups of a prototype installation. We must know what our partners in the construction industry are really doing. This requires a new level of communications and information exchange between manufacturers and, frankly, manufacturers have not been accustomed to working at this level.

Probably the best example of coordination on the SCSD program was the service sandwich. The sandwich is one space between the ceiling and the roofdeck and measures, approximately, 36 inches in depth. It illustrates the development of a freeway for the duct system and an additional freeway for the plumbing and the electrical system as well (Figure 3). If these components can be organized and can assume their own individual locations without interfering one with the other, then we have taken a giant step forward in coordinating the trades. There are many examples that we can see in virtually any building around us where we have had serious interference between the installer of the duct work and the installer of the piping. These interferences are not only expensive, but, frequently, they seriously affect the operation and quality of the system.

One method of coordination between component manufacturers, which has been used quite successfully, is the pre-bid conference. This is a meeting in which all of the trades are requested to come in, sit down, and discuss the complete design of the building. Slides, movies, and blackboards are used, and it generally is best to have the architect and the engineer present. What this accomplishes is the removal of much of the mystery and many of the contingencies

Figure 3
Diagrammatic section of an integrated
HVAC system.

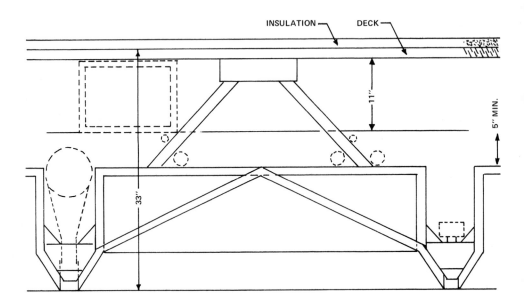

that normally are plugged into the costing of any job. This was done
in Chicago, Illinois, at the Barrington School. Interestingly enough,
three of the contractors that attended the pre-bid conference were
all within a maximum span of 5 percent on their bidding. Two other
contractors did not attend because they felt they really had great
experience and did not need to sit through a session of this type. Both
of these contractors were well over 10 percent above the highest
of the three low bidders; i.e., there was a very clear separation between those that attended the pre-bid conference and those that
did not. We have repeated this pre-bid approach with similar success
in other parts of the country. This, I believe, is as much a part of the
systems concept as the development and interfacing of hardware.
Educational work with the various trades is extremely important, and
the manner in which you attempt to develop this educational program becomes quite critical.

Another area of system development with industrialized components
is the development of a transportation system to get the product
from the point of manufacture to the job site. The particular product
we developed for SCSD was the largest product that we have ever
made. This was a 22-ton piece of rooftop equipment. In order to ship
this product in quantity to the West Coast, we developed special
racks on railroad cars in which the units could be triple-decked,
somewhat like the automobile-transportation rail cars. We have also
developed a special truck-and-trailer arrangement on which we can
double-deck these units and supply four of them on each trailer. To
show you just what this means, it allows us to schedule within a
matter of a very few hours of the time that a product is needed on a
job to the time we can actually set that product on the roof. By
controlling this with our own facilities, we are completely independent of the delays that occur utilizing conventional trucking systems.

Another subject which comes up, when discussing industrialized
systems, is the question of esthetics. One might well ask, what have
esthetics got to do with heating, ventilating, and air-conditioning
equipment? Esthetics are an important aspect of mechanical units
which are located on the roof of the building. The marriage of odd
shapes and sizes can create a jumble of confusion on the roof, and,
frequently, this appearance is quite apparent to those who observe
the building. The "what-the-hell" approach sums the basic impression that esthetically unrelated components convey. On the other
hand, one can design a package system which operates perfectly
well—it heats, it cools, and it looks good, illustrating that, perhaps,
by working with the architect and getting some ideas on exterior
design, an envelope can be developed that contains all the functions
and still has clean, crisp lines and actually complements the structure, rather than confuses it.

A complete thesis could be written on the subject of open systems, as compared and contrasted to closed systems. The industrialization of the building system could well fall into either category; in fact, examples of both open and closed systems can be cited. The industrialized box or module could be a closed system where specialized components are developed to achieve a maximum level of compatibility. At the same time, a building system can be considered an open system and still have industrialized components which make up the subsystem (Figure 4). The only necessity here is that the designer has available to him a selection of several subsystems in the same category, which are all compatible, and which have all had a minimum level of coordination developed in relating all subsystems to each other. There will be much more heard on this subject, and we find that supporters of both approaches can become quite emotional in promoting their particular philosophies.

Getting into a specific building system, I would like to explain some of the details on the Montreal School Building System or, as it is known, the RAS Project. This Montreal system was developed for the Parochial School Program. Its target was about $18,500,000 worth of contracts for, basically, five component suppliers. By specification, they indicated that they wanted a consortium or a group approach, which, in effect, called for a number of competing closed systems. It is my belief that this project represents virtually a quantum jump in systems developments over anything we have seen in any area. This is a concrete system inasmuch as they had a three-hour fire ruling and, also, a multistory requirement. The structural system with beams with programmed openings was developed by the Francon organization in Montreal. One of the very important elements in the development of this system was the use of a well-qualified coordinator. This coordinator was a former quantity surveyor, a gentleman by the name of Robert Hughes. There were also structural engineers, mechanical engineers, accoustical engineers, and architects who worked hand in hand with the entire group, so we should not be misled and feel that a systems development is just a straight industrial approach excluding the professionals. The professionals were very much a part of this project. Every one of our drawings submitted was reviewed by a professional mechanical engineer and contained the engineer's stamp on it, indicating that he worked alongside of us.

Basically, the structural members were relatively simple and few in number. The mechanical system was contained in core area of 20 feet by 20 feet. The corners of the space were notched and the electrical services, plumbing, and so forth, were routed through these openings in a vertical fashion. The mechanical unit was set on the 20 by 20 slab while the slab was still on the ground, and all of the connections were completed. The mechanical core slab had openings for ventilation and for exhaust air which penetrated vertically through the mechanical core. On a multistory building, the mechanical cores

Figure 4
Section perspective. Illustrating the
subsystem of roof deck, partition walls,
structure, mechanical components,
lighting, and floors juxtaposed in an
"open systems" approach to the bidding
procedure and building process.

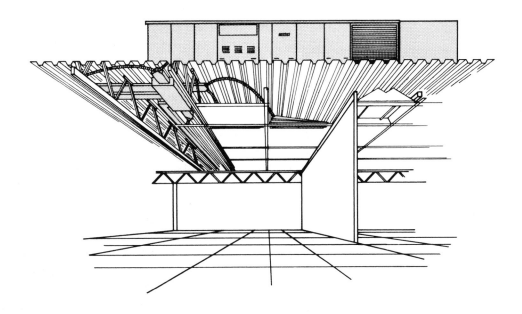

were stacked vertically, which allowed the ventilation and exhaust air ducts to be exactly in line in a vertical manner. Each one of these mechanical areas is designed to serve 16,000 square feet of building, so it becomes a relatively simple matter of looking at the mechanical core as a modular divisible situation. The building is simply divided up into modules, or areas, of 16,000 square feet each. In these areas, there is much of a repeatable nature in the air distribution system and other subsystems. Flexibility and ease of installation was one of the important elements of the performance specifications.

To discuss a bit more detail of the mechanical approach each 20-foot by 20-foot mechanical core area, or module, had the capability of handling 48 different control zones. This was a maximum number, however. Any lesser number could be utilized and, if additional control zones were required at some future date, these could be added very easily. The precast-concrete members had openings programmed in them to allow the duct work to pass through the structure out into the building space. At this point, an interesting relationship was developed between the lighting elements. A method of dropping down out of the ducts with a tube that came down and distributed air at the intersection of a structural member was worked out. A snap-on cover over this structural section routed the air out to a diffuser allowing the air to go in any one or more of four directions. The diffuser was a completely new development and did not exist before the project began. The diffuser was made up of a simple aluminum extrusion, and permitted full control of both volume and directional flow of the air. There were some minor areas of coordination in the development of the diffuser and the duct system which allowed the bracket which supported the lighting coffer to also serve as a support for the duct work. This, in itself, might not sound important, but I mention it only to indicate the level of detail which was considered in developing this system.

Some people have the mistaken idea that the primary function of a building system is to simply reduce costs. While costs have been reduced in many of the subsystem areas, the two things that we are looking for, at a cost not to exceed conventional building, is a higher level of quality and flexibility and, also, a substantially shorter construction time. I think the element that is underrated as one of the key benefits of a building system is the time that can be saved in the process of constructing a building. With the interest rates at the level that they are today, a reduction in construction time from one year to six months can become a very significant economic factor. Also, the orderly flow of material into the construction process is possible, due to a high level of coordination prior to the beginning of construction. This will reduce the delays in the construction schedule and will allow the contractor to figure actual costs without involving expensive contingencies. The advantages of this will accrue only after repeated experience in using a building system. Once we are operating on a more favorable portion of the learning curve, the dollar savings can be quite impressive.

The Lockheed Aircraft Engineering Building in Marietta, Georgia, is an example of speed of construction that a system can bring to the building processes. This building was designed and built for engineering personnel, and a high level of lighting intensities and flexibility was required. Fifty-four thousand square feet of this building were erected and completed and occupied within 88 calendar days of the beginning of the design. Ultimately, a total of 306,000 square feet were completed in 196 calendar days. We can relate this rate of construction to virtually any job of similar size in your own community and compare the construction time using conventional procedures. This Lockheed building actually cost $15.10 a square foot three years ago, which was a normal price even considering a normal escalation. At today's figures, this is still an extremely low price.

The Europeans have been in the building systems business considerably longer than we have, and experienced people from Europe report that the integration of mechanical subsystems and structures can result in a 50 percent saving in electrical cost alone and about a 20 to 25 percent saving on heating and plumbing. Admittedly, this is a broad statement; however, even if we can cut these projections in half we still have a very promising savings picture. Looking at the school market and observing what has happened to costs, the publication *School Management* states that "if you peg a figure of 100 to the year 1957, the overall cost of the building index is now at 134.2, but the cost of materials in 1969 is at 112.1." It is interesting to note that the materials of the HVAC systems, at the time of this report, was indexed at 96.5, which means that it is actually cheaper in 1969 for the materials for heating, ventilating and air conditioning than it was in 1957. However, the picture of on-site labor is quite another story. On-site labor is at 162.1, and I think this quite clearly indicates where we must begin in an attack on this problem of spiraling costs with industrialization of prefabrication. Call it what you will, it is through this type of effort that we will bring as much labor back into the factory, where better quality-control and cost-control procedures can be exercised. This is where the major savings will accrue. This actually is what, at least to me, the term "industrialization" means; simply putting the work, to a much larger extent, in an organization, a roofed area, or, in other words, a manufacturing facility.

14
Performance Codes

Charles Topping

There might well be a question raised about why we talk about codes in these meetings which concentrate on technological improvement, whereas building codes, to say the least, are rather unscientific. Most code discussions are pretty dismal and depressing. They are often highly exothermal, and they're of low efficiency on a light-to-heat basis. People are not very objective about them because there aren't too many people who know a lot about them. In fact, I once calculated, on the basis of 33,000 full-time code people, that only one person in 6,000 really knows very much about codes.

I would like to make three points.
1. Building codes don't affect the sales price of homes as much as is claimed.
2. We will not have performance codes or any other dramatic improvement in building technology until we have developed a fairly complete measurement and evaluation methodology.
3. Specification building codes as they now exist are not unsurmountable barriers to economy and innovation if good engineering and good management are used.

Building codes are generally accused of being archaic, unchanging, and rigid. In fact, there exists a new phrase. One has to say "archaic codes," and, today, the word "archaic" generally has the word "code" after it. Tom Rogers, the first Director of Research and Technology of HUD said, "Institutional restraints, such as building codes, are one of the greatest obstacles to low-cost housing and new building technology."

However, I'd like to raise the question of how much building codes can affect the sale price of a house. Table 1 is a price breakdown of a typical conventional $24,000 single-family house. This is a compilation and average of some well-known, but frequently forgotten, figures. FHA has the same figures; NAHB has them; most builders know them; and they are usually ignored when someone wants to make a point which the figures refute—which is often. The principal point I want to make is based on the first number in the right-hand column, which represents the percentage of the cost of the building itself—not the land, not the financing, not the overhead, and not the profit. The cost of the building itself amounts to only 56 percent of the sale price of the house. That figure may vary 3 or 4 percent, depending upon the price of the house, the location, the builder's efficiency, land prices, etc. But, anyway, it's not much more than half the sale price of the house. So, if you want to reduce the price of a house by 10 percent, you must reduce the cost of the building 20 percent. Now, figure out how often that's possible.

Presented to the 1970 session. Charles Topping is a consultant to the building industry.

Table 1   Price Breakdown of a
Typical Conventional $24,000
Single-Family House

Item	Percent
Building	
Material for structure	24 } 36 }
Labor	12 }
Material for plumbing, heating, air conditioning, electricity	14 } 20 } 56
Labor	6 }
Land and Improvements	23
Street paving	
Sidewalks	
Sewers	
Water	
Financing	8
Builder's overhead and profit	13
Design	
Estimating	
Supervision	
FHA survey and inspection	
Permits, building, sewer, electrical	
Insurance, advertising, selling expense	
	100

This is my first point—that the base of structural cost is small, considering the sale price. You are not going to change the sale price of a house significantly if you invent a new version of one thing out of the hundreds that go into a house. As I implied before, the knowledge of the breakdown is important in understanding the effect of codes. Actually, building codes, when properly used, can influence the cost of the building only slightly, and the sale price of the building very, very little. Knowledge of the breakdown is important in analyzing cost reduction through technological improvement. It is important in understanding the HUD Operation Breakthrough program because HUD is putting most of its emphasis on technological improvement. It is also significant in evaluating much nonindustry sponsored research and political ballyhoo.

Later, I shall talk about whether codes are archaic or not. Codes are newer than you think. Most codes are quite new or have been revised lately. Age of codes is not the problem. The term "archaic" is just handy; it isn't realistic.

I shall also talk about the real problems connected with the use of building codes. One is ignorance. It's a rough term, but I mean it. We don't know enough to know how to write good codes. The second, and equally important, is political pressure.

Codes are legal standards governing various aspects of our controlled environment. States, and not the federal government, are the sources of authority. This makes it very difficult to have a national code. Many states delegate their authority to municipalities. The authority is enforced by police power. At least 13 states have either mandatory statewide or optional codes for adoption. The federal government, however, plays a part in codes; I shall discuss this federal role later. There are five main types of codes and some others.

Zoning codes govern land use and the types of buildings permitted, whether they should be residential, institutional, commercial or industrial, the specified density, location on the lot, how much of the lot can be built on, the height and the type of structure, style, appearance, and materials, whether prefabricated or modular. Zoning codes are frankly, flagrantly, and purposely restrictive. They have no other purpose than to restrict. They are designed to enhance and protect the interests of property owners. They are almost impossible to write and administer logically, fairly, and for the greatest benefit of all. They are not building codes.

Housing codes, which are fairly new, govern living and sanitary conditions, healthful and decent shelter. Housing codes are usually locally written, and they aren't too troublesome except to slum landlords. They are referenced to the American Public Health Association. They are not building codes.

Plumbing codes are designed to insure health. They are sponsored by the American National Standards Institute. Three of the model codes have plumbing-code sections. Plumbing codes are closely allied to building codes.

Electrical codes are designed for the safety of people, to prevent electrocution and fire. The national Electrical Code is sponsored by the American Insurance Association and written under the administration of the American National Standards Institute. Electrical codes apply to electrical work in all types of buildings, and they are closely allied to building codes.

Building codes are what I'm really talking about. Their purpose is safety of people. The best explanation of building codes is D. E. Parsons' pamphlet, *Building Codes and the Producers of Building Products*. Building codes apply to institutional, commercial and industrial buildings and to housing in urban locations of more than four stories and of high density. They often do not significantly affect single-family suburban housing.

The best count of the number of building codes was by the Douglas Commission of Urban Problems. Of the 4,073 cities of over 5,000 population, 80 percent, or 3,273, had building codes. One-third of these were home-made and two-thirds, 4,200, were based on one or another of the four so-called model codes, most, however, with substantial changes.

What are model codes? Well, there are four, more or less, proprietary codes intended as models for widespread adoption. Dozens of experts are involved in writing these codes. They're about as complete and as well researched and as well written as available data permits. The staffs are alert to well-thought-out improvements. Most of the model codes are revised annually, and are widely respected.

Their faults are recognized. They are fairly clean as they are written. However, they are proprietary. A high degree of emotion and chauvinism are involved in their acceptance. Model codes are usually adopted by reference, but problems are often involved. Modifications and outright opposition are introduced by affected local groups. Failure of local boards of appeals is another place where they break down.

I think you know what the model codes are. There is the Basic Code of Building Officials Conference of America, the Uniform Code of the International Conference of Building Officials (ICBO) (mostly used in the West), the Southern Code of the Southern Building Code Conference. The National Code, the granddaddy of all building codes, is the work of the American Insurance Association.

The Minimum Property Standards (MPS) of the Federal Housing Administration, while not a code, comprise a very influential set of documents that are probably more influential in the construction of houses than any building code, simply because people building low-cost houses have to be prepared for a buyer who will rely on an FHA guaranteed mortgage. The MPS have been lately superseded, I believe, by the first version of HUD's minimum property standards.

There is a new sun on the horizon, however. The National Council of the States on Building Codes and Standards is an organization without very much structure, but which is made up of building officials appointed by the governors of the various states who are getting together and trying to write similar state building codes. More about this later.

The generation of codes is pretty difficult. There is really little valid data. Most of the knowledge in the building industry is empirical. Everybody has his own idea and his own interpretation, so that the writing of codes is torn by conflicting beliefs. Usually, the individuals or groups who start out to write codes are sincere, honest, and fair in their intentions. Trouble starts when people with axes to grind offer their "help." The dull-ax owners are often the affected labor trades, some of the affected trade subcontractors, and some of the affected building product manufacturers. In the ax-sharpening process, a fairly good code may be sabotaged. The code very often becomes, not a building code, but a list of permissible products and labor trades involved in building.

Hal Colling, Director of the International Conference of Building Officials, wrote in *House and Home* (April and June, 1964) of the 40-year guerrilla war between code-writers, administrators, labor and certain building product industry associations. He said that in five annual meetings between 1957 and 1961, from 35 to 52 percent of the floor time was used by lumber and steel industries battling code changes. Much of the rest of it was taken up with arguments by labor. Completely absent from this list of people who write codes are the ones most affected—architects, owners, and general contractors. They never get to write a word in codes. Thus, the legitimate purpose of building codes has been subverted by certain building industries and certain labor groups, in order to maintain markets and jobs. This is half of what is wrong with codes.

Codes have lately received so much criticism that some reform is being undertaken cautiously. "Modernization" is the key word for it. Parsons, in the previously mentioned study, said that a 1948 survey of 4,000 municipalities of more than 2,500 population, showed 46 percent of their codes had not been rewritten in 15 years. In a similar survey in 1955 and 1956, this figure dropped to 26 percent. The Douglas Commission found in 1968 that just under two-thirds of the codes they surveyed were either new or revised in the previous six years. And 37.5 percent were new or revised in 1966 and 1967. This is why I say that codes are not "archaic" in all cases. They have been revised, they are relatively new, and they're still not very good. But they are not old. What is being done is to try to improve the fairness and to take out the prejudices.

However, they are not being made less strict in their technical requirements. Quite the contrary. Because as we go through life, experience builds records of disasters. It doesn't erase records of disasters; it adds them to the list. Escapes are less dramatic; only the engineers know about them. But the disasters are supported by emotion and codes are becoming more and more strict, probably, in certain instances, because they should be. An example is the first anti-noise provision in the United States in the New York City code. This was right. We needed it badly. There is a new hope that large corporations getting into real estate may de-emphasize single-line products, and this may provide a better atmosphere for code-writing.

Uniformity in Codes

There is a considerable body of argument in support of uniformity in codes. However, uniformity, whether in a federal or an independent single national code, is actively opposed by many industries and labor. A massive code is thought to be too difficult to control or manipulate; too difficult to circumvent. The domino theory is used by some to build up numbers of approvals, first by smaller, then by larger and larger code administrations. Some believe that regional codes can better accommodate climatic and geologic differences. However, such accommodations have been made in model codes which are widely applicable. Model codes are a form of uniformity and slowly closing the gaps. But Gaylord Clayborne, Technical Director of the Building Officials Conference of America (BOCA), said that labor is the largest group at model code adoption meetings, and it is usually in opposition because adoption means a form of uniformity.

I said I would tell you about the National Conference of States for Building Codes and Standards. Several groups a few years ago rediscovered the states' authority for codes. But the states had no way of talking to each other. The Building Research Division of the National Bureau of Standards had a man who had considerable experience, and he suggested an exploratory meeting which was finally held in 1967. The Governor of Wisconsin called an organizational meeting in 1968. Seventeen states accepted, and the Building Research Division accepted the Secretariat. I want to say right here and make it perfectly clear: the Building Research Division of the National Bureau of Standards is not writing a code. They are simply acting as a Secretariat for this group of states who are, themselves, seeking ways to get some uniformity in codes and some acceptable way of writing good codes.

Inspection

The National Conference of States are also trying to solve the problem of inspection, which is particularly important in industrialized modular housing and standardization. Part of this problem boils down to a little local building inspector's reluctance to trust a factory inspector passing the building for which the local inspector has ultimate responsibility. The problem is to get a system set up where a valid inspection, no matter where it is conducted, will be accepted in whatever community the industrialized building is finally located.

The National Council of States for Building Codes and Standards is believed to be a new white hope because it's probably big enough to be above the level where affected parties can interfere. It will be be politically too hot to do so. A BOCA survey of state activity in 1969 turned up the information that 13 states, as I said before, have adopted state building codes. Sixteen have such legislation pending, 11 have clauses which make their code compulsory for municipalities within their borders, 15 have legislation pending that would require municipalities to accept the state code, and 22 have the whole problem under study. So it is rather widespread.

Uniformity, while it is highly desirable by itself, is not enough, as

I've pointed out, because all the knowledge with which we write the codes is based on an empirical background. We do not know what is needed because there exists no building science per se. Also, there is no building science because we do not have adequate methods of evaluation and measurement. A science cannot exist without a complete system of measurement. It is so essential, that the Building Research Division of NBS has recently adopted, as its primary mission, the development of a complete methodology for measurement and evaluation for the building industry. I served on an advisory committee to the Building Research Division for the past six years, and I consider the adoption of this mission to be the most important step taken toward long-range improvement of our industry.

Typical existing building codes specify acceptable construction in terms of space, strength, fire behavior, health, and safety. They rarely state what is not acceptable. Most codes, including the model codes, have preambles stating that alternatives are permissible when the administrator considers that the alternatives satisfy the requirements. Problems arise in finding bases for making such decisions. Codes containing such preambles often are called "performance codes." This is ridiculously dishonest. They are not performance codes in any sense of the "performance" concept.

Calling them "performance codes" is like the sales manager who had to put on a training program for his salesmen. He was searching for a theme and went for a walk after lunch. He met some Girl Scouts selling cookies. Still searching for his theme he asked one little girl why she wanted to sell him cookies. Smiling up at him sweetly, she replied, "Because you're so handsome." So he bought two dozen boxes and returned to the office having decided on his theme. "The brightest tools in the salesman's kit are truth and honesty."

Now at last I'm going to talk about performance codes. Everybody wants performance codes, and they want them so badly that they will accept anything in the name of performance codes.

I'm going to quote from a masterful study by the Building Research Division of the Bureau of Standards called *The Performance Concept — A Study of Its Application to Housing*: "Those documents which have been prepared in the recent past, based on the performance concept, fall short of the mark, not because their writers were insincere, but because the sum of knowledge now available is not sufficient for the task. Our general conclusion is that we are a long way from having adequate performance specifications. The obvious needs of individuals and families who live in houses have not been explicitly stated or systematically identified. The art of planning houses for meeting humans' physiological, psychological and sociological needs is largely one of intuition and perpetuation of existing solution patterns which have been apparently satisfactory. This apparent satisfaction has resulted in a lack of motivation to support research which makes these needs more explicit and has tended to concentrate measurement techniques and specifications on physical properties of housing elements."

The performance concept requires new nonphysical "intellectual technology," the application of the new intellectual techniques of systems analysis, simulation, and operations research to problem solving—the systems approach.

Figure 1 and the following explanation are taken directly from the BRD's previously mentioned study on the performance concept, because I believe this is, by far, the best statement made to date.

The first block of Figure 1 is "Performance Requirements." At the fundamental level, these are derived from the characteristics of users which the physical environment can affect such as physiological needs or life processes; psychological needs or the mental processes; and sociological needs or the interactions between people and groups and the effects of commonly held beliefs. Needs are not dependent on particular materials, devices or systems, but derived from the following questions: What is the use or the function being considered? For whom is the requirement posed? Why is there a need? This helps explain the background of considerations out of which the need has grown, and will assist in determining the anticipated benefits. Where will the needs exist, what are the limits and context of the needs? When will the needs exist and for how long?

The next block is "Performance Criteria." These are attributes or characteristics which are to be used in evaluating whether or not the requirements are being met. They may or may not be measurable in any rigorous way, but can be evaluated by some appropriate method. There are secondary, but imperative, criteria with respect to public health and safety that may be present because of the context of the requirements. There are secondary but *desirable* criteria related to the interface between solution and the larger subsystems or systems of which they will be a part. Criteria related to *costs* of alternative solutions will enter into the evaluation of performance potential versus benefits.

The third block is "Performance Evaluative Techniques." Once criteria are identified, there is a need to develop some method of evaluating solutions advanced to meet the requirements against such criteria. The most reproducible evaluative techniques are those based on physical tests. However, some criteria do not lend themselves to numerical evaluation, so that simulation techniques will

Figure 1
The performance hierarchy. Source:
*The Performance Concept – A Study of
Its Application to Housing*, Building
Research Division, National Bureau of
Standards.

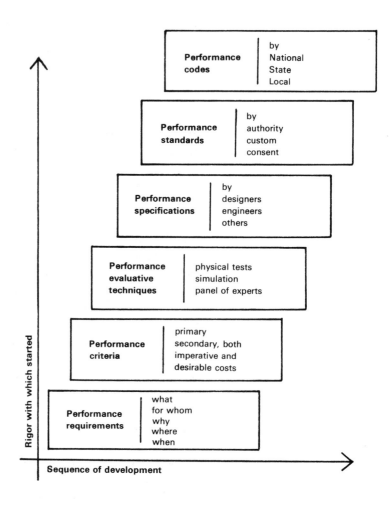

Delivery system. Proponents of the light-weight monolithic box have always dreamed of aerial delivery of assembly-line-produced dwellings directly from the factory to the homesite. Courtesy of Sikorsky Aircraft.

Building element. The demand for brick construction in tradition-oriented communities has resulted in this solution—a precast panel with bricks cast into its facade. The lack of talented masons and the cost of manual labor has forced this particular technological feat in Sweden. Courtesy of Tegelindustrins Central-kontor.

have to be utilized to answer simply that the solution is satisfactory or unsatisfactory. In other cases, the judgment of experts may be the only evaluation possible.

The fourth block is "Performance Specifications." These are statements which are rigorous enough to indicate which criteria are to be considered and how they are to be measured. Upper or lower limits, established according to the selected measurement technique, are used to indicate the range of values of the criteria which are considered acceptable or unacceptable. They may be used or required by owners or their agents, including architects and engineers.

The fifth block is "Performance Standards." If the measurement techniques are reproducible and the requirements are reasonably common ones, a duly constituted (authoritative) body may issue the specifications as a standard to be referenced by others, or it may become a de facto standard by common usage.

The sixth, and final, block is "Performance Code." This is a collection of specifications and standards, which have been adopted by a process of law and which can be enforced by the police power of a government. Codes are promulgated by national model-code groups and state and local governments. A code is usually intended for impartial regulation of an area of activity, the purpose of which is the protection of the safety, health, and general welfare of the public.

The Building Research Division's mission is now principally directed toward development of the evaluative techniques which, we hope, will become the heart of building science and the steps just described will become, at least, a part of the framework of a building science.

This is my second point. We will not have performance codes or any other dramatic improvement in building technology until we have developed a fairly complete measurement and evaluative methodology. We have a big job to do. All the little improvements that we do along the way are fine, but we must set up a foundation of measurement and evaluative techniques.

15
The Labor Movement and Industrialized Building

Reese Hammond

The labor movement is concerned with the application of the concept of industrialized building, i.e., that point in time when on-site work starts or when off-site work, preparatory to on-site work, commences. The theoretical definition of any building project includes all construction projects for which performance standards can be developed, but a practical definition is more restrictive and narrows down the application of the concept to components that can be mass-produced to provide end products with a mass market. If we accept this definition, then in its early applications systems building would be restricted to certain types of buildings and highways. If this is the practical definition of industrialized building from the labor movement's point of view, then the labor movement should analyze the contract-construction outlook for the decade of the 1970s. Responsible authorities dealing with construction projections have indicated that heavy construction will increase 145 percent from 1970 to 1980; that transportation facilities will increase 135 percent between 1970 and 1980; that electricity, gas and communications will register a 103 percent increase for the decade; that residential building—excluding one- and two-family homes—will increase by 63 percent during the same period; and that nonresidential building will increase 77 percent during the period. Most people, including Secretary Romney of the Department of Housing and Urban Development, are discussing the application of system building only as it applies to building construction.

A more detailed split-out of this suggested market has even more significance. Projections are that apartment construction will increase 55 percent during this period, arriving at a $12 billion annual gross product by 1980. If we add to this the market for one- and two-family homes, which has been estimated at roughly for twice the number of multi-family starts, we find 60 percent more construction for a $24 billion gross product by the end of the decade. In a less dramatic area, college dormitories will increase 233 percent to $3 billion, while hotels and motels will increase 100 percent to $1.5 billion. This will result in a total residential market, in 1980, of some $40 billion, as opposed to the 1970 market of $24 billion. If we add to this the possible (but by no means *probable*) increase in government subsidized housing, this becomes an extremely enticing prospect. If you add to that the commercial, educational, and medical services, as well as the government structures that should be built during this decade, the prospects cease to be enticing and become phenomenal. But even if we deal only with the more modest residential building program of $40 billion, we should look at the reaction of the building-trades unions to such a building program.

Some of this work is under union control. Urban housing, particularly

Presented to the 1970 session. Reese Hammond is Director of Research and Education, International Union of Operating Engineers.

high-rise housing, is pretty well controlled by the building trades unions. The majority of the commercial work is controlled by the construction trades, and government work—particularly in those areas that are well organized—is controlled by the trades. On the other hand, much of the work included in this projected $40 billion package is not under control. Uncontrolled work includes previously mentioned types of work in nonunion areas, and the 80 percent of the one- and two-family homes which are built nonunion. The federal government may some day deliver on the often-promised program of subsidized housing to meet the somewhat hoary, but still urgent, goals of the 1949 Housing Act, and in that event, the program could very well include techniques that are radically different than current methods—techniques, skills, and workers that would not necessarily be under the control of union contracts. If these techniques should provide some answers to seasonality, then there could be a whole new work world opened for construction workers who currently spend the winter months on the bench.

The prospect of organizing those geographic areas that have historically been nonunion, of making substantial inroads into the one- and two-family home market, and controlling new techniques that may emerge as a result of achieving a mass market for housing, coupled with the availability of tens of thousands of skilled mechanics in the winter months (when construction is normally at a low ebb) has a lot of attraction for all construction unions. These possibilities must be measured against the history of the American trade unions. A look at union philosophy in the United States will give us some insight into the possible response of organized labor to such opportunities.

Unions were, and are, a response to industrialization. They have historically responded to the dehumanizing influence of the factory system. Conditions of work and conditions of life at the turn of the century prodded workers into collective action. The guild system, transferred to the colonies before the revolution, emerged from the crucible of nineteenth-century industrialization in the form of craft unions, while industrial unions—those organizations encompassing all workers in an industry in one union, such as the United Automobile Workers—had their base in the socialist movement. In 1969, these organizations have, in general, lost many of their original characteristics as our increasingly abundant society has required considerable modifications of union strategy. The principal characteristic of the American trade-union movement has been a down-to-earth realism. A matter-of-fact, practical response to problems is a chief characteristic of the American Labor Movemement as we enter the 1970s. There has been no attempt to establish a labor political party, such as exists in Western Europe and there has been no simplistic overall economic dogma, but, rather, a continual upgrading of attainable goals which have been changed from time to time as progress has been achieved and new objectives set. One student of the labor movement has described the American Federation of Labor as an organization with its feet planted firmly on the ground and its head reluctantly in the sky, and the Congress of Industrial Organizations as a group with its head firmly in the clouds with its feet reluctantly placed on the ground. The significance of the development of the American labor movement is that, as new conditions arise, new responses will be forthcoming. Certainly, industrialized building, as it has been discussed in this conference, represents an entirely new set of conditions in the construction industry and properly deserves a new response.

With this background, I think it is important to move on to a look at the composition of the building and construction trade unions. There are characteristics peculiar to the construction unions that are important to know in order to deal realistically with them. Local unions affiliated with the Building and Construction Trades Department have strong local autonomy which is jealously guarded and stringently preserved. This is because of an old truism—control of any organization rests where the money rests. Local unions in the building and construction industry have a surprisingly low per capita tax. A per capita tax is that portion of dues paid to an international union. In my union, the Operating Engineers, for example, local union dues run eight to twelve dollars per month, of which ninety-five cents goes to the international union for operation and administrative expenses at the international level. Obviously, most dues money remains in the local union to provide direct services to local union members. In contrast, industrial unions generally have a relatively high per capita tax, and provide services from a central point, i.e., from the international or regional office. The significance of these facts is that craft unions follow international leadership because they *want* to and are convinced that they should, not because they *have* to for financial reasons.

To provide a little more insight into the seventeen international unions that are affiliated with the building trades and which, with the Teamsters, make up the unions that represent workers in the construction industry, we can look at the composition of these international unions. Certain large unions, such as the Teamsters, the International Brotherhood of Electrical Workers, and the Carpenters, serve a number of different industries. The Teamsters, in addition to construction, serves the baking industry, the dairy industry, the breweries and over-the-road trucking; the IBEW, in addition to the construction industry, serves the manufacturing industry and public utilities; while the Carpenters has a large membership in the manufacturing of wood products, millrights who perform rigging, and workers in lumber yards as well as in the timber operations in the Northwest. In contrast are the small internationals which serve only the construction industry, such as the Roofers and the Asbestos

Workers. The seventeen international unions that are affiliated with the Building and Construction Trades Department in Washington, D.C., have local unions chartered with craft and geographic jurisdiction. These local unions affiliate with local Building and Construction Trades Councils. An international union such as the Painters and Allied Trades may have several locals in the same Building and Construction Trades Council because their jurisdiction is subdivided into local unions covering glaziers, painters and floor coverers. This is true also of the Carpenters, which has local unions in the same geographical area chartered over different types of work, such as pile driving and commercial building; and the United Association of Plumbers and Steamfitters, which—almost without exception—has different local unions chartered for their steamfitters' jurisdiction and their plumbers' jurisdiction. In general, it can be stated that the real strength and the real centers of power in the construction trades rest in the local Building and Construction Trades Councils. Those local unions whose members work side by side, day after day, and week after week, are more responsive to the daily needs of their organizations and carry much more influence with their members than a periodic policy statement that may be issued by their international union, or by the Building and Construction Trades Department in Washington. Recognizing that there are three distinct levels of policy and authority in the unions with jurisdiction in the construction industry—i.e., the Building and Construction Trades Department, the international union and the local union, through its affiliation with a local building trades council—it is apparent that the implementation of any new policies must take place at all three levels.

I suggest that the initial attempt at establishing a new policy should take place with the Building and Construction Trades Department, where the diplomatic, academic, and intellectual argument in favor of a new policy should be presented, with the immediate goal in mind of coming out of such a meeting with no opposition. From that point, an approach should be made to the international unions. The arguments presented at this level should be the politic and polite arguments regarding the merits of the new system and what they have to offer to the individual international unions. The goal of this type of meeting should be to come out with approval of the concept and, possibly, a national agreement with each international union which puts the imprimatur of the international union on the new process. But it would be both incorrect and incomplete for you to feel that your efforts would be finished after approval from the international union.

If you want to get where the action is—if you want to cause the crunch, rather than get caught in it—if you want to hang in, rather than hang out—then you should present your arguments to the local building and construction trades council and the unions affiliated with it. And the objective which you should seek at this level is a project agreement for all trades, with common expiration dates and clear-cut jurisdiction, or a clearly established policy for resolving jurisdictional disputes. The exercise that I have suggested, through three levels of union hierarchy, has a real logic—a logic based on practical considerations.

A systems builder has a multiplicity of problems, other than labor-force problems. Before you even discuss the role which workers play in an industrialized building operation, you will have spent countless days with architects, consultants, clients, owners, real estate interests, financiers, local-government code agencies and your contractors. Resolving these problems will take a long time and a lot of work. Before you get off the ground with any systems operation, large capital investment will be required to assure the necessary financing and land acquisition. With the exception of small modular residential homes, it is improbable that a single systems sponsor would have more than one or two operations underway at one time simply because of the large cost involved in the factory and other financial commitments. When the total effort is considered, the amount of time spent in negotiations with the building trades unions should fall into perspective, and I believe you will find it not unduly excessive.

If you have decided that you're willing to invest all this time and patience dealing with the building trades unions, you will be concerned with the response that you may expect at the bargaining table. That response will be determined by at least six factors. First, if half of the films that have been shown during the past week are accurate, there will be a significant reduction in total construction costs; and construction unions, representing members who need housing, understand the social significance of lower construction costs, not only for themselves, but also for the less affluent in the nation. Second, aside from the economics in *construction* cost, is the reduced *total* cost because of the immediate occupancy that results from the timely construction of an industrialized home. Construction-loan money is transferred to mortgage money, carrying a lower interest rate in a shorter period of time than would be the case under conventional building. Third, and quite pragmatically, industrialized building offers the construction trades substantially increased membership. Most of this potential membership will not conflict with existing union membership, although there will be some displacement as has been pointed out clearly in the Battelle Report. The fourth factor that has attraction to the trade-union movement is the possibility of continuity of employment promised by both the off-site operation and in the on-site, or erection, operation. The fifth factor would be the promise of supervisory positions to the skilled journeyman mechanics, both on-site and in the factory, because of the need for personnel who understand the end product of the operation as well as the day-to-day process. That I see a sixth advantage of industrialized building may be due to a rather provincial outlook on my part. Certainly for my organization, the Operating Engineers, there will be increased job opportunities on-site, as large modules require power-assisted equipment to be placed. If these six factors have attraction to the craft unions, you then may wonder what form the response to this abundance will take. I think you can reasonably expect a rather abbreviated period of conflict and adjustment; this expectation is given credence by the comments in the Battelle Report that indicate there will be a substantial adjustment in some trades when on-site work is transferred to the shop, or, as you would have it, to a factory. I believe also, though, that there will be ultimate recognition of the new conditions that exist in industrialized building. I believe this because the record clearly demonstrates that craft unions have developed wage rates and working conditions commensurate with skill requirements and conditions in a wide variety of industries. Certainly the electrical workers don't get construction wages in their industrial operations; the sheet metal workers have secondary rates established in job shops where employment conditions are substantially different than in construction; and, in my own union, it is widely accepted that, under certain conditions, secondary wage rates exist in the sand pits, quarries, and equipment shops. In general, the secondary nature of the wages is compensated for by the continuity of employment. If industrialized building, therefore, offers continuity of employment at the factory, then appropriate wage rates can be expected. However, in this period of adjustment, there will be a series of problems to overcome. I suggest that they fall into three areas. One is the leadership of the international unions and, to some extent, the local unions. These organizations are, in general, still led by men with a depression-based outlook, who recall, all too vividly, the scarcity of jobs, the terrific cyclical and seasonal employment, and other conditions which have resulted in construction workers suffering double the national unemployment rate. But I would suggest that within the next five years, considerable attrition will take place, both at the international level and the local level, and the personalities and leadership with whom you will be dealing will be more receptive to the promise, if not to the guarantee, of year-round employment. Beyond the problems involved with the leadership at all levels of the trade-union movement will be a problem directly involved with the membership. That problem is twofold. Initially, our members will be concerned about the total number of jobs available, but this should be a short-lived fear as total employment will probably be affected very little by industrialized building. Their more legitimate concern will be over new methods. Your discussion this week has probed deeply into the possible changes in construction methods. I suggest that any campaign to sell a local union on systems building should include a training component which will assure older members that they will have the opportunity, should they desire, of learning the new skills required in the new systems. The third problem area is the almost unbelievable vacillation of

government programs. To say the least, it has been disturbing to
hear Pat Moynihan, a top White House aide, indicate that, with the
winding down the Vietnamese war, there probably would be little,
if any, new money available for a concerted attack on this nation's
social problems and the building that must be associated with their
resolution. The National Housing Program has been a statement of
record for some two decades, but has been little more than a statement, as neither authorizations nor appropriations have been made
to fulfill the promise of the 1949 Housing Act. There must be some
method developed to transfer the twenty-year-old *promise* of decent
housing into a *guarantee* of decent housing. Something may be
gained from reviewing the highway trust fund set up under the inter-
state program in 1956.

If you are willing to deal with the multi-level problems of the construction trades, and *if* you are ready to pursue implementation of
new policies through these levels, and *if* you accept the logic of local
negotiations, and *if* you believe that industrialized building does offer
substantial opportunities to the craft unions, and *if* you believe that
the unions will respond as I have suggested, then you may reach
what I believe are the ultimate results. I feel that craft unions will
fight for potential job opportunities, as well as protect existing job
opportunities. I think this is clearly indicated by the actions of the
Carpenters with their contract with Stirling Homex, the contract of
the Detroit Building Trades in Michigan and the tripartite agreement
of the Carpenters, Plumbers and Electricians.

Construction workers have and will accept technological change.
The single most significant area of change in construction has been
in earthmoving—an operation important to my union. We have progressed as technology has progressed. We have not objected to the
introduction of money-saving machines. Contrary to the public image
spun by those whose interests are to weaken the most powerful
unions in the country, the construction industry has been innovative
and has accepted change, but not under unilaterally imposed conditions. We've been successful in trading off technological change for
money—a major role of a union to play as it represents its members.
If the offer is attractive and the price is right, the worker will buy it.

In conclusion, I would suggest that in the construction industry we've
come a long way since the height of an electrical outlet was determined by the length of the handle of an electrician's hammer. Dr.
Bates of the Office of Standards Policy of the National Bureau of
Standards has stated: "I can cite every major institution affecting
building. Every one of them must undergo an evolution which takes
them out of the past to the future. . . ." I believe that includes our
unions. From time to time as I discuss this exciting topic with my
colleagues, both within the labor movement and within the building
industry, the question has been posed as to who will be the moving

force in systems building. Some have suggested the architect; some, the engineer; some, the contractor; others, the government; or, perhaps, even some of the manufacturers. However, I've never heard anyone suggest that the unions will be the boss. That decision rests with you gentlemen, and I'm happy to leave it with you.

Glossary

Action Radius	Efficient service radius (from the production facility) of the manufacturer.
Basic Module	A unit of dimension used to coordinate the size of components and of building elements.
Building Process	The entire process which embraces every step from the conception to the total satisfaction of all building requirements.
Closed System	A building system having interchangeability of *its own* subsystems and components only.
Component	An industrial product which is manufactured as an independent unit capable of being joined with other building elements to make a whole.
Dead Load	The weight of all permanent construction including walls, floors, roof, partitions, service equipment and other integral building parts.
Dimension	A distance between two points, lines, or planes.
Geometry	The aspect of building design related to the spatial and dimensional characteristics of the completed structure.
Grid Line	A line in a reference pattern (See: *Planning Grid*).
HUD	United States Department of Housing and Urban Development.
Industrialized Building System	The total integration of all subsystems and components into an overall process fully utilizing industrialized production, transportation, and assembly techniques. This integration is achieved through the exploitation of the underlying organizational principles—rather than the external forms—of industrialization, mechanization, and programming to structure the entire building process.
Interface	The point of contact or blending of two objects, systems, or activities.
Joint	The space between and the meeting of two or more building elements, the connection point(s).
Live Load	The weight superimposed upon a structure by the use and occupancy of the structure, not including wind loads or dead loads.
Mobile Home	A portable structure built on a chassis or a frame and designed to be hauled to a site and used with or without a permanent foundation as a dwelling unit when connected to utilities.
Modular Coordination	A method of sizing the dimensions of building components and of building on the basis of a basic module.
Module	A convenient size (usually a volume) that is used as an increment or coefficient in building design and construction.
Open system	A building system, designed to have interchangeability of its subsystems, components, or building elements with like subsystems, components, or elements of other systems.
Planning Grid	A reference grid pattern used for the presentation of plans and elevations of buildings.

Prefabrication	The fabrication of building elements before they reach the building site.
R.F.P.	Request for Proposal (United States Government research terminology).
Subsystem	A complete, physically integrated, dimensionally coordinated, series of parts which function as a unit.
Tolerance	An allowance for the lack of accuracy which must be accepted for the positioning of a component, whether on-site or in factory production.
U-Factor	A coefficient of heat loss.
Wind Load	The lateral, vertical, or uplift forces due to wind blowing in any direction upon a structure.

Selected Bibliography

Bemis, Albert Farwell
The Evolving House (Rational Design, vol. 3). Technology Press, Cambridge, Mass., 1933.

Bender, Richard
Selected Technological Aspects of the American Building Industry: The Industrialization of Building, prepared for the National Commission on Urban Problems, New York, 1968.

Blachère, G.
Savoir Bâtir, Habitabilité, Durabilité, Economie des Bâtiments, Editions Eyrolles, Paris, 1966.

Brooke, Henry
Flats and Houses 1958: Design and Economy, H.M.S.O., London, 1958. Written for the Ministry of Housing and Local Government.

Carreiro, Joseph, et al.
The New Building Block, A Report on the Factory-Produced Dwelling Module, Research Report No. 8, Cornell University, Ithaca, N.Y., 1968.

Cutler. Laurence S.
Industrialized Building Systems (Urban Affairs Cassette Tape), McGraw-Hill Book Company, Hightstown, N.J., 1970.

Deeson, A. E. L., editor
The Comprehensive Industrialized Building Annual, Products Journals, London, issued annually.

Diamant, R. M. E.
Industrialized Buildings, Volumes I, II, III, London, Iliffe Books Ltd., 1968. Published under the auspices of *The Architect and Building News.*

Dietz, Albert G. H.
Future Potential of Building Systems, American Society of Civil Engineers, Pittsburgh, September, 1968.

Ecole D'architecture, Montreal, and Washington University.
"Communicating industrialization: two courses and a symposium," *Industrialization Forum*, January, 1970.

Grumman Allied Industries
Modular Low-Cost Housing System Feasibility Report, Grumman Aircraft Engineering Corp., Bethpage, N.Y., 1968.

Guy, R. B. et al.
The State of the Art of Prefabrication in the Construction Industry, Battelle Memorial Institute, 1967.

Harrison, H. W.
Performance Specifications for Building Components, Watford, England, 1969. Written for H. M. Ministry of Public Building and Works.

H.M. Ministry of Housing Local Government
Homes for Today and Tomorrow, H.M.S.O., London, 1961.

———
Co-ordination of Components in Housing: Metric Dimensional Framework, H.M.S.O., London, 1968.

H.M. Ministry of Public Building and Works
Dimensions and Components for Housing, H.M.S.O., London, n.d.

Hoffman, Hubert
Row Houses and Cluster Houses: an International Survey, Frederick A. Praeger, New York, 1957.

Institute of Building Types Design
Building Industrialisation Technical Design Typification in Hungary, Budapest, 1969.

Institution of Structural Engineers
Industrialised Building and the Structural Engineer, London, 1966.

| Interbuild Prefabrication Publications Ltd., | *Europrefab Systems Handbook, Housing*, 1969. |

Jeanneret, Charles E. (Le Corbusier) — *The Modular—A Harmonious Measure to the Human Scale Universally Applicable to Architecture and Mechanics*, Harvard University Press, Cambridge, Mass, 1948.

Kelly, Burnham — *The Prefabrication of Houses*, Technology Press of the Massachusetts Institute of Technology, Cambridge, Mass., and John Wiley & Sons, New York, 1951.

Marchand, P. Eugene — *Report of the Canadian Technical Mission on Prefabricated Concrete Components in Industrialized Building in Europe, September 2–22, 1966*, Department of Industry, Ottawa, 1967.

Martin, Bruce, editor — *The Coordination of Dimensions for Building*, Royal Institute of British Architects, 1965.

McGraw-Hill Book Company — *Time Saver Standards*, New York, 1966.

Notter, George, comp. — *Comparative Housing Study*, Harvard School of Design, Cambridge, Mass., 1958

Pratt Institute — *Cost Reduction Methods for High-Rise Apartments*, Brooklyn, 1967.

Rowland, Norman — *Reston Low Income Housing Demonstration Program*, Washington, D.C., 1969. A report on factory-produced multifamily housing utilizing light-gauge steel modules.

Royal Institute of British Architects — *The Industrialisation of Building, An Appraisal of the Present Position and Future Trends*, 1965.

Royal Institute of British Architects and National Building Agency — *Industrialised Housing and the Architect*, London, 1967.

Schmid, Thomas — Systems Building, Frederick A. Praeger, New York, 1969

Second CIB Congress — *Innovation in Building*, Elsevier Publishing Company, Amsterdam, 1962.

Swedish Industries' Building Group — *The New Building Market: Product Responsibility, Competition, Continuity*, Stockholm, 1969.

Third CIB Congress — *Towards Industrialised Building*, Elsevier Publishing Company, Amsterdam, 1966.

Thomas, Mark Hartland — *Modular Design of Low-Cost Housing*, United Nations, New York, 1966.

United Nations — *Modular Coordination in Building*, New York, 1966.

——— Modular Coordination of Low-Cost Housing, New York, 1970.

United States Commission on Urban Problems — *Building the American City: Report to the Congress and to the President of the United States*, Washington, 1968.

United States Department of Housing and Urban Development — *Bibliography of Housing, Building, and Planning*, Washington, D.C., 1969.

——— *Developing New Communities: Application of Technological Innovations*, Washington, D.C., 1970.

——— *Housing Markets: Selected References*, Washington, D.C., 1967.

	In-Cities Experimental Housing Research and Development Project, Phase 1, Washington, D.C., 1969.
	Industrialized Building, A Comparative Analysis of European Experience, Washington, D.C., 1968.
USSR	*Industrialised Techniques in Housing*, Moscow, 1963.

Index